Dollars & Sense *for* Kids

What they need to know about money—and how to tell them

JANET BODNAR

Senior Editor, *Kiplinger's Personal Finance Magazine*

KIPLINGER BOOKS, Washington, D.C.

Published by
The Kiplinger Washington Editors, Inc.
1729 H Street, N.W.
Washington, DC 20006

Kiplinger publishes books and videos on a wide variety of personal-finance and business- management subjects. Check our Web site (www.kiplinger.com) for a complete list of titles, additional information and excerpts. Or write:

    Cindy Greene
    Kiplinger Books & Tapes
    1729 H Street, N.W.
    Washington, DC 20006
    email: cgreene@kiplinger.com

To order, call 800-280-7165; for information about volume discounts, call 202-887-6431.

Library of Congress Cataloging-in-Publication Data

Bodnar, Janet. 1949-
    Dollars & sense for kids: what they need to know about money--and
    how to tell them/Janet Bodnar
      p. cm.
    Includes index.
    ISBN 0-93872-1-67-4 (paperback)
    1. Children--Finance, Personal. 2. Saving and investment.
    I. Title.   II. Title: Dollars and sense for kids.

HG179.B5669   1999
332.024--dc21

                                              99-40649
                                                CIP

This publication is intended to provide guidance in regard to the subject matter covered. It is sold with the understanding that the author and publisher are not herein engaged in rendering legal, accounting, tax or other professional services. If such services are required, professional assistance should be sought.

First edition. Printed in the United States of America.
9 8 7 6 5 4 3 2

Dollars & Sense *for* Kids

Acknowledgments

When I first started writing about kids and money nearly 10 years ago, I knew a fair amount about money but I was still learning about kids. Since then my children have taught me a lot, and in this book they have pride of place.

First and foremost then, I'd like to thank John, Claire and Peter, my long-suffering money-smart kids, for giving me the best financial advice and letting me share it with the world.

I'd also like to thank:

My husband John, for cooking me a spaghetti dinner tonight;

My parents, Renie and Ed Bodnar, for never having any doubts that this book would get done;

My sister, Priscilla Jackman, for always getting me over the rough spots;

The parents, students and teachers of St. Camillus School, especially Glen Mayers;

All the family members, friends, co-workers, casual acquaintances and Dr. Tightwad correspondents whose anecdotes enliven these pages;

David Harrison of Kiplinger Books, who always knows what to say and how to say it;

Christy Pulfrey, Cindy Greene and Allison Leopold for keeping me honest in getting the facts straight and the words spelled right;

Heather Waugh, Dan Kohan, Cynthia Currie and the other members of the Kiplinger art department for putting it all together so beautifully;

And Jennifer Robinson. There never was a better editor or friend.

Contents

INTRODUCTION ix

QUIZ: Test Your Money Smarts 1

CHAPTER 1: The Perils of Being Dr. Tightwad 7

CHAPTER 2: A Kid's-Eye View of Money 17

CHAPTER 3: The Adman Cometh 25

CHAPTER 4: The Apple Doesn't Fall Far from the Tree 39

CHAPTER 5: Small Change: The Preschool Years 61

CHAPTER 6: Surviving with 'Tweens 71

CHAPTER 7: Why Is Money Green? 91

CHAPTER 8: Allowances: A Hands-On Experience 103

CHAPTER 9: Penny Wise: Kids & Saving 131

CHAPTER 10: Your Kid, the Investment Guru 145

CHAPTER 11: Of Lawnmowing & Milkshake Stands 177

CHAPTER 12: Teens: The Early Years 201

CHAPTER 13: To Work or Not to Work?......................**225**

CHAPTER 14: Off to College & On Their Own (Sort of) **243**

CHAPTER 15: Giving & Getting with Grace & Gratitude........**255**

CHAPTER 16: Girl Scout Cookies & Other Sticky Situations ...**273**

CHAPTER 17: Money-Smart Grandparents......................**287**

CHAPTER 18: Dr. Tightwad's Final Rx...........................**299**

INDEX **301**

Introduction

In all of history, no children have had more money of their own, more pressure to spend it, and less guidance in how to do it than the kids of America at the dawn of the 21st century.

"Today, more than ever, children must learn about money, for it is both a source of confusion and an indispensable tool they must learn to use." Those words made a lot of sense back in 1950, in a *Kiplinger's* magazine article entitled "Will Your Child Know the Value of a Dollar?" And they're even more true today.

Decades ago, it was a lot easier to raise children as responsible money managers. When young people worked for pay, they typically contributed most of their earnings to the family kitty, to help make ends meet. Consumer credit was not widely available, so people saved up for major purchases. Before TV, kids could covet only what they saw at their friends' homes or in a magazine.

Today money is more abstract—plastic credit cards, electronic transfers, cash spewing from an ATM slot. Many teens work not to help support their family or save for college, but purely to fund their own discretionary purchases. Some develop an appetite for clothes, entertainment and consumer goods that they will have difficulty affording when, as young householders, they will have to pay for their own rent, food, car, insurance and other basics of life.

The challenge for parents today is to teach restraint and responsibility in a society that doesn't put much value on those traits. This new book, Janet Bodnar's *Dollars & Sense for Kids*, can be a big help.

As the mother of three, Janet has lots of experience

in handling real-life money issues. Under the nom de plume of Dr. Tightwad, she began writing kids 'n' money advice in 1992, in the pages of *Kiplinger's Personal Finance Magazine*, of which she is senior editor. There followed a best-selling book, *Money-Smart Kids (And Parents, Too!)*, a newspaper column syndicated by The New York Times Syndicate, and countless appearances on national TV and radio programs. In a few short years, Janet has become the Dr. Spock of money-smart childrearing.

Her new book offers astute, practical advice for parents of children ranging in age from preschool through college: Advice on allowances and family chores. Advice on teen employment. Ideas on how kids can get started as savvy savers and stock market investors. Tips, too, on how parents and grandparents should make gifts to their young ones.

In all of this good counsel, one theme keeps recurring: the importance of communication. Effective parents include the kids in discussions and solicit their ideas, even though the parents make the final decision. And they try to set a good example in their own money management, because children learn more from our deeds than our words.

If all goes well, your kids will grow up with a healthy attitude toward money and the ability to manage it. They will become fulfilled, competent and financially secure young adults. And they won't land back on your doorstep after you thought the nest was empty.

KNIGHT A. KIPLINGER
Editor, *The Kiplinger Letters*
Editor in Chief, *Kiplinger's Personal Finance Magazine*

Test Your Money-Smarts

Warm up your parental reflexes with these 20 kids-and-money situations—common experiences, at least in principle, for most parents. Once you've identified your level of parental agility and authority, read on; you'll find plenty of my strategies and ideas for teaching your kids the value of a dollar. Remember, raising money-smart kids starts with you.

1. Your 7-year-old daughter loses the $5 she got for her birthday from her Aunt Mary. You:

a. ask Aunt Mary to send another $5.
b. tell your child she should have put the money in the bank.
c. let her do chores to make up the $5.
d. tell your child she should have been more careful.

2. Your 14-year-old son has been saving half of his allowance and money earned from neighborhood jobs. Now he wants to use the money to buy a $200 compact-disc player. You:

a. allow him to buy it.
b. offer him your old turntable instead.
c. tell him there's no way he can touch his savings.
d. buy it for him as a birthday gift.

3. Your daughter has mowed your lawn since she was 12. Now 14, she wants to make money by mowing neighbors' lawns. She also wants to be paid to do your lawn. You:

a. say, "Okay, and go ahead and use our mower and gas."

b. hire a neighbor's kid to do your lawn.

c. tell her to forget it because mowing your lawn is her job.

d. say, "Use our mower and pay for the gas you use. We'll pay you half of what you charge neighbors."

4. You usually pay $50 for your son's sneakers. Now he wants a pair of $200 inflatable high-tops. You:

a. chip in the $50, and let your child come up with the balance.

b. say "I'll buy a $50 pair, or you can still wear your old ones."

c. buy them, because "everyone else has them."

d. buy yourself a pair, too (everyone else has them!).

5. Your 15-year-old daughter gets an allowance for which she is expected to help out around the house. She has ceased to help. You:

a. hire a neighbor's kid to help clean the house.

b. stop the allowance altogether.

c. continue to pay until the child turns 18.

d. tie the allowance to financial responsibilities, and make chores a separate issue.

6. You're trying to teach your 16-year-old about the stock market. She invests her own money in a stock you selected. It loses money. You:

a. make up the loss.

b. hire a neighbor's kid to make future stock picks.

c. say, "That's how the market works. Too bad."

d. share the loss with her, and help her figure out what to do with the remaining stock.

7. Your son is getting his driver's license, which means that your insurance will go up. You:

a. sell your car and buy bicycles for the entire family.

b. pay the increased premium—he is part of the family, after all.

c. make him get a job and split the increase.

d. pay the increase but make him pay for his own gas.

8. You finally allow your daughter to shop for her own school clothes. She comes home with the ugliest clothes you ever saw. You:

a. let her keep the clothes, but have a discussion about buying clothes that suit her and will last.

b. grin and bear it, because at least she likes the clothes—and bought them on sale!

c. say, "I knew I couldn't trust you with that much money."

d. make her return the clothes—with you in tow.

9. Your 10-year-old took on a paper route to earn money but is getting lazy. He's in danger of getting fired. You:

a. hire the neighbor's kid to help him out.

b. tell him to do the job right or not at all.

c. pick up the slack by getting up early to help him deliver papers and collect fees.

d. warn him that he's likely to lose his job and income, and then allow him to do so.

10. You're standing in a toy store and your son is insisting that he needs a $60 video game. You:

a. fork over the cash to avoid a scene.

b. fork over the cash but tell him next time he'll have to pay part of the bill.

c. don't fork over the cash, and otherwise proceed as in step b.

d. proceed as in c, and suggest that he try the game over at the neighbor's to see if he really likes it before he buys it.

11. After telling your children that they absolutely, positively cannot have Super Nintendo, their doting Auntie Mame arrives and presents them with one. You:

a. tell Auntie Mame that the kids can't accept the gift.

b. grit your teeth and accept the gift.

c. sit down and start playing.

d. thank Auntie Mame for the gift, and at a later date, ask her to consult with you before purchasing expensive gifts for the kids.

12. Your daughter receives a $20 birthday check in the mail from her grandparents. You:

a. let her spend it as she wants—it's a gift.

b. deposit the check in the bank for your daughter.

c. tell your daughter to save $5 and let her spend the rest.

d. call Grandma and tell her $20 doesn't buy much nowadays.

13. You bought your 16-year-old a car on the condition that he not leave the school grounds during lunch hour. He does, and totals the car. You:

a. tell him to get his bicycle tuned up.

b. ground him for a month and limit him to using the family car at your discretion, provided he pays for his gas.

c. buy him another car.

d. you'd never be in this predicament, because you'd never buy a 16-year-old a car in the first place.

14. Your son is on his way out the door for a date when he casually asks for $20. You:

a. tell him you didn't know he had a date, and ask him where he he's going.

b. give it to him, plus an extra $10 for gas.

c. tell him that date and gas money come out of his allowance, as previously agreed.

d. give him $10 for gas.

15. It's your preschooler's birthday, and he gets so many presents from family members that he quickly gets bored and toddles off to play. You:

a. give the remaining gifts to the neighbor's kid.

b. put the gifts away to open another time.

c. proceed as in b, and determine that you will set up a college fund for your child and ask relatives for contributions in lieu of gifts.

d. open the rest of the presents yourself.

16. Your 17-year-old works three nights a week and weekends, and his grades have dropped significantly. You:

a. hire the neighbor's kid to do the homework.

b. make him quit the job.

c. don't do anything; he's almost an adult, and his grades are his responsibility.

d. tell him to pull up the grades and consider cutting back on hours, or face quitting altogether.

17. Your 5-year-old wants everything in sight when you

go to the supermarket. He begins to make a scene when you say no. You:

a. wear ear plugs and let him scream his little lungs out.

b. leave him home from now on.

c. buy him what he wants.

d. let him choose one item.

18. Your son is heading for college in the fall and will need spending money. You:

a. tell him that if he stays in his room and studies, he won't need spending money.

b. agree to send a weekly allowance.

c. tell him to get a summer job.

d. discuss his needs, see what he has available from jobs and savings, and agree to supplement that with an appropriate allowance.

19. Your 22-year-old son quit his first post-college job and has moved home "temporarily." You:

a. agree on a combination of chores and a contribution to household expenses, and mutually set the date by which he will move out on his own.

b. tell him that he's an adult now and he has one week to get his act together and leave.

c. give up your home office temporarily so he can have his room back.

d. ask him to do some chores around the house.

20. Your kids, 6 and 8 years old, ask you what would happen if you died: Where would they live, who would take care of them? You:

a. tell them you aren't going to die and there's no need to discuss it.

b. ask them if they would like to live with Uncle Eddie (as your will currently specifies).

c. tell them that they would probably go to live with Uncle Eddie and his family (but you don't have a will and haven't discussed it with Uncle Eddie).

d. proceed as in b, and take the opportunity to write a letter to Uncle Eddie outlining how you would like the kids raised in your absence.

Answer Key

Add up the point values of your answers to get a sense of where you stand.

1. a. 0, **b.** 1, **c.** 2, **d.** 3   **11. a.** 1, **b.** 2, **c.** 0, **d.** 3
2. a. 3, **b.** 0, **c.** 2, **d.** 1   **12. a.** 3, **b.** 1, **c.** 2, **d.** 0
3. a. 2, **b.** 0, **c.** 1, **d.** 3   **13. a.** 1, **b.** 2, **c.** 0, **d.** 3
4. a. 3, **b.** 2, **c.** 0, **d.** 0   **14. a.** 1, **b.** 0, **c.** 3, **d.** 0
5. a. 0, **b.** 0, **c.** 0, **d.** 3   **15. a.** 0, **b.** 2, **c.** 3, **d.** 1
6. a. 1, **b.** 0, **c.** 3, **d.** 2   **16. a.** 0, **b.** 2, **c.** 0, **d.** 3
7. a. 0, **b.** 1, **c.** 2, **d.** 3   **17. a.** 2, **b.** 1, **c.** 0, **d.** 3
8. a. 3, **b.** 2, **c.** 0, **d.** 1   **18. a.** 0, **b.** 1, **c.** 2, **d.** 3
9. a. 0, **b.** 2, **c.** 1, **d.** 3   **19. a.** 3, **b.** 0, **c.** 1, **d.** 2
10. a. 0, **b.** 1, **c.** 2, **d.** 3   **20. a.** 0, **b.** 2, **c.** 1, **d.** 3

SUMMARY

0-10 Either you should adopt the neighbor's kid or you just like taking tests.

11-29 Keep this up and your kids will still be living at home when they're 30.

30-49 You're on the right track, but you could use a consultation with Dr. Tightwad.

50-60 You and your kids are well on the way to being money-smart. Compare notes with Dr. Tightwad to learn how you can fine-tune your approach.

The Perils of Being Dr. Tightwad

On February 5 I left a note at my 16-year-old son's place at the breakfast table, reminding him to write thank-you notes for his birthday gifts.

His birthday was November 19.

While John's younger brother and sister, whose birthdays are also in the fall, had faithfully written their notes, John's had somehow been neglected in the holiday hustle. But because I've gone on record about the importance of kids' sending acknowledgments when they receive gifts, I was determined that John would get his out, even if it was three months after the fact.

As "Dr. Tightwad," I have been dispensing advice on how to teach kids the value, and the values, of money for nearly ten years. What started as a humorous but helpful alter ego in *Kiplinger's Personal Finance Magazine* has taken on a life of her own. In addition to my monthly "Money-Smart Kids" column in *Kiplinger's*, I write a weekly column called "Ask Dr. Tightwad" that is syndicated nationally by The New York Times Syndicate and appears on our Web site, www.kiplinger.com. And I've written two books on the subject, *"Dr. Tightwad's Money-Smart Kids"* and *"Mom, Can I Have That?"*

But the trouble with being "Dr. Tightwad" is that I feel a responsibility to raise money-smart kids of my own. And a heavy burden it is. People often assume I have a magic system for calculating just the right amount of allowance (I don't), and that my own kids never spend a penny (they spend plenty). And for the record, I am *not* a tightwad.

Actually, I tell people, all the advice I give has been used successfully by some parent—though not necessarily by me. Writing about children and money has made me more conscious of the subject, but, like any family, we've had our successes and failures.

For example, once when we were on vacation, my then 9-year-old son Peter had to wrestle with the moral challenge of "finders keepers." One day in Toronto, Peter spotted a $20 bill in the street near the curb. While he waited for traffic to pass so he could pick up the money, a woman jumped out of a car and grabbed the bill. "Is this yours?" she asked. "No," he replied. She pocketed the money and sped away.

At an amusement park a week or so later, Peter walked onto a ride and found $23 on the floor. "Is this yours?" he asked the child who had just vacated the spot. "Sure," said the kid, and pocketed the cash.

Several rides later, Peter clambered into a bumper car—and found $4 on the seat. With no obvious owner in sight, he turned the money in to the ride operator—only to be hooted down by his cousins, who speculated on how the operator would spend his windfall.

"Losing" $47 within a week would be a blow to any 9-year-old with millionaire aspirations. But though his shoulders were slumped, I told Peter he could hold his head high because his honesty was unsullied and his pride intact. To make the point, I gave him a $4 reward—and his shoulders snapped squarely back into place.

I consider that one of our family's success stories. Another is our $50 sneaker rule. I won't pay more than $50 for a pair of sneakers—even John's size 11s. If the kids want something more expensive, they make up the difference.

As a result, they have rarely paid more than $70 or $80 for a pair of shoes—not cheap, granted, but not extravagant by today's standards. And they don't turn up their noses at buying last year's styles on sale.

To avoid the grocery-store gimmies when my children were preschoolers, I told them they could choose one treat, and one treat only, on our shopping expeditions. I have never had to deal with a tantrum in the store, and the kids still play by the rules.

Getting Organized

On the other hand, one of my most glaring failures was my total inability to remember to give my kids their weekly allowance on time. I always ended up handing over two or three weeks worth at once, which was a pain in the neck for us to keep track of. Also, the kids would go several years without getting a raise. When John headed off to high school, with all the new expenses that entails, it seemed an appropriate time to rethink our system.

After considering the alternatives, I decided to go with a kit called ParentBanc. The kit gives children their own checkbook in which they credit deposits (allowance, gifts, earnings) and then write checks when they want to make withdrawals (payable by mom or dad). It's up to the kids to keep the check register up to date.

I paid $7.99 each for the kits in Toys "R" Us; you can buy a slightly fancier version (with a more substantial checkbook cover and a Velcro closure) for $14.95 by ordering direct (800-471-3000). Extra checks (personalized in the child's name) cost $6.95 for four pads (100 checks). Of course, you could save money by creating a similar system on your own with a ledger or leftover checks.

I liked the idea behind ParentBanc because it relieved us of having to remember to fork over money each week. Because our children were a little older when we started the system (15, 13 and 9), we felt we could get away with crediting an allowance monthly, rather than weekly, and we wanted the children to learn how to write a check and balance a checkbook. ParentBanc suggests depositing all the child's money, including gifts and earnings, in the account, but we decided to limit the account to allowance only.

Once we decided on a system, we had to negotiate how much each child would get and what their financial responsibilities would be. We had already decided the kids were due for a raise. But how big?

As a starting point, we used average allowances as reported by the Nickelodeon/Yankelovich Youth Monitor survey. At the time, the average for 14- and 15-year-olds was roughly $9 per week, and we thought that made sense for John.

But Claire balked at the $7 figure for kids her age. Since there's only a two-year age difference between her and her big brother, they have always gotten the same allowance and had similar expenses. We compromised on $8.

The average for 9-year-olds was about $4 a week. Peter immediately protested that he was making less than half as much as his older brother, and wanted to know if he would have to pay for less than half as much stuff. We compromised on $4.50.

With this significant increase in their income came a significant increase in their financial responsibilities. I spent several days writing down a list of expenses appropriate for kids their age: for example, movie tickets (and popcorn), rounds of miniature golf, after-school snacks, and extra caps and goggles during the swim season (they belong to a swim team). The older two would have to buy birthday gifts for their friends, as well as tickets to school football games and dances. If they ran short on cash they could always earn additional money by doing extra chores.

I didn't require that they give a certain percentage to charity, but I strongly recommended that they contribute to church every Sunday. If they have money left in their account at the end of the month, I agreed to pay one-half per cent interest, twice as much as they'd get in the bank.

DEAR DR. TIGHTWAD

Q. Every week I take my daughter out for lunch at a restaurant. I limit how much she can spend, but sometimes I worry that I'm spoiling her.

A. Dr. T has a confession to make: When my three children were in the same school, I took them out to lunch, too. We went to a fast-food place and the tab usually came to about $13 ($10 if we went to Taco Bell). And if anyone was spoiled, I was.

We took our time eating and caught up on the week's news. When my eldest went off to high school, he left our group and we missed him. His presence was worth more than the $3.49 I customarily spent on his Extra Value Meal.

Treating your kids is part of the fun of being a parent. As long as your daughter doesn't expect to feast on filet mignon, don't feel guilty. Enjoy your time together, and *bon appetit*.

What We Wrought

It only took a month or so for our new system to yield results—though not necessarily the ones we had expected. Our kids turned amazingly, incredibly, cheap. Perhaps because they could see their account balances shrinking before their very eyes, they became reluctant to spend money.

They used to beg to go 7-Eleven after school for a soft drink; now that the drinks were on their dime, they decided they weren't so thirsty. Movies on Friday night? There just didn't seem to be anything they wanted to see.

All of the children had money left at the end of the month, so I credited the promised one-half per cent interest. The eight cents my older son earned seemed paltry even to me. But I wasn't ready to raise the rate just yet.

John spent more than half of his $36 allowance, an amount that seemed in line with his expenses as a high school freshman. Claire spent a smaller percentage of her money, but ended up buying more holiday gifts for friends, so it evened out.

And Peter, usually the first to part with his cash, carefully parceled out his birthday money so that he could put off tapping his account.

Six months into the system, John had figured out how to use it to his advantage. Even when he needs cash at the end of a month, he holds off on writing a check until after the interest has been credited.

After depleting her account buying holiday gifts, Claire slowly built it back up again by taking on a few babysitting gigs and carefully managing her cash. She hates to spend money (both hers and mine) on herself, and is willing to wait patiently till her birthday or Christmas to get something she wants.

Peter, meanwhile, needed help with both writing checks and balancing the account. If he weren't a typical younger sibling, always wanting to imitate his older brother and sister, I probably would have kept him on a weekly cash allowance (which he admits he'd prefer).

Two years later, our system is still working. The kids' friends sometimes think it's a little weird when our kids whip out their checkbooks to get cash before heading out to the movies or the music store, but our children never complain when they dutifully make the subtractions in their check registers. I finally caved in and upped the interest rate to a whopping 5% a month on their savings so they could see some measurable results. I've asked the kids to give me a little notice before they write a check so I can have cash on hand, and I try to keep small bills—ones, fives and tens—in my wallet.

As for my own faulty memory—I still forget to credit the kids' allowance on the first of the month. They tease me, but my memory lapses aren't as big a bone of contention because the kids usually don't run out of money. I can always consult the check register to see when I last paid them—and John has taken on the task of catching up the bookkeeping when I fall into arrears.

New Challenges

My biggest challenge now is that the children are forever putting me on the spot to make spur-of-the moment decisions about who should pay for what—and how much.

For example, now that John has his driver's license, should he pay for part of the $1,600 a year he has added to our insurance bill?

Does it qualify as a "family movie night"—with admissions paid by Mom and Dad—if Mom goes but not Dad?

Should we pay for John to go on an optional trip with his high school swim team over winter break?

Some decisions are easy. That trip, for instance, was out of the question; we told John he'd have to pay for all or part of any extracurricular travel (the looser the connection with academics, the more he'd pay). It was decided that both parental units would have to be present for an official family movie night (but I treated when I took my two teenagers to see *Shakespeare in Love* because it was my idea).

The jury is still out on car insurance because John doesn't have a paying job, although he does pay for gas out of his allowance and takes turns driving in the family car pool.

I always advise parents to take stock of their children, no matter what their ages, and picture them going off to college and managing a semester's worth of money on their own. Despite our rough spots and false starts, I'm confident my own kids wouldn't bounce checks or overdose on credit. And in my book, that is a pretty good definition of a money-smart kid.

By the way, John sent those thank-you notes on February 8.

A Game Plan for Parents

So what does all this mean for you? It means you should take heart. Even in this age of consuming passion you can still teach your kids to be savvy shoppers, super savers and cautious users of credit. You just need to find a successful strategy, and the time to use it.

Of course, what works for you won't necessarily work for your neighbor. Your family values and financial circumstances, as well as the personality traits of your children, may be quite different. But there is a common theme in how you should teach your kids about money: Be candid, be consistent and use your own good common sense.

Beyond those general guidelines, this book can help you fill in the particulars. Within it you'll find suggested solutions to the problems that plague parents: how to cure a case of the gimmies, set up a workable allowance plan, cultivate the savings habit. And you will see how you can do it with a minimum of time and effort—for example, by turning everyday encounters with cash machines into mini lessons on money management.

You'll also find guidance on how to help your kids cope with the economy at large by holding down a job or starting a business of their own. You'll hear from the people who study kids and money, as well as the real experts out there in the trenches—parents and kids themselves. You'll get answers to financial questions of interest to kids—when they must pay taxes, how to set up an investment account, how babysitting money can be turned into a retirement fund. As frazzled parents, you're likely to feel overwhelmed by the task of turning your children into financial whiz kids. But the job is a lot more manageable if you forget about raising a future Peter Lynch, Sam Walton or Bill Gates. Instead, focus on your top priority, whether it's encouraging your kids to give to charity or standing firm on not buying what everyone else has. You're the parent; that's your job. You're in charge, and if you set the tone in even one area, it will echo throughout your child's life.

That's often difficult to remember nowadays, when changing mores and increasing affluence undermine parents' confidence and weaken their will power. It's easier to buy kids the stuff they want—and buy into the consumer culture as well.

I don't pretend to have all the answers. The advice dispensed here can't create more money in households where there's simply not enough. The prescribed strategies won't work unless parents are willing to talk with each other and with their children. And some problems are beyond the scope of this book. If you suspect that a child is using his allowance to buy drugs, for example, how much of an allowance to give is the least of your worries. Cut off all funds and get professional help.

But after fielding hundreds of questions from parents in my "Dr. Tightwad" columns, and speaking to dozens of parent groups, I know what's on parents' minds when it comes to teaching kids financial values. And I've collected dozens of valuable strategies that have worked successfully for families (even mine!). In this book, my aim is to offer reasonable solutions in a readable form that real people will find useful—and even entertaining.

Why You Need a Snappy Comeback

Sprinkled throughout each chapter in this book you'll find a selection of questions from parents. But I've also learned over the years that kids have questions, too. In fact, when it comes to money, kids ask the darnedest things. Parents on the receiving end find their children's queries:

- **Exasperating:** "Mom, can I have that?"
- **Amusing:** "How much will I get from the tooth fairy?"
- **Puzzling:** "Why is a nickel bigger than a dime?"
- **Awkward:** "How much money do you make?"
- **Embarrassing:** "How come you two are always fighting about money?"

It's from family discussions about subjects like these that children will learn their most lasting lessons about the value—and the values—of money.

Unfortunately, kids and their questions can't be scripted. On the contrary, you can count on them catching you off guard, when you're least prepared to answer. Ill at ease or in a hurry, we've all given our kids the bum's rush at one time or another, with an abbreviated, even abrupt, response—usually along the lines of "Yes," "No," or "Maybe."

Yes, No, Maybe

In the "yes" group are parents who take the path of least resistance—or maybe they just like to spend money. "Since she's been born, I've hardly bought myself anything. I'd rather spend on her," one parent told Forbes magazine in an article titled "Babies As Dolls," about the booming market for infant clothing and equipment. Said another parent, "My kids have tons of stuff, but if they want something I just don't know how to say no." And these kids are barely old enough to ask a question. Imagine the scene when they really turn up the heat at age 8 or 13—or 21 or 35.

At the other extreme are parents who respond with a knee-jerk "no" that's commendable but ineffective. Their strong stand is undermined by a shaky foundation because they don't bother to explain why they're denying whatever it is their kids want.

In the vast middle—and we've all been there—are the wafflers, who, when put on the spot, respond with a resounding "maybe" in any of its forms: "We'll see." "I don't know." "Go ask your mother/father." "Do you think I'm made of money?" For lack of a great comeback, we take refuge in the flip response, the old cliché, the evasive answer—anything to avoid the question. And we miss a golden opportunity to teach a mini-lesson in money values. Besides, kids are people, too, and they deserve to have their questions taken seriously and answered thoughtfully.

So at the end of many chapters you'll find questions that, in one form or another, you're bound to hear sometime. For each question, I'll give you a response that will get you out of a jam, fill a void, smooth over an awkward moment, satisfy your children's curiosity and leave them with something to think about so they're less likely to bring up the subject again.

A Kid's-Eye View of Money

With all the other demands on your time, teaching your kids about money has all the allure of cleaning out the basement: You know you should do it, but you just never get around to it.

And time isn't the only factor. Money is one of the last great taboos; nowadays, parents may find it easier to talk to their kids about sex and drugs than to tell them how much money they make. To complicate things even further, money matters can't always be reduced to a "common cents" discussion. Within a family, parents can wield money as a weapon, flaunt it as a symbol of power or use it as a stand-in for love. And looking at how you manage money can reveal things about your own personality that you'd rather not face. If you're an unreformed shopaholic, for example, you may feel understandably ambivalent about urging your teens to stay within a clothing budget. And so, like the basement, you leave it for another day.

Even if you're willing to take on the task, you face the same problems as you do when trying to discuss sex: How much do your kids already know? Not nearly as much as they should, according to a slew of studies that measure the financial savvy of young people. In a test of high school seniors conducted by the Jump$tart Coalition for Personal Financial Literacy (a group of government, educational and financial organizations led by the Federal Reserve Board), the average score was 57%—less than a passing grade.

A snapshot of teen finances in two other reports—the Youth & Money Survey by the American Savings

Education Council (ASEC), which interviewed students ages 16 to 22, and a Merrill Lynch poll of teens between the ages of 12 and 17—showed that while teenagers do save money, they need to learn more about how to invest for the long term (and how to stay out of debt). Here's a closer look at those findings:

In the ASEC survey, 49% of those interviewed said they save some money whenever they receive an allowance or get paid; in the Merrill Lynch study, 56% said they usually save half and spend half of their money. That's good news, but I'm a little concerned about the 18% of kids in the Merrill survey (up from 12% in a previous study) who confess to spending most of their money as soon as they get it.

Although lots of teens have jobs, a whopping 86% of those in the Merrill survey get their money as handouts from parents when they need it. Unfortunately, only a minority get a regular allowance, which I think is a far better way for both parents and kids to keep track of all that cash.

Relatively few kids say they stick to a budget or written spending plan—23% in the ASEC survey, 14% in the Merrill Lynch poll. Given their age, that's not surprising—and probably not much worse than their parents' record.

Wall Street is still foreign turf. In the ASEC survey, only students earning $5,000 or more per year were likely to invest in stocks, mutual funds, or even bank certificates of deposit. In the Merrill poll, 11% of teens said they own stock. Most significant to me is that nearly half of those questioned by Merrill Lynch said they're "totally unfamiliar" with investing in the stock market.

Most kids in the Merrill study reported having household discussions about money, yet 68% said they never talk about using credit cards responsibly. That could reflect the younger age of Merrill respondents, but it could also explain ASEC's finding that 9% of all students—representing 28% of students with credit cards—roll over credit card debt each month.

Dr. Tightwad Takes a Field Trip

To get a kid's-eye view of personal finance, I did some field research of my own with a group of middle-school students. When my daughter was in seventh grade, I accepted the invitation of teacher Glen Mayers to spend a morning interviewing small groups of students in her class at St. Camillus School, in Silver Spring, Md.

We talked about how the kids spend money, and how they save; what they want to be when they grow up, and how much they think they'll earn; which commercials they like, and whether they actually buy the products.

My sample wasn't scientifically selected, but it did represent an ethnically and economically diverse group of kids in a major urban area. And early teens have certain advantages as subjects: They're old enough to know something about money, but not so old that they think they know everything.

On most of the topics we chatted about (the stock market being the notable exception), the children had a good grasp of basic money-management skills—up to a point. For example, they knew enough to be wary of credit cards but were a little fuzzy about what evil fate would befall them if they didn't pay their bills in full.

The good news for parents and educators is that it wouldn't take much to fill the gaps in kids' knowledge. For example, the children knew what interest was in connection with a savings account but had never heard of dividends paid to stockholders, so a few simple definitions would help. Using examples to illustrate how fast savings will grow or how long it will take to pay off debt will hold their interest longer than a lecture on the evils of borrowing and the virtues of thrift. Many kids admitted to taking buying cues from their peers, but were open to a discussion on how to resist peer pressure.

Small lessons can yield a big payoff when it comes to making children financially literate and fostering a healthy attitude toward money.

But let's listen to the kids (with asides from me).

ON SPENDING. Thirty expectant faces, each with a name attached: Bridget, Dave, Anthony. Thirty pairs of shoes, many with a name attached: Pippen, Jordan, Penny (as in Hardaway).

Normally these students wear uniforms (hurrah!) and regulation black shoes to school. But on this day they've been given special permission to come in their civvies because they're going to talk with a visitor about their spending habits.

And if there's anything kids like to spend money on, it's clothes—often expensive articles of clothing bearing names other than their own. Bridget said her glittery silver Pippens cost $95, "but if they were a bigger size they'd probably be $120."

The kids were blunt about what clinches the sale. "Most people consider you cool if you wear clothes like Tommy Hilfiger or Nautica," said Safiya. Added Abdul, "I just buy what everybody else wears."

But it's encouraging to know that kids don't always feel obliged to go along with the crowd: "What you wear doesn't determine who you are," insisted Mia.

So don't hesitate to sell your children on daring to be different. They'll be willing to listen (and buy cheaper clothes as a result). "I don't think you should spend $17 on a red shirt that says 'Tommy' on it when you can get a red shirt for $4 or $5," said Kendra.

If kids must look like everyone else, at least once in a while, there are less expensive ways to do it. "You can buy a 'Tommy' sweater for $75 or a fake 'Tommy' for $10, and nobody can tell the difference if you cut out the tag," advised Ashley.

A sure way to help kids kick the brand-name habit is to make them kick in for their clothes. Would Bridget have bought a pair of $95 shoes if she had had to spend her own money? "No (giggle)."

ON MARKETING. When it came to spending money, the kids showed healthy signs of growing into skeptical consumers, wary of being talked into buying things they didn't want or need.

Take commercials, for example. All of the children had a favorite. One popular choice was a Sprite ad in which a cartoon sun leaps from a Brand X drink container and runs amok through the house, terrorizing a family. Sprite to the rescue.

The commercial sent the kids into gales of laughter, but did it persuade them to buy Sprite? Not necessarily. "I buy Sprite because I like it," said Mia. "I like the commercial because it's funny."

A couple of children did admit to having been victims of marketing ploys—but sometimes they were willing victims. For instance, John let himself be talked into paying 50 cents extra for a super-large drink at the movies, only to find that "it wouldn't even fit in the drink holder."

So was it a bad deal, especially because he could have gotten free refills on a smaller drink? Maybe not, said John. "You'd have to leave the movie to get the refill, and you'd probably miss one of the good parts."

And Claire thought that an extra 50 cents is a small price to pay: "You can never have too much soda at the movies," she reasoned.

ON CREDIT CARDS. None of the kids had actually used a credit card, and they disagreed about whether they'd want to. Eric, for one, was reluctant: "I like to spend, so I'd probably max it out." Anna, on the other hand, was willing to take a chance because "I think I'm pretty good with money."

While the kids had a general grasp of the perils of credit, they weren't quite clear on the fine points—for example, what happens if you don't pay your bill in full. "You have to take stuff back," said Eric. "They take your limit down a little," said Chris. "The repo man comes," said Abdul.

Only one of the children knew that you're charged interest on any unpaid balance, and none knew what that interest rate might be. The consensus guess: 10% to 15%.

The next time your kids overhear you complaining

about the size of your credit card bill, be specific about the consequences of carrying a balance. A little numbers game would help make your point.

Let's say your son spent $300 on designer clothes, and when the bill came he made the minimum required payment of $11 on a card with an annual percentage rate of 21%—not an uncommon rate for a first-time cardholder. At that rate, it would take 38 months to pay for the clothes—by which time the wardrobe would be history.

To have fun with their own numbers, kids can check out the financial calculators at www.kiplinger.com (click on "Calculators").

ON BANKS. Nearly all the kids had savings accounts, but they didn't always know what their balances were or how much interest they were being paid—or that banks would also charge interest (at a higher rate) if you took out a loan. And the only CDs they'd ever heard of are the ones that play music or computer games.

But the kids could explain how a checking account works and, at least in theory, knew that you couldn't keep writing checks just because you had them in your checkbook. "You can't spend more money than you have in your checking account," said Allison, "and every time you write a check, you subtract it."

When it comes to money, never assume that children will pick up even the most basic facts on their own. It's up to you to tell them exactly how much interest banks pay on a savings account, how much they charge for a loan, and how much you'll pay if you bounce a check. As kids get older, knowing that a bank CD pays twice as much as a regular savings account should be music to their ears.

ON THE STOCK MARKET. When I asked the kids what it means to own a share of stock, few would hazard a guess. Andrea had the right idea, if an exaggerated order of magnitude: "If you buy a share of stock in McDonald's, you say to the company, 'If you earn a million dollars, I want to get at least one-third of that, or one-half.' " No one could define the word dividend.

You wouldn't expect most kids this age to know much about the stock market—not because it's too complicated for them to understand, but because adults think it's too complicated and don't bother to discuss it. I've found that kids who do follow the market are an enthusiastic minority, often inheriting their interest from parents and grandparents.

If you own stocks, don't sell your children (or grandchildren) short. Encourage them to pick a company or two and follow the stock price in the newspaper or online. Better yet, buy them shares of their own.

ON JOBS. Several of the children were already in the labor force, and a couple were entrepreneurs (a word which Eddie can even define). Stephen pet-sits when his neighbors go on vacation but is timid about setting a price for his services. "They just offer me money," he said.

If they get a part-time job when they're older, the kids guesstimated that they would earn anywhere from $3 to $8 an hour, but they weren't sure about taxes. "I don't think children would have to pay taxes like adults because adults have to take on more responsibilities," said Andrea. (Working-age kids should know that the minimum wage is $5.15 an hour but that if they work ten hours, they won't actually take home $51.50. Sorry, Andrea, the IRS doesn't let kids off the hook.)

These children know what they want to be when they grow up: lawyer, pediatrician, engineer. But they were a little shaky on how much they could earn: "$35,000 a case"; "I don't know"; "at least $1,000 a year."

They didn't think it fair that some athletes are paid more than others—"They play in the NBA, they play on the same team, they should all get the same amount of money," said Nick—or that athletes in general are paid more than teachers. But they had a glimmer of understanding about why that is: "Entertainment," said Andrea.

ON RELATIVES. When the kids want something that

they can't afford and their parents won't spring for, they have no qualms about appealing to other family members. Grandparents are considered a particularly soft touch.

"I'm into really baggy pants, but my dad doesn't like them because he says I look like a thug, even though I don't mean to," said Eric. "So I ask my grandparents, and they'll go out and buy them because grandparents spoil you to death."

Grandma, you've been warned.

Teaching Financial Literacy

With financial literacy becoming an increasingly hot topic, the Jump$tart Coalition has set a goal of financial competency for high school graduates by 2007. The coalition has even developed teaching guidelines for personal-finance topics in grades K-12, along with a clearinghouse for teaching materials (888-453-3822; www.jumpstartcoalition.org).

While any help from the classroom is a bonus, all the studies about kids and money show that young people overwhelmingly depend on their parents as their prime source of financial information. Financial facts kids learn in school need to go hand-in-hand with a healthy attitude and open communication about financial matters at home. That's my prescription for financial literacy.

The Adman Cometh

ow you have a rough idea what your kids know—or think they know—about money. And you're willing to take on the task of filling in the gaps in their knowledge, because you know that what you don't teach them, their peers—and the media—will. And what an education it will be: that clothes make the woman and sneakers the man, that video games and cable TV are their birthright, that credit cards will satisfy every need and gratify every wish. They will learn, in short, that money really *does* grow on trees. So let's take a look at their financial reality—their income, their spending patterns, and the influence they have on how you spend your money.

Money Really Does Grow on Trees

You can't blame kids for buying into that myth when they're buying so much else these days. Studies done by James McNeal, a faculty member at Texas A & M, show that kids between the ages of 4 and 12 have annual income of more than $27 billion, of which they spend around $23 billion. Parents are totally in charge of their kids' purchases only up to about age 3; after that, children are given choices—what kind of beverages to drink, ice cream to eat, toys to play with. At around age 2, many kids begin asking for things on their own, either because they've seen them in the store or on TV. From that point on, children are a recognized consumer force. By age 3½ kids are selecting the things they want and watching their parents buy them (typically cereal, toys and snacks, in that order); by 5½ the kids are making the purchases (toys, snacks and gifts for others) and the parents are watching. By age 8 children make independent (unassisted) purchases while shopping with their parents.

For the most part, kids are doing all this consuming with their parents' blessing. Children are getting more money at a younger age than they did in the past, and letting them make purchase decisions is seen as a way of teaching them to be self-reliant. That's also a big help to frazzled moms and dads, many of whom are single parents or part of a dual-earner household. So it's not surprising that in addition to the money children spend directly, they have an enormous impact on what their parents buy. It's been estimated that children between the ages of 4 and 12 *directly* influence adult purchases to the tune of more than $187 billion a year in dozens of different product categories—everything from food to clothing to sports and recreation equipment.

The more expensive the purchase, and the more adult in nature, the less their influence. But nowadays kids even have a say when it comes to buying cars. I can attest to that. Knowing my bias against trendy sport utility vehicles, my children didn't even try to talk their father and me into an SUV when we bought the latest family car. But they didn't hesitate to voice their preferences for our new minivan: quad bucket seats and a CD player, preferably with a juiced-up sound system. When I later sat in on a panel discussion with mothers and their children about how the kids influence their parents' purchases, I could sympathize with the mom who said she

---

ZILLIONS FOR KIDS

You can help your kids develop smart consumer habits early with a subscription to *Zillions: Consumer Reports for Kids*. A single issue of this lively magazine, published by *Consumer Reports*, offered comparison-test results for hamburgers, milkshakes and bubblegum; gave advice on surviving a haircut and getting respect from store clerks; and featured an exposé of sneakers. *Zillions* should appeal to the late grade school and junior high crowd (six issues per year, $16; Subscription Dept., P.O. Box 54861, Boulder, CO 80322; 800-388-5626). You'll find other magazines listed in the box on pages 80-81.

and her husband had sold their minivan after just two years because it didn't have two-zone air conditioning and "the kids were miserable."

Teenagers are spending close to $85 a week of their own and their parents' money, according to Teenage Research Unlimited in Northbrook, Ill.; that's $141 billion coming out of the pockets of 12- to 19-year-olds. Boys spend $59 of their own money and $25 in family money; for girls, the figures are $53 and $30. As they have for generations, teens arc buying clothes, cosmetics, snack foods and movie tickets. What's different today is that they're spending more on electronic gear and other big-ticket items. In addition, more than half of the girls and more than a third of the boys do some grocery shopping every week to help out those frazzled moms and dads.

An Advertiser's Dream

That kind of buying power is simply too tantalizing for advertisers to ignore, and increasingly, they're bypassing parents and making their pitch directly to children. Retailers of all kinds are targeting them directly year-round, not just at the holidays or back-to-school time. In particular, they have set their sights on Generation Y, today's 4- to 21-year-olds who will eventually replace the Baby Boomers as the financial and cultural powerhouse generation.

In an effort to capture the brand loyalty of budding households, retailers are stretching the definition of school supplies to pitch sofas, chairs and other housewares to college kids. At the younger end, some clothing chains are growing as fast as their prime customers—girls age 7 to 14.

"Kids enjoy new things and they aren't set in their ways, so they're an ideal target," said Irma Zandl, who heads The Zandl Group, a New York City research firm that studies the youth market. If sneakers had been sold as an adult product, according to Zandl, they never would have become a multi-billion-dollar business.

Over the years, the list of products that owed their success to kids has been long and varied: string cheese and individually wrapped cheese slices; fruit snacks; Old Navy clothing stores; Sony PlayStation. After Jolly Rancher candy repositioned itself to appeal to the "tweens" market (kids around ages 9 to 12), it became a hit with an age group that craved its super-fruity flavor. Kids wield such clout that 1- to 3-year-olds are now a market segment. "It's staggering to see how brand-aware 2-year-olds are," said Paul Kurnit, president of the advertising agency Griffin Bacal. "The marketer who gets there first and best gets there to stay."

While adults might be health- or price-conscious, that kind of appeal won't work with kids. Advertisers have to be careful not to offend parents, who are still, after all, the biggest spenders in the house and the ones who ultimately make most purchase decisions. But advertisers' main goal is to hit kids where they live: sports, music, an overwhelming desire to be cool and fit in. And they're getting through.

HOW *NOT* TO TEACH YOUR KIDS FINANCIAL VALUES

1. Ignore the whole subject. Money should be neither coveted nor feared, but treated as a useful tool.

2. Indulge your kids. Love does not equal stuff.

3. Send mixed messages. Don't deliver a lecture on the wastefulness of a new video-game system and then treat yourself to a new CD player.

4. Be inconsistent. If you've made it a rule not to lend your kids money, don't waffle the first time they ask.

5. Quit before you start. Children will accept any system of managing money as long as you set one up.

6. Fling platitudes. Of course your kids don't understand the value of a dollar (unless you teach them).

7. Fail to listen. If your kids ask questions about money, give them an answer, not a brush-off.

8. Relive your childhood. Be realistic about how far a dollar will stretch nowadays.

9. Overload your kids with information. Don't tell them how much you make until they're old enough not to blab it around the neighborhood.

10. Gripe too much about your job. You'll turn your kids into cynics about the world of work.

Nike athletic shoes offer another classic example of marketing to teens, according to Zandl. Teenage boys are preoccupied with performance; when asked who they'd like to meet, they tend to cite people who are outstanding in their fields. So Nike used celebrity endorsers like Michael Jordan and stuck with them for years, to the extent that the company "totally meshed itself and the celebrity in the eyes of young consumers," said Zandl.

The Difference Between the Sexes

One truism about advertising to kids: Sexism sells. The Zandl Group regularly conducts nationwide surveys of young people between the ages of 8 and 24 on products that they buy. In reading the anonymous responses, "you'd never for a minute confuse male and female," said Zandl.

Girls liked water and iced tea; boys liked root beer and Mountain Dew. Girls watched *Dawson's Creek* and *Friends*, boys watched *The Simpsons* and professional wrestling. Boys used no-nonsense toiletries like Pert Plus and Head & Shoulders, girls preferred beauty brands like Clairol Herbal Essence and Pantene. Asked to name their favorite supermarket department, girls chose health and beauty aids, boys chose frozen foods.

In a recent study by the Kaplan Educational Center, a national test-prepping company, high school girls picked *Seventeen* as their favorite magazine, while boys chose *Sports Illustrated*. If they had to choose, most boys said they'd rather be rich than smart, followed by athletic. Girls, on the other hand, chose to be smart, wealthy and pretty. So it's little wonder that boys respond to ads that are sports-oriented and aggressive; girls respond to ads that are, well, cute. One of their favorites was a carpet commercial featuring a baby zooming around in a walker. With girls, supermodels have always had more influence than athletes, but perhaps that will change with the success of the U.S. Women's soccer team.

How Kids Trick Their Parents

If kids are tempted to consume conspicuously, indulging their wants as never before, advertising isn't totally to blame. Advertisers may be pulling children but parents are pushing them simply by making so much money available and giving them so much leeway to spend it.

At a Consumer Kids marketing conference, the panel discussion with mothers and their children that I mentioned earlier was a highlight for those in the audience, who were obviously interested in how to get the attention of the kids for their products, yet still get past Mom, who remains the gatekeeper. As a parent and as an adviser to parents on how to resist sales pressure from their kids, my own loyalties were divided. When, for example, one woman complained that her son will eat only one kind of sandwich—Louis Rich plain oven-roasted turkey on white bread—and confessed that she no longer tries anything else, as a parent I had to agree it would be pointless to waste money on food that wouldn't be eaten.

But when a young man confided that his strategy for getting the things he wants is to "trick" his parents by promising to pay them back and then hoping they forget about the debt, I wanted to stand up and shout, "That's why you should never advance your kids money to buy something—or if you do, at least hang on to the item until they come across with the cash."

The kids candidly revealed other tricks: "I beg," said one forthright youngster. "I tell her I'm not going to move till I get it," said another. "I go to my Daddy," confessed a third.

And the moms admitted that those tactics often work: "Older kids have a lot more influence because they're louder and in my face more," said one. "I can spend twice as much money because of what she sees on TV," said another. "I've lost control," admitted a third.

The parents were surprisingly willing to give their kids a say in spending decisions that ranged from vacations to home decor ("I'm glad my daughter is out of her silver phase," said one mom.) But they weren't pushovers, and they had their own strategies for nego-tiating with their kids: "When we disagree about a pur-chase, we have a cooling-off period and wait for a day." "I give them choices that I can live with." "I won't buy Lunchables."

Marketers attending the conference were as fasci-nated as I was by the interaction between generations as they peppered the panel with questions. "How do you decide which restaurants to eat at?" someone asked. "Mom makes us agree on one," answered one kid. "We rotate around," offered another. But Paul Kurnit, of ad agency Griffin Bacal, who was chairman of the conference, stressed that marketers "have to take a responsible view of nurturing and protecting kids," even while selling to them.

TEN FINANCIAL MOVES YOU MUST MAKE FOR YOUR KIDS

I. Get your child a social security number. Even infants must have social security numbers to be claimed as dependents on your tax return.

2. Make a will and name a guardian. Without a will, children face the possibility of having a court-appointed guardian and court supervision of their property.

3. Buy enough insurance. Parents of young children need life insurance equal to between five and ten times their annual income.

4. Start saving for college. Don't be intimi-dated by the big bucks you'll need years from now. Focus instead on the small amount it takes to get started.

5. Talk about money, part I. If you never do anything else to teach your children about money, treat it as a natural part of everyday life. It can't buy happiness but it can create choices.

6. Revise your will and other beneficiary arrangements. Revise your will every five years or so, and after certain life events: the birth of a child, divorce, remarriage or a move to a new state.

7. Talk about money, part II. Don't sud-denly clam up about money when your kids leave home. Now's the time to share with them provisions of your will, or plans for suc-cession in a family business.

8. Save for your own retirement. Financ-ing an independent retirement for yourself is one of the greatest gifts you can give your kids.

9. Give some money to your children. Assuming you intend to pass along assets even-tually, you might want to do it during your life-time to help your children buy a home or to realize estate-tax benefits for yourself.

10. Spend some money on yourself. After all you've done for your children during your lifetime, don't assume you have to enrich them even more after you're gone. With the help of this book, they should be able to make it on their own.

Most heartening to me, however, were the results of an online survey by Griffin Bacal of what's on the minds of children ages 10 to 14. They were interested in making and saving money, but even as the millennium approaches they expressed old-fashioned concerns about family issues, such as wanting to get along better with their siblings and worrying about the health of their grandparents. And Mom and Dad are still bigger heroes than Michael Jordan, Kurnit said.

After the parent-child panel, I asked the no-Lunchables lady how she makes her rule stick. "We just don't buy them," she said. And are her kids willing to go along with that? "If you put your foot down, they are. You just can't do it all the time. You have to pick your battles." That's worth shouting about.

Are Kids Savvy Shoppers?

Children nowadays may be sophisticated consumers, but they themselves confess to sometimes being naive and even gullible shoppers. In *Zillions*, the consumer magazine for children, a group of kids recite their worst "buying blunders": Maggie plunked down $20 for a board game that looked exciting in TV ads but turned out to be boring; Jonathan handed over big bucks for sneakers that didn't help him improve his basketball game; Becky bought a shirt at one store and later saw it at another store for half the price; Theresa bought a cheap squirt gun that broke the first time she used it.

But thanks to the efforts of the Jump$tart Coalition and lots of others in the financial-literacy movement, the number of school-based and independent programs to teach kids about money is growing by leaps and bounds. Look around the country and you'll see that where kids are given the incentive and opportunity to learn, they're catching on quickly:

At Young Americans Bank in Denver, where all the customers are under age 22 and come from all 50 states, the average loan customer is 17 years old and has borrowed an average of $2,000 to buy such things as cars or musical instruments. Kids may not understand the term "annual percentage rate," but somewhere along the line they've picked up the notion that it's a good idea to repay a loan. (For more on Young Americans Bank, see Chapter 9.)

In a class on economics, fourth graders in Wilmington, Del., rattle off terms like "market clearing price," "factors of production" and "opportunity cost" as they discuss marketing strategies for the new products they have cooked up: the "super-duper spaghetti scooper" and other gizmos for making it easier to eat spaghetti (see Chapter 11).

In a discussion about money with a third-grade class in Maryland, kids want to talk about everything from collectibles to currency exchange rates to the Great Depression.

Despite their reputation as yuppie puppies, schoolchildren around the country socked away more than $125 million in 18 years as part of Save for America, a reincarnation of the old school saving program (see Chapter 9).

Each year, teams of high school students come to the Federal Reserve Board in Washington, D.C., and argue their case for which direction the Federal Reserve

DEAR DR. TIGHTWAD

Q. To keep my 7-year-old daughter from spending all her money every time she goes into a store, I gave her some advice that works for me. I told her that whenever she's deciding whether to buy something, she should say, "If in doubt, don't buy." Now when she goes to a store and looks at all the items she "really wants," she often walks out without buying anything. At first she was kind of disappointed, but then I pointed out that when she really wanted something, she'd have more money and no doubts.

A. There's no doubt parents and kids can learn a lot from your experience.

First, you had a sound money-management tip. Second, you took the trouble to communicate it to your daughter. Third, she listened to you. Fourth, it worked. Fifth, you followed up, so the point will probably stick. Sixth, it didn't take a lot of time.

Lots of similarly frustrated parents would have lectured, yelled or thrown up their hands and watched their kids fritter away their money. You've shown there are simple yet effective alternatives.

Board should take in setting monetary policy. Winners of the Fed Challenge receive thousands of dollars in scholarship money, courtesy of Citibank.

James McNeal, who has done considerable research on the kids' market, finds that most college kids would be hard-pressed to figure out the unit price of a six-pack of beer. But his observation is that, overall, children "manage to spend and understand money and the marketplace system reasonably well." Even the kids in the *Zillions* article learned some valuable lessons: Maggie tries out a new board game at a friend's house before springing for it herself, Theresa took back her broken water pistol and got a refund, Becky looks around for bargains instead of buying something at the first place she stops and Jonathan is practicing harder to improve his game.

A Different Kind of "Peter Principle"

My own optimism about kids' ability to catch on is based on the counsel of my most trusted financial adviser: my son Peter. Mind you, he's not the most frugal child. But you won't find a more reliable guide to what's on a kid's mind when it comes to money.

When I need a child to test a financial game, review a book, or watch a videotape, I seek Peter's advice. His spontaneity is priceless. Once, when he was trying to decide which pair of sunglasses to buy, he looked at me and wailed, "You write books about this. Tell me what to do."

He's also a free spender, so when his eyes widen I get a clear view of which ads and products capture a kid's fancy. Sitting on my lap one lazy summer Sunday, he suddenly blurted out that when he makes his first million dollars he couldn't possibly spend it all in one day. Tops on his wish list was a $300 baseball bat (to help him hit higher and farther), but he would also buy "a lot of stock in things that have gone down, because they have to go up again."

The other day Peter voluntarily picked up one of the kids-and-money videos I periodically review and watched it. Afterward he pronounced it "pretty good," but noted a flaw or two: "They showed 17-year-olds who didn't know that you have to pay bills, or that taxes are taken out of your paycheck. When you're 17 you should know that."

How Does It All Translate to Your Kids?

So, faced with a marketing blitz, what are parents to do? With strength in numbers, sales resistance could be stronger if they were to band together in a kind of PAC—Parents Against Conspicuous Consumption. Unfortunately, being a parent is often a lone-wolf operation.

But moral support is at hand from an unlikely source—children themselves. Surveys indicate that they're not necessarily suckers for every sweet-talking marketing campaign that sashays into the mall.

In the American Express Retail Index, an annual survey of more than 1,300 consumers, 66% of teens questioned said that "there is too much pressure to wear the 'right' clothing." In a study on gender-based marketing, Saatchi & Saatchi's Kid Connection found that boys and girls look up to their parents and use them as role models. "I think Mom has combined work and family very well," said Betsy, 12. "She takes her job seriously, but she always has the time to be with me and my sisters."

Parents, you still have influence. Don't be afraid to use it.

A Word About the Web

The Internet has opened up a whole new world of opportunities for marketers to target children. But even newfangled technology hasn't taken the place of old-fashioned values. Take the case of one teenager I know who was deeply enmeshed in an online game and frustrated by busy signals when he tried to log on and play. He finally got a connection by choosing an alternate phone number in his area code. When his parents got their phone bill a month later, they found an unexplained (to them) charge of more than $200. When they tracked it down, they found that while the phone number for their son's game connection was in their area code, it was a toll call. Their solution: Get their son to work off the bill by doing extra jobs around the house and kidsitting for his younger brothers.

Even more direct are new Web sites that give kids the opportunity to buy stuff online without using a credit card (www.icanbuy.com; www.doughnet.com; www.rocketcash.com). Instead, parents are encouraged to use their own credit cards to set up an account the kids can draw on. Parents can limit the amount spent, and the set-up is billed as a money-management system for kids, who can sometimes use money in their accounts to make deposits in an online bank and contribute to certain charities and causes.

Now, there's nothing wrong with kids spending money online. They do it every day at shopping malls, movie theaters and fast-food restaurants, so why not on the Web? But as a money-management tool, I'd rather have parents start with something more hands-on than clicking a mouse.

When kids make purchases, for example, the transaction is more real if they actually hand over hard cash to a sales clerk—or even to their parents in repayment for a specific item the parent ordered for the child online—instead of simply drawing down a virtual account for which their parents pay the bill. And parents shouldn't begrudge the extra time and effort the personal touch requires. In one newspaper story, a father sang the praises of the online sites because in managing his shopping account his 10-year-old son now had to consider extras such as shipping costs. Before, Dad would ferry his son to the store and pay for whatever video game the boy chose. His son had no concept of sales tax, Dad complained.

But Dad could have accomplished the same result offline simply by making his son pay for the video game—and the sales tax—with his own money.

And while its time has certainly come, retailing on the Web isn't about to replace hanging out at the mall or even shopping by catalog. When my son Peter used the Toys "R" Us Web site to help generate his last Christmas list, he pronounced it "pretty good" because he could click on exactly the department he wanted. But searching took time, and he kept getting bumped offline by other members of our one-line household who wanted to use the phone.

The Sears Wish Book, on the other hand, was independent and portable, so Peter could take his time comparing prices with circulars from Kmart and Best Buy, and fine tune his list in the back seat of the car. But flipping through 300 pages was inefficient. "It should have an index," he concluded.

The Apple Doesn't Fall Far From the Tree

Author Suze Orman has brought personal finance to the masses by milking our psychological hangups about money. Those hangups, Orman insists, have their roots in our "early formative experiences" with money, memories of which are "riddled with self-doubt, unworthiness, insecurity and fear."

Whew! I'm not willing to admit that an adult's feelings of inadequacy can be traced to not getting a raise in her allowance. But if early money experiences don't scar you for life, they do leave their mark. Kim Hutchins, my son's third-grade teacher, has never forgotten that when she was a kid, her father made her account for every penny of her allowance in a ledger (which she still has). She found the exercise so tedious that when she got older, she vowed never to keep such close track of her finances.

With my own kids, I sometimes goof by not following my own advice. I have preached ardently and often that because children will take you literally, parents should never respond to their kids' comments about money with a glib answer that can be misunderstood. Yet when my daughter, Claire, and I were chatting recently about how much she had spent on books for high school, I commented (jokingly, or so I thought) that she was sending us to the poorhouse. Claire blanched. "That's not true, is it?" she asked. When I assured her it wasn't, she responded, "Don't ever say that to a kid." And she's right.

The message to parents is to be careful what you say to—and in front of—your kids when you're discussing money with them, or with your spouse. Kids will take you literally, reacting and reaching conclusions you hadn't bargained for and may not be aware of until years later. Even if you never sit your kids at your knee and lecture them on the birds and bees of finance, they'll get an education just by watching and listening to you.

Do you scold your spouse for spending too much money—and are you chided in return for being too stingy? Within your family, do you talk freely about money or are you secretive? Is money a lightning rod for emotional as well as financial tensions? Parents can wield money as a weapon, as in the case of the higher-paid breadwinner who metes out financial crumbs to other family members to keep everyone in line. They can flaunt it as a symbol of power—as do the Joneses with whom everyone is always trying to keep up. Or they can use it as a stand-in for love by substituting presents for their presence.

Your children's attitude toward money will be shaped by nature—what they inherit from you—and nurture—what the pick up along the way. Despite the heavy influence of their peers, it's likely they'll end up much like you. So have a go at picturing yourself as they see you and tune in to the message you're sending.

Careful, the Kids Are Watching (And Listening)

Parents who grew up during the Great Depression spent a lifetime trying to teach a new generation of children what it was like to have to save coffee grounds. Wealthy families with mixed feelings about their money often overemphasize the virtue of not having any. The self-made man, on the other hand, sometimes insists that his children follow his example. Because circumstances can't be duplicated, those are unrealistic expectations. Yet they can have an effect on you, even if, as in Hutchins's case, it is precisely the opposite of what your parents intended. You're likely to return to your roots eventually, however, even if you feel inclined to stray in between. Although she no longer keeps a written record of her expenses, Hutchins admits that when she got older those early ledgers helped her keep mental track of where her money was going, and she's a smarter money manager as a result.

When I was a kid I didn't get an allowance. Instead, my parents gave me money when I needed it. A sure prescription for creating a spoiled brat? On the contrary. One reason I didn't get an allowance was that we didn't have a lot of money. I didn't have an outside job, but I was responsible for doing much of the housework while my mother worked. Today I'm much more comfortable financially, but I still spend carefully and save a lot. By not giving me an allowance or making me get a paying job, my parents probably broke some rules about teaching me money management (and I admit I could have used more experience handling cash). But it was the atmosphere at home that counted most in shaping my conservative money habits as an adult.

Gender Differences in Managing Money

Whether by nature or nurture, your sex is likely to have an influence on your attitudes toward money. It starts slowly but shows itself early. Among children between the ages of 4 and 12, James McNeal's studies showed, girls save a slightly larger proportion of their income than boys do. McNeal is at a loss to explain the difference except to guess that boys are permitted more freedom in their activities than girls, and therefore they spend more. "Even in Mom-only households, boys seem to be on a longer rope than girls are," said McNeal.

The disparity continues when kids become teenagers. Overall, guys spend more of their own money each week—$59—than do girls, who spend $53.

According to the Bureau of Labor Statistics, girls between the ages of 16 and 19 who work at jobs earn 88.5 cents for every dollar paid to their male counterparts.

On the whole, though, McNeal didn't find significant differences in the consumer behavior of young girls and boys. "There's a kid culture before there's a gender culture or even a national culture," he said. It's a culture that values play above all else, and the more outrageous the plaything the better. Parents might be attracted to toy kitchens or cars—scaled-down versions of adult products—but kids are enamored of slime in any form and characters of indeterminate origin that go by names like Pokemon and Furby.

In adolescence, however, boys and girls show definite—and traditional—preferences in the things they buy (see Chapter 3). Irma Zandl of the Zandl Group, which researches the youth market, thinks human nature makes them favor what they do just as it accounts for other differences. "If you ask kids between 13 and 15 about their favorite times in history, over 30% of the boys list periods of war. Girls just don't do that," said Zandl. But culture, and peer pressure, may have something to do with it as well. If girls have a natural inclination to wear tiny crop tops and paint their faces, TV and print images certainly encourage it.

DEAR DR. TIGHTWAD

Q. One of our kids is conscientious about saving and budgeting, but the other can't seem to save anything. What are we doing wrong?

A. The only thing you're guilty of is having children.

To a great extent, a child's attitude toward money is shaped by his or her own personality. And as every parent knows, kids within the same family can have very different personalities. The shy, serious oldest child may be diligent about saving, while the carefree, gregarious little brother spends every cent he gets his hands on.

You can't change your kids' birth order or personality, but you may be able to modify their behavior. By requiring them both to save part of their allowance, you can guarantee that each has at least some money put aside.

Right now your words may seem to be falling on one pair of deaf ears, but kids do remember what they've been taught. Sometimes it just takes a while for the lesson to sink in.

By the time they're young adults, both sexes are showing more fundamental differences in their attitudes. A University of Maryland study of upper-level college students (most of them in their twenties) found that women were more likely than men to believe that getting rich isn't a realistic investment goal. They were also more likely to consider investing in stocks too big a gamble, to be unwilling to go for broke and to seek help with their finances.

Men were more likely to read financial journals, believe they have adequate financial resources and prefer selecting their own investments. They also had more confidence in their knowledge about money and their ability to manage it.

Even after marriage, differences persist. A nationwide survey of 2,000 people by Oppenheimer Funds showed that while women are more likely than men to manage financial matters in most families, men have more confidence than women in their knowledge of investing and their ability to invest a $10,000 windfall. And more men than women say they know how a mutual fund works.

But the gap has narrowed since Oppenheimer did its first gender study in the early 1990s. Of the women surveyed today, 64% said they are more interested in investing today than they were five years ago. And among women ages 21 to 34, more than half report that they were encouraged to learn more about investing while they were growing up, versus just 35% of women age 55 and over. The survey indicated a "leveling of the playing field by gender," said Oppenheimer president Bridget Macaskill.

Even in the Maryland study, there was common ground. Men and women were similar, for example, in their priorities: "Being in control" and "knowing where I stand" ranked first, followed by "working for an improved standard of living" and "saving regularly."

Still, family squabbles about money are all but guaranteed. Disputes about money are among the leading causes of divorce in the U.S., and it's easy to understand why—men and women don't always see eye to eye. In the Oppenheimer study, 44% of the men surveyed thought the husband was more likely to manage financial matters in most families, compared with 31% who cited the wife. But the women surveyed had a different point of view; 52% said the wife was more likely to be in charge, versus 28% who selected the husband.

Your Money Profile

Your basic money personality overshadows even your sex in determining your attitude toward money. See if you recognize yourself in the following portraits.

The Accountant. You keep your checkbook balanced, and one of your greatest thrills is watching your savings account grow. You blanch when your spouse spends impulsively on a piece of furniture or a set of golf clubs. You're a downer to live with, but you'll never be broke. For you, money means security.

The Social Worker. You regard money as filthy lucre, and the quicker you wash your hands of it the better. You are, however, willing to spend it on the people, and causes, you love. You're the one who gets suckered into hosting the family dinner every Thanksgiving, and you probably have a "Save the Whales" bumper sticker on your car. For you, money means affection.

The CEO. You own a BMW and a Mercedes, live in a house you can't afford and are planning to remodel the kitchen with your next bonus. When your kids bring home a good report card, you write them a check. Your motto is, the one with the most toys wins. For you, money means success.

The Entertainer. Every Friday afternoon you have a couple of drinks with the gang from the office and you pick up the tab. Every Saturday night you go out to dinner with the neighbors and you pick up the tab. You never balance your checkbook and can't be bothered saving receipts. You drive your accountant spouse crazy but your neighbors and co-workers love you. For you, money means esteem.

You can probably place yourself and your spouse in one of these four broad categories but not necessarily in the same one. Show me a couple who don't fight about money, goes the old one-liner, and I'll show you a couple on the way to their wedding.

Olivia Mellan, a Washington, D.C., psychotherapist who specializes in trying to resolve money conflicts, breaks down money personalities further into types that are polar opposites:

Hoarders vs. Spenders. Hoarders find it difficult to spend money; Spenders can't seem to hang on to it. A subspecies is the **Binger**, a combination of hoarder and spender who saves up pennies only to blow them all at once.

Money Monks vs. Money Amassers. Monks feel anxious when they have too much money; Amassers feel anxious when they don't have enough.

Money Worriers vs. Money Avoiders. Worriers balance their checkbook over and over and finish their taxes in January. Avoiders ignore the checkbook and can usually be found licking the stamp on April 14.

Risk Takers vs. Risk Avoiders. Takers relish gambling on the stock market and even more exotic investments; Avoiders are reluctant to venture forth from the security of bank certificates of deposit.

Even if you and your spouse are similar, one of you will tend to take on the role of foil. In a family of hoarders, for example, someone has to spring for living-room furniture and clothes for the kids. If you're both spendthrifts, one of you will feel the need to play guardian of the checkbook. Either way, some conflict is certain, and your children are bound to pick up on it. In extreme cases, children may take the side of the preferred parent, choose the position that will win them the most affection or simply leave the field altogether and refuse to have anything to do with money.

Kenneth Doyle, a financial psychologist at the University of Minnesota who deals with such problems, recalls a poignant personal experience. After he and his wife divorced, he took his then-10-year-old daughter to a fair. While they were strolling through the booths, she suddenly realized that she had forgotten to bring her own money to spend—and worried that her father didn't have any. "She had picked up my stress and was hoarding her cash to take care of dad," said Doyle. "So we worked on convincing her that I was all right, and that she should keep her money and learn to spend and enjoy it."

Ways to Meet Each Other Halfway

None of the money personalities described above is necessarily bad; all have their good points. In fact, your spendthrift spouse probably secretly admires your self-discipline. What you need to do is keep from getting too far out of balance. The key to resolving potentially tense situations is to know what makes your spouse crazy and resolve, if not to change your ways completely, at least to meet your partner halfway.

In her book *Money Harmony* (Walker), Mellan recommends a series of weekly exercises in role reversal, or practicing behavior that's out of character for you. For example, in the case of a money monk married to a money-amasser, the monk should try splurging on something that he or she would otherwise consider selfish or decadent, while the amasser sets aside a day on which he or she doesn't spend, save, invest or deal with money at all. They write down their feelings and reactions, give themselves a reward, and continue the exercise for several weeks—long enough, ideally, for it to make a permanent difference in their behavior or for them to at least appreciate one another's position.

Does This Sound Familiar?

Here's a look at some other key flashpoints guaranteed to ignite financial fireworks in a marriage, with suggestions on how to defuse them.

He: "You're always spending money we don't have."
She: "You're so tightfisted we never have any fun."

Try shock therapy. Present the spendthrift with your paychecks and your bills and let him or her handle the budgeting. For cases in which spending has gotten seriously out of control, you may have to consult an organization such as the National Foundation for Consumer Credit (8611 Second Ave., Suite 100, Silver Spring, MD 20910; 800-388-2227) or Debtors Anonymous (General Service Office, Box 92088, Needham, MA 02492-0009; 781-453-2743)

Remember, though, that the spender isn't necessarily the one who is at fault here. Sometimes the sober half of this duo is simply afraid to part with money. When that's the case, it might help to lay out your financial goals—retirement, children's education, a major vacation—to see whether you're on track toward achieving them. Once you see where you stand in dollars and cents, one spouse may be convinced that you need to spend less or the other might feel more comfortable about spending more. "People are willing to change their behavior as long as they don't feel like they're being blamed," said one family counselor.

This kind of exercise can be invaluable for kids, too. One reason they seem to think money grows on trees is that they have no experience in setting goals and making choices. They just don't understand why they can't have everything they want when they want it. It helps them to hear that you're holding off on buying the new car because the house needs painting or forgoing dinners out to help pay for your vacation at the beach.

One mother recalls the day her 12-year-old son announced that he wanted to play lacrosse and presented her with a list of equipment adding up to more than $200. She told him she didn't think lacrosse was in the cards, and she told him why: He had never played before, and it seemed like a lot of money to spend on something he wasn't sure he'd stick with. He ended up agreeing, mainly because "he heard me say

what I was thinking and not just, 'we can't afford it,' "
said his mom.

She: "Our money's just sitting in the bank. We ought to invest."
He: "Yeah? You want to end up like Charlie, who lost his shirt in the market?"

The ticklish problem of different tolerances for risk can be easily resolved if you both realize you don't have to commit to all or nothing. If one of you must take risks, do it with 10% of your assets instead of 100%. If you're reluctant to move beyond the safety of a bank, take it one step at a time by investing in a relatively safe utility stock or blue-chip company instead of an aggressive-growth mutual fund. If you each have your own IRA or 401(k) tax-favored retirement plan, each of you can decide how to invest the money.

If you still can't reach an amicable agreement, you might seek help from a neutral third party, such as a financial planner, who can recommend investments and act as a buffer to absorb some of the worry (and the blame).

He: "How can I balance the checkbook when you can't even hold on to an ATM receipt?"
She: "I've got more important things to think about."

Whip the disorganized spouse into shape by starting small: Get him or her at least to toss receipts into a shoebox. Move on to assigning specific tasks—who's going to balance the checkbook, who's going to monitor credit card charges so you don't use up your credit line. Set aside one day a month to talk about family finances. Then switch bill-paying responsibilities every six months.

If all else fails (and it just might), be prepared to go it alone. One couple settled their squabbling when the wife officially hired her husband to be her bookkeeper. Now that they've made it a business arrangement, she takes their finances more seriously and he's less resentful.

If you're the one who's stuck with keeping the

books and the very word "budget" sets your teeth on edge, make it easy on yourself. As long as you're meeting your savings goal, you probably don't need to fiddle with a budget at all. If you aren't, you don't have to keep track of every nickel and dime. Instead, make a guess about what your expenditures are and then compare your estimates with the bills as they come in. That will show you where your spending is out of line and you can focus only on those areas where you want to cut back.

She: "Your kids are already costing us a bundle in child support. Why do you have to spend so much on them when they come to visit?"

GOLDEN RULES FOR FENDING OFF FIGHTS

For richer or poorer, in good times and bad, it's possible for spouses to avoid, or at least defuse, many of the most common disputes about money by adding the following resolutions to your marriage vows:

- **Talk about money openly** and matter-of-factly. Silence is not golden and could lead to unpleasant surprises later.
- **Settle the issue** of joint versus separate checking accounts. Either system will work if you both accept it. Or both of you could chip in to fund a third kitty for household expenses.
- **Designate which spouse will pay bills,** balance the checkbook and handle investments. Whether you pool your money or keep separate accounts, someone has to do the financial housekeeping.
- **Know where your money is.** Even if your spouse is the numbers whiz, you can't afford to tune out. Touch base periodically so you know how much you owe on your credit cards and how much is in your retirement accounts.
- **Don't begrudge your spouse** small indulgences. Each of you should have some money to spend, with no explanations needed.
- **Consult with each other** on purchases of, say, $500. That counts as a big indulgence, and your partner deserves a say.
- **Don't criticize your spouse** about money in front of others. Talk openly, but talk privately.
- **Coordinate your responses** when your kids ask for something, so they don't play one parent against the other. If Mom says no, Dad says no.
- **Discuss your goals regularly,** preferably at a time when you're not under the gun to solve a money problem. Even when you keep separate accounts, you need to coordinate financial plans—if you hope to retire together.

He: "They're my kids—I'll spend as much as I want."

Court-ordered child support is one thing, but what often rankles a new spouse is unanticipated demands on the noncustodial parent's pocketbook. One solution is to set aside a certain amount for extra child-related expenses. But money may not always be the problem. The new spouse may simply want reassurance that he or she is top priority, and you may get better results by expending a little extra time and attention rather than cash.

Kids and money are often at the center of other prickly problems involving divorce and remarriage. "Whatever money means to you and your spouse will be magnified if you go through a divorce," said Doyle. (For a more extensive discussion of some of the problems and solutions, see Chapter 16).

He: "You spent $120 on a pair of sneakers for Johnny? You're spoiling those kids rotten."
She: "I'm only buying them what the other kids have. Besides, we can afford it."

It's the sociological phenomenon of our time: Love equals stuff. The more stuff our kids have, the more we must love them—and the better parents we must be. It's exacerbated by parental guilt about not being around more and by the very natural desire for our kids to fit in.

The solution is both breathtakingly simple and excruciatingly difficult: Just say no. Your kids will still love you in spite of your refusal to gratify their every wish (or perhaps because of it). If you think those $120 sneakers are an outrageous purchase, put your foot down and tell your son that they don't fit into your budget. If you're inclined to compromise, tell him how much your budget does allow for sneakers and let him make up the difference. In our house we have a $50 sneaker rule (see Chapter 1), and it works like a charm.

Use the same strategy even when you can afford the shoes and it's the principle, not the cash, that is at stake. Never lie to your children and tell them you can't afford something when you can. Be honest and tell them why you don't choose to buy it or why you'd prefer to spend your money on something else.

One child psychologist tells the story of well-to-do parents who had given their teenage son a car, with the understanding that he not use it to leave school at lunch time. Sure enough, the son flouted the rule and smashed up the car to boot. His father's response was simply to buy him another one, thereby teaching his son a lesson that would "damage his perception of money for the rest of his life."

Mistakes to Avoid

You probably won't be able to change your attitude toward money. The idea is to reach a happy medium, or at least be aware of and honest about your shortcomings. If you have a tendency to pinch pennies, let your kids in on the secret and tell them why you consider it a good—or bad—trait. If you're a shopaholic, tell them you're not the world's greatest authority on budgeting. They'll appreciate your candor and learn from your experience.

In talking to your kids about money, follow these other golden rules:

Don't Duck the Issue
Whether they're pressed for time or they're just reluctant to bring it up, parents often give the subject short shrift. But children do think about money and sometimes they get some cockeyed notions about it. One woman recalls that when she was in elementary school she wanted more than anything to take an after-school class in horseback riding, which cost $80 at the time. Her middle-class parents could probably have afforded the lessons, but she didn't dare ask for them. "It sounded to me like $80 would plunge the family into poverty...like it was the end of the world," she recalls.

Another woman recalls that when she was in the

second grade she was "overwhelmed by the abundance of crayons, stars, paper and pencils in my teacher's supply cabinet. I couldn't imagine that my parents could ever afford to buy me those kinds of things, so I stole a bunch." Her parents, of course, made her return them and 'fess up.

When kids raise some issue involving finances, even if the connection seems tenuous to you, don't ignore them or give them a curt response. Before you speak, try to imagine what you'd say to a neighbor's child, recommends Harold Moe, who chronicled his experiences with his own children in *Teach Your Child the Value of Money*, because "we tend to treat the neighbor kids a little more kindly than we do our own, and we're not as abrupt."

Be Consistent

If you've decided to give your kids an allowance and you've made a "no advances" rule, don't waffle—standing firm one week and handing over extra money the next. Your child will never learn the discipline of living within a budget if you keep expanding the limits. Today she's getting an advance on her allowance, tomorrow she'll be using one credit card to pay off the balance on another.

Repeat the following sentence ten times: "I will never tell my children, by word or example, to do as I say and not as I do." Your lecture on the wastefulness of scrapping a perfectly good video game system just to get the latest model will be in vain if you regularly trade in a perfectly good car just to get a new one with the latest bells and whistles.

Don't Be a Cynic

For adults it's de rigueur to complain about their jobs and criticize their bosses as a way of releasing tension. After venting their spleen, they usually go back to work and forget about the incident. But for kids who witness the outburst, the memory can linger, with destructive consequences, according to Peter Spevak, director of the Center for Applied Motivation, a psychology practice in Rockville, Md., that counsels underachieving teens. In his work, Spevak said, he encounters many 17- and 18-year-olds who have become "incredibly cynical" about the working world because they have been exposed too early to a negative attitude instead of the enthusiasm and inner satisfaction they need to see. If your kids ask whether you make as much money as your boss, don't answer, "I wish," as if you're somehow being shortchanged. Better to respond, "No, but someday you will."

Kids also need to start learning, by word and example, how much things cost, as well as how to use money, earn it, save it and keep it in perspective. The following chapters will give you ideas on how to tackle that task with kids of different ages.

Turn page for Kids' Questions→

KIDS' QUESTIONS

Q. "Dad, can I have $15 for a new CD? Mom says no, but all the other kids have it."

A. Stand by your spouse. Tell your child that if Mom (or Dad) says no, the answer is no. There are lots of other issues here—whether you can afford the $15, whether you should cave in to your child's peer pressure, whether your child should be buying the CD with his or her own money (all of which are covered elsewhere in this book). But in a situation like this, your most important consideration is to keep up a united front. If you do, chances are you won't hear this question again. If you crack, your action (and your kid) will come back to haunt you.

If you really disagree with your spouse, or if your child is exploiting a sore spot between the two of you, you and your spouse should talk it over afterward to agree on a response. But this is one discussion that doesn't have to take place in front of the children.

Q. "Why do you two always fight about money?"

A. You may not always fight about money, but your kids are obviously getting a different impression.

Don't overreact or go on the defensive. Instead, ask your children to describe a time when you and your spouse fought about money. What they define as "fighting" might simply be a run-of-the-mill parental discussion about whether to get the car fixed or buy a new one. If that's the case, you can reassure your kids by bringing them in on the discussion, which is critical anyway if they're ever to learn how to make such decisions themselves. If they're old enough to eavesdrop, they're old enough to participate.

If your kids were right on target and you are always fighting about money, you may have to seek outside help from a marriage mediator (contact the Academy of Family Mediators, 5 Militia Drive, Lexington, MA 02421; 781-674-2663). "Fighting in front of the kids isn't bad as long as the kids see you finding a solution," said one mediator.

Q. "How come you and Dad went out to dinner and a show but you won't buy me rock concert tickets?"

A. Go ahead and tell it like it is: You earned the money and you can spend it any way you want.

Kids shouldn't be so selfish as to presume that they always get first dibs on the family's resources. You don't need to justify your actions to your children, but it doesn't hurt to remind them that your family's income has to be divided among lots of different expenditures, one of which is R&R for Mom and Dad. You might also remind the child that while you may not choose to buy concert tickets, you did spring for an electric guitar (or whatever) on his birthday. Then go off for your night on the town.

In the future, you can head off this question by making concert tickets and other expenses part of your children's budget, to be paid for out of their own allowance or earnings.

Q. "How come you bought David a new jacket and you didn't buy one for me?"

A. What parent hasn't been tempted to retort, "because we like David better than we like you." Actually, that's not a bad comeback—assuming it isn't true and you're smiling while you say it. Meeting your child's unspoken criticism head-on with a little humor can defuse the tension and give you a chance to explain that you intend to buy your whole family new jackets eventually, but you just happened to find one in David's size that was on sale.

Children are sensitive to what they perceive to be favoritism, whether real or imagined (and let's hope it's usually imagined). To the extent it's possible, follow the one-for-all rule: When you buy something for one of your children, buy one for all of them. That's easy enough to do with small items—books from the bookstore, treats at the dollar store, even souvenirs if you go on a business trip (save the bags of peanuts from the plane or the good-night mints on the pillow in your hotel room). A little extra money buys a lot of good will.

If you're going to be shopping for back-to-school clothes and you don't want to take all the kids along at once, let them know that they'll each have a turn. If you're buying a new ball for your young basketball player, it isn't unreasonable to consider a new glove for your baseball player. Of course, if she doesn't need a new glove there's no reason to spend the money. But as long as you've created an overall atmosphere of fairness, she won't feel slighted.

Q. "Kids cost too much. I'm not going to have any when I grow up."
A. This isn't exactly a question, but it does demand a response. Somewhere along the line, your kids got the idea (incorrect, I hope) that they're undesirable. Tell them that the rewards of having children far outweigh the expense.

Remember that talking to your children about money will set them straight about what it can and can't buy, but talking about money over their heads as if they weren't there is simply asking for trouble. It may seem that all your children want to do is spend your money, but often they do worry about whether your family

has enough:

- Watching her mother write a $65 check for a month's worth of piano lessons, 10-year-old Michele looked soberly at her mom and asked, "Can we afford this?"
- A fifth-grade teacher arranged a special field trip for her class to a nearby aquarium. When she told her students that it would cost $12 each, several of them came up to her and told her that the trip was too expensive and they probably wouldn't be able to go.

It's true that money is tight in many households. But in these cases it's likely that the kids' fears were out of proportion to the costs involved. That's not unusual, since children aren't always clear on the difference between $65, $650 or $6,500. Kids need to develop a sense of relative costs and values, so that they know which expenses might be expected to fit into your budget and which would be a stretch. In the case of the piano lessons, for example, the mom could have explained that music lessons are a worthwhile expense, and $65 a reasonable cost. But if the child also wanted to take dancing lessons for $65 a month, she might have to choose between the two.

Kids also need to know that they're not a burden but a responsibility that parents (presumably) have taken on willingly.

Government statisticians routinely calculate the cost of raising a child from birth to age 18. Parents often read the number, shake their heads and sigh, "If I had only known…" But even if you had known, you probably would have gone ahead and done it anyway.

Q. "Who will take care of us if you die?"
A. There's nothing wrong with reassuring your kids that they shouldn't worry because "that's all been arranged"—assuming it's true. But it would be even better if you could tell

your kids whom you have named as their guardians should anything happen to you. And if you haven't named any guardians, your child's question should be the encouragement you need.

Many parents rely on informal arrangements—"My wife's sister has agreed to take care of our children in case my wife and I die." But if both you and your spouse should die before your children are grown without formally naming a guardian, the courts will decide who's going to bring up your kids. And you can't count on your wishes being honored. A judge who doesn't know your children and family could choose the one relative you wouldn't want.

In fact, for parents of minor children the single most important reason for making a will is to name a guardian for the kids. Many parents put off writing a will because they see it as a downer—a way to dispose of your assets after death. Think of it instead as a way to protect your most precious assets.

Q. "How much money do you make?"
A. Instead of dismissing the question with an abrupt, "That's none of your business," go with an answer that's vague but more polite, as in "More than some families but not as much as others." That's a nicer way of not answering the question, which you shouldn't feel obliged to do. When it comes to teaching kids about money, parents have lots of responsibilities. Telling your kids how much you make isn't necessarily one of them.

For one thing, no matter how much you make, whether it's $30,000 or $130,000, grade-school kids (and even high-schoolers) will have trouble putting it in perspective. It will sound like an enormous sum to your children—certainly more than enough to buy the $100 bicycle or

$200 video-game system they want. For another thing, you have a right to your privacy. While it's certainly desirable to talk with your kids about money (that is, after all, what this book is about) you can't be blamed for not wanting your affairs blabbed around the neighborhood—which your kids will almost certainly do, if only in innocent conversation.

Besides, when young children ask this question chances are they don't care about the numbers anyway. They're just trying to get an idea of your relative wealth and where you stand vis-a-vis other families. They'd also be relieved if you assured them that you're not at risk of being turned out into the street.

As your kids get older you may choose to be more forthright about how much you earn. But it will make more sense to your children, and be more comfortable for you, if you put your income in the context of your expenses. Kids need to know, for example, that after taxes your take-home pay is a lot less than your actual salary. They need to know that you can't spend money on just anything because you have to cover certain fixed expenses first, such as the mortgage and the car insurance. One dad gave his teens a crash course in household finances by converting his pay into dollar bills, stacking the money on the table and inviting his kids to watch the pile dwindle as he paid the monthly bills.

Some parents have even turned over the bill-paying chores to their kids. "For several years, since Mary was 12, I have given her the bills and the checkbook and she does the rest," one mother wrote to me. "I just do a quick review and sign the checks." What many adults would find tedious Mary finds fascinating, says her mom. "From this experience she not only acquires the skill of managing a checkbook, but also gains a real sense of what it costs to run a household on a month-by-month basis."

Q. "Are we poor?"

(Often preceded by "You never buy me anything.")
A. It's easy enough to snap, "We would be if I bought you everything you asked for," but that's probably not the case. Typical middle-class families aren't poor (even though it sometimes feels that way), and it would be misleading and unfair to let your kids think you are, even unintentionally.

But your funds are limited, and kids don't understand the concept of limits, especially as it applies to them. Explain that watching where your money goes doesn't mean you're poor. It just means you have to parcel out your income to cover lots of different expenses.

A variation of this question is, "Why are you so cheap?" Assuming that your child is being serious and not merely fresh, explain that shopping for the best price or deciding not to buy something doesn't mean you're cheap, just that you want to make your money go as far as it can.

It might help to give your kids more hands-on experience in the art of managing money. The next time you buy the kids' back-to-school clothes, for example, tell them in advance how much you can afford to spend and then let them have a hand in choosing the wardrobe without busting the budget.

If your children must have a misconception about your financial status, it's healthier for them to think you're poor and cheap rather than rich and extravagant!

Q. "Are we rich?"

A. If the first thing that pops out of your mouth is "Whatever gave you that idea?" think for a minute. *You* may have given them that idea. Even if you don't feel rich, you probably live comfortably enough that your kids think you are. Or maybe their curiosity was piqued by a specific event—you bought a new car, for

example, remodeled your house or got a job promotion.

In any event, answering the question with one of your own isn't such a bad idea. It gives you a chance to find out what's on your child's mind, and gives you a few seconds to get your thoughts together. "Are we rich?" is similar to "How much do you make?" in that it demands a diplomatic answer that will still satisfy the children. One mom didn't miss a beat when her 6-year-old put her on the spot. "We're not rich," she replied, "but we have enough money to buy the things we need and some left over to share."

Now, if your name happens to be Rockefeller, you'll eventually have to tell your kids that you are, in fact, rich. But the rest of the advice in this book should be as helpful to you as to any other parent.

Q. "How come we don't have a big-screen TV like the Joneses?"

A. On hearing that one, many parents would be inclined to offer to let their disgruntled offspring move in with the Joneses. Unless you really expect that to happen (and a big-screen TV can be very tempting), stick to answering the question, whatever the answer may be: "Because we can't afford a big-screen TV," or "Because we're saving our money for a trip to Disney World next spring," or "Because we think a big-screen TV is a waste of money." Kids are willing to accept the truth when it's offered.

Sometimes a question like this is just an attempt by your kids to make you feel guilty. But sometimes kids are genuinely curious about where you fit in on the scale of wealth compared with other families. In that case, take the opportunity to explain that different occupations pay different salaries. That in turn can kick off a discussion of jobs and careers, such as why basketball players are paid more than teachers, why someone might want to be a writer rather than a doctor even though doctors earn more, or why being your own boss might be attractive.

Explain that some people might choose a lower-paying job because it suits their talents or gives them more satisfaction—or be forced into one because they don't have the skills or training for anything better. Now is a good time to make your pitch about getting a good education if your kids want to be able to afford a big-screen TV or a trip to Disney World when they grow up.

Q. "Why do you have to go to work every day?"

A. Don't respond with a flip but familiar remark about "putting bread on the table for you." A response like this makes it sound as if you're literally a step away from starvation—and it's all their fault.

Tell your children instead that you work to earn money to pay for all the things your whole family needs and wants. Tell them you work to earn money to save for the future—to pay for next year's vacation, or a new car. Tell them you work because you're good at what you do. Tell them you work because you enjoy it.

Children don't always hear a dispassionate discussion of adult jobs. They're more likely to overhear you grousing about the boss or yearning for early retirement.

It's healthier for all of you to get your children involved with what you do. Take them to work on a regular work day so they know where you go every day. Talk about the people you work with and what your job involves.

You may spend more of your waking hours on the job than with your children. So anything you can do to make your kids feel more a part of your mysterious outside life is bound to bring you closer together, make you less resentful of the time you spend apart, and make your children less fearful of the day when they'll have to go to work to put bread on the table.

You can also have a big influence on their career choices. One study of children from kindergarten to sixth grade showed that more of them wanted to follow in Mom's footsteps than in Dad's. Among fifth-graders, 33% of the girls—and 30% of the boys—said they wanted to have the same job as their mother. Only 11% of the girls, and 13% of the boys, cited their fathers' jobs. The study concluded that the kids choose Mom's field more often because women tell their children more about their jobs, and are more likely to take their children to the place they work.

One woman who runs a business out of her home even took her two children on a tour of her home office and carefully explained that that's where she goes to do her job and earn money. Several weeks later she mentioned that she was short on cash and would have to make a trip to the bank, when her son piped up, "Mommy, you can just go into your office and make some."

Q. "Why do you have to get a new job so far away and make us move? I don't want to leave my friends."

A. Instead of setting yourself up as the bad guy, emphasize that you're all in this together. Acknowledge that the move will be an adjustment for you, too, and even a little scary. But your new job will make it easier for your family to buy the things they need (including, presumably, things the kids want). If you've been out of work prior to the move, your children have probably sensed your tension and felt the financial pinch, and may actually be as relieved as you are that you have found work.

It's true, though, that long-distance moves get more difficult as your kids get older. "The ultimate nightmare is to take a kid away before senior year," said one child psychologist. If you're in that situation, try to defuse possible conflicts by letting your kids know as early as possible that a move is in the works and bringing them in on discussions about buying houses and choosing schools. You might even consider taking them with you on a scouting expedition to your new home.

Q. "If you lose your job, how will we get money to buy food?"
A. You mean well, but if you say "Don't worry about it. That's my problem," you're actually being too reassuring. If your job's in jeopardy, of course your kids will worry. Even if they're not quite sure what it means to be unemployed, they can sense you're upset and they're going to pick up on your cues. It's easy for them to imagine that things are worse than they are.

Be as straight with them as you can about how a job loss might affect your finances, but don't burden them with problems they can't handle. You can tell them, for example, that you'll get money from unemployment benefits without telling them that those benefits will eventually run out. Tell them that many people nowadays lose or change their jobs, and explain how you're going to go about looking for a new one. Tell them you'll have to cut back on spending for a while, and ask for their suggestions.

Whatever you do, don't try to shield the children by continuing to spend money you can no longer afford. Kids are surprisingly adaptable to economic circumstances. A survey by the American Board of Family Practice showed that, to help their families through a financial crunch, a majority of teenagers were willing to get jobs, buy fewer clothes and give up some of their allowance.

Small Change: The Preschool Years

Perhaps the shortest question I've ever received was this one-liner: "At what age do you start turning an ordinary little child into what you term a money-smart kid?"

The one-line answer is, at whatever age an ordinary little child starts showing an interest in, and asking questions about, money. I feel compelled to add, however, that far from pushing kids to grow up faster, I consider myself a pulling parent, keeping them young as long as possible. As I said at the beginning of this book, there's no point in trying to make your child into a little Peter Lynch or Bill Gates, or in running your family like an accounting firm. When it comes to financial issues, as in everything else you discuss with your kids, your role is to satisfy their curiosity in an honest and age-appropriate way.

Dealing with money is such a natural part of life that you don't even have to set aside extra time to talk about it. Instead you can take advantage of situations that crop up every day. When your child begs to press the buttons on the ATM, use the opportunity to tell her how the money got there in the first place. Dragging your children to the supermarket becomes more pleasant for all of you if you keep them busy scouting out the best deals. A visit to your office opens the door to a discussion of where the money comes from to pay the household bills.

Your ultimate aim is to turn out independent adults who know how to manage money and have a healthy regard for what it can and can't buy. But with preschoolers you'll have to start with a less lofty goal—like how to tell the difference between a penny, a nickel and a dime.

Let 3-year-olds choose among those three coins and they'll almost invariably choose the nickel because it's bigger. Let them choose between a quarter and a dollar bill and they'll take the quarter, which, after all, you can spin, flip, drop into a bank and stack with other coins. Let them choose between a dollar bill and a $50 check and they'll take the dollar bill, which at least looks like money. Abstract concepts are beyond the grasp of most preschoolers. They focus on the concrete and so should you, showing them what coins look like and how they can be exchanged for other things.

Not that preschoolers aren't capable of some surprisingly sophisticated behavior. Laurie Fratangelo was floored when her son, Jake, then 4½, announced that he was going to open a business selling lollipops—and save his profits to buy a car. Fratangelo operated her own home-based business selling children's clothing, and Jake had observed with more interest than his mother realized. He began asking his mom's customers to buy lollipops and eventually got his grandfather to

---

DEAR DR. TIGHTWAD

Q. The other day I went to pick up my 5-year-old from school and her teacher handed me $32. Apparently my daughter had taken $33 from my purse and spent $1 on candy before her teacher spotted what was happening and took the rest of the money. How should I handle this?

A. Keep calm. You're dealing with two situations here. The first is that your daughter took money from your purse; the second is that she took a *lot* of money from your purse.

In the first case, let's assume your daughter wasn't being sneaky but simply going straight to what she knows to be the source of cash. This is potentially the more serious problem, but it can be handled by telling your daughter that helping herself to money is a no-no. She has to ask.

As for the amount she took, children this age often don't understand the abstract value of money; three $10 bills are the same as three $1 bills. They'll know better once they learn about money in school. You can help things along by counting out exact change when your daughter handles money so she knows how much she needs to buy a candy bar.

With any luck, this will turn out to be an innocent—and isolated—incident.

build him a plywood stand from which he could conduct his business. Then he decided he wanted to expand into selling juice as well.

Of course, there were a few snags in the operation. At first Jake wanted to sell the lollipops for $14 each, until he was talked down to 3 cents. And his mother said it took him a while to grasp the concept of paying his supplier.

It wasn't surprising that Jake apparently pulled the $14 figure out of the air. One parent once told me that she was at her wit's end because despite her best efforts to teach her 5-year-old about money the child thought everything cost $64. Where had she gone wrong, the mother wanted to know. She hadn't, of course. To her daughter the $64 figure was simply a tangible symbol of money—an idea she would grow out of as she got older and and more sophisticated and learned more about money in school. Until then, you can take advantage of lots of everyday activities to familiarize your preschoolers with family finances.

At the Grocery Store

Most children get their first look at the world from the seat of a shopping cart. So learn to make the most of the opportunity, and avoid some nasty scenes as well. For example, present your children ahead of time with several coins (adding up to 50 cents, $1 or whatever you deem appropriate) and tell them they can spend the money on something of their own choosing (for more tips on how to forestall a bad case of the gimmies, see the questions on page 70).

As you cruise the aisles, let the children toss your items into the cart and count them as they go in. Keep the children busy hunting for the brand of soup or crackers that you buy, or let them choose between two different kinds of cereal. If they decide to buy something from a vending machine, let them put in the coins and scoop out the change.

Watching Television

If your kids spend part of Saturday morning in front of the television, make it a point to join them to see what kinds of commercials are being pitched their way. Preschoolers can't always tell when the television show ends and the ad begins. They need you to explain to them that when they hear the voice saying, "We'll be right back after these brief messages," they're about to hear a sales pitch for something you may not want them to have.

A spokesperson for the Children's Advertising Review Unit (CARU) of the Council of Better Business Bureaus, suggests that parents show their kids this demonstration of how to be a "TV star": Take three apples that look similar. Then "dress up" one of them by sticking raisins or marshmallows into it, putting it into a colorful box or shining a flashlight on it. Ask your children which they'd be inclined to buy. If they choose the spiffed-up apple, have them take a bite out of each one. Does the "star" actually taste any better?

Don't be surprised if despite your best efforts your preschoolers still want it all. Don't panic, either. At that age, it's natural for them to ask for everything they see—and promptly forget about it as long as you don't feel obliged to buy it for them. In fact, it's important for kids this age to get used to hearing you say "no." Don't fall into the parent trap of giving in to your kids out of fear, guilt or pure indulgence.

Sounds easy, but in today's world that often takes an iron will, a stiff backbone and a tight fist. For instance, I once read a newspaper report on the booming sales of designer clothing—for young children. It seems that a growing number of parents think nothing of spending hundreds of dollars on a kid's version of a

---

SEEING THROUGH THE HYPE

The Children's Advertising Review Unit (CARU) of The Better Business Bureau was established by the advertising industry to promote responsible children's advertising and to respond to public concerns. CARU publishes a parent's guide, *Advertising and Your Child*, which discusses how you can monitor and explain advertising to your children; and for advertisers, *Self-Regulatory Guidelines for Children's Advertising*. To order, contact CARU (845 Third Ave., New York, NY 10022; 212-705-0124).

Moschino jacket or a skirt and jacket by Versace. Asked how she came to fritter away $20,000 on a closetful of clothes that her 2-year-old rarely wore, one mother's response was enough to take your breath away: "I can afford it, so why not?"

After catching my breath, I can think of plenty of reasons why not—starting with the simple fact that no child needs a $250 black motorcycle jacket. Period.

If this book came equipped with a sound card you would hear teeth gnashing (mine) and bones rattling as I figuratively took the parents of America by their shoulders and gave them a good shake. Since that's not possible, here's a verbal shoulder-shaking should you ever be tempted to drop a bundle on designer duds (or their equivalent) for toddlers:

- **The only name** on kids' clothing labels should be their own.
- **Don't kid yourself** into thinking that you're buying this stuff for your children; you're buying it for yourself.
- **If you lead your children** to believe that spending money on expensive clothes buys happiness, they will end up broke and sad.
- **Parading kids around** in miniature versions of adult outfits is not cute. They grow up fast enough without being pushed.
- **Dressing for status** is a no-win game. Someone will always be able to go you one better.
- **Simply having money** at your disposal is never a good reason to buy something.
- **If you buy your 4-year-old** a $300 jacket and $99 jeans, he or she will never learn either the value, or the values, of money.
- **Every family needs** at least one adult, and that person should be you.

Far from doing your children a favor or helping them get on in the world, you're doing them a disservice by teaching them the shallowest of lessons: that clothes make the kid, that it's fine to cave in to peer pressure, and that you're willing to pay the price. You'll still be paying when your child is 44.

Lending a Hand

Children this age are old enough to pick up toys, put away clothes or help make the bed. They probably won't do any of those things, of course, unless you make the demands manageable, stick to them and give your kids a hand. For kids, chores become less work and more play if they're doing them with mom or dad. Settle on one chore a day and let them choose which one it will be. Present it as a privilege that they enjoy now that they're growing up (they're still young enough to buy that).

Of course, you can offer a little incentive as well. It can be as simple as a chart showing the chores to be done and the days of the week. Each time a job is completed, your daughter gets to stick a star on the chart. Seven stars and you might buy her a small treat—an ice cream cone or a drink at the corner store. Think of it as a reward—positive reinforcement for doing something good—rather than a bribe—a payoff for not doing something bad. (For more on rewards and when to give them, see Chapter 8.)

Whiling Away a Rainy Afternoon

You have to figure out something to occupy the kids' time anyway, so once in a while you might as well kill two birds with one coin by occupying your kids with money-related games and activities. There are, of course, old standbys such as playing store. I personally like the idea of letting kids play with one of the nifty savings banks you can buy nowadays—everything from motorized coin sorters to talking ATMs (for a selection, visit www.eToys.com). And if you're looking for an excuse to get out of the house, why not an excursion to a dollar store, where the price is always right for kids.

In her book *Moneyskills: 101 Activities to Teach Your*

Child About Money, author Bonnie Drew offers lots of other ideas. Here are a few games from Drew's book that are appropriate for getting preschoolers used to handling coins. I like them because they're manageable, short and fun.

STORY TIME. Let your children handle a penny, a nickel, a dime and a quarter. Show them the pictures on each coin and tell a story about each one. (Remember, it's Lincoln and the Lincoln Memorial on the penny, Jefferson and Monticello on the nickel, Franklin D. Roosevelt and the torch and olive branch on the dime, and Washington and the American eagle on the quarter.) Then let them make impressions of the coins in clay. Hint: Kids especially like the new commemorative state quarters .

TREASURE HUNT. Fill a box or dishpan with sand, rice, beans or packing peanuts, hide five pennies in it and ask your children to dig for the "treasure." Have them count out the coins. You can add other coins later and ask the kids to sort them into groups.

HEADS UP. Start with five nickels and five pennies. Explain that the side of the coin with the man's head is called "heads" and the other side "tails." Show your children how to spin and roll each coin and ask them to guess which side will be showing when it lands, heads or tails. Have them balance a nickel on the tip of a finger and see how far they can walk across the room. When the coin falls, let them call heads or tails.

ANIMAL CRACKERS. Place five pennies and a nickel on the table and explain that five pennies are worth the same as one nickel. Then break out a box of animal crackers and let the children "buy" them for one cent per cracker; let them buy five crackers at once with the nickel. Pour a small cup of juice and pretend that it costs five cents. Let your children choose to buy the juice with either five pennies or one nickel. Then eat and drink up.

TOY STORY. Aside from homemade activities, there's an increasing number of financially-oriented toys on the market these days—everything from old favorites like "Monopoly" to solar-powered cash registers and, for a short time, that infamous Barbie doll with her own credit card. Money-related toys can be great teaching tools for kids—if you choose them wisely.

For instance, some toys aimed at preschoolers, such as cash registers or supermarket shopping sets that come with scanners and groceries, generally teach positive lessons and are harmless enough. I do have a sneaking suspicion, however, that to a kid this type of toy can be a bit like pleasant-tasting medicine: Parents give it and kids are willing to take it, but they don't necessarily ask for it on their own.

More controversial are toys such as "Mall Madness," the shopping game, or that credit-card-carrying Barbie, which teach lessons you may not want your kids to learn. At the very least, you'll have some explaining to do—and if you feel a toy is so objectionable that it requires a warning, why buy it in the first place?

My favorite money toys for kids are board games. Even as I'm writing this, I'm looking at "Monopoly" and a stack of other games that my children and I have played, plus a few new ones we haven't gotten around to yet. Games bring family members together in a fun activity while giving kids a painless lesson in personal finance. But there's a big difference between "The Game of Life" (our family's personal favorite), which introduces kids to college loans, mortgages, insurance, dividends and taxes, and "Easy Money," in which players can win wads of cash simply by making bets—it's fun, but parental guidance is required (for more on financial fun and games, see Chapter 6).

What You Can Expect

You'll be surprised at how fast preschoolers catch on. It didn't take long for Jake Fratangelo, the lollipop tycoon, to figure out that there are five nickels in a quarter and four quarters in a dollar. At this age, if you've accomplished that much, you've accomplished a lot.

Don't be upset when your 4-year-old tears open birthday cards, shakes them to see if there's money inside and immediately asks to be taken to the store to spend it. You're not raising a greedy little kid, just a normal one. For preschoolers, spending is more immediate than saving. If your child knows that money can be exchanged for things, you're off to a good start that you can build on.

Turn page for Kids' Questions→

KIDS' QUESTIONS

Q. "Can I have a cookie?"

(Your 4-year-old in the grocery cart)

A. Often, parents will agree to this because it seems a small price to pay to head off a tantrum. But give in that easily and in the next aisle your child will want a sweet cereal, in the next aisle a candy bar, in the next aisle a frozen yogurt.

Next time, try leaving your child home. Failing that, lay down the rules in advance. Tell your kids they may each choose one treat—either a cookie *or* a candy bar *or* a box of sweet cereal *or* whatever else is appropriate. If they settle on the first thing they see, remind them that they get only one choice and they might want to think about other possibilities before making a final decision. That should keep your kids busy and get you off the hook. They'll be so eager to see what new goodies are waiting around the next corner that, with luck, you can hold off buying anything until your shopping trip is just about over. One mom actually puts a small carry basket underneath her grocery cart and tosses in items her kids say they want. When they get to the checkout counter, the kids get to keep one thing from the basket.

It isn't saying no that brings on a temper tantrum. It's saying no after a string of yeses that tempts your kids to test your sincerity with a stream of tears. They'll soon tire of the tactic if they know the rules ahead of time and are convinced you'll stick to them. Setting limits early and often heads off bigger confrontations later.

Q. "Can I have one of those big Barbie convertibles [or Batmobiles] that runs on batteries so I can sit behind the wheel and drive?"

(Your 5-year-old watching a commercial)

A. This is a much bigger item, and a much bigger issue, than a cookie at the store. I personally don't think preschoolers have any business in a vehicle that's powered by anything but their feet, so I'd answer this question with a simple "no." But you can always improve on a negative response by telling your children why you're denying their request. If you think self-propelled vehicles are too dangerous, too expensive, or just plain too grown-up for kids who should be getting around via pedal power, say so. Your kids will know you've given your response some serious thought and aren't just trying to put them off—and they won't harbor secret hopes of finding a convertible under the Christmas tree or on their birthday.

Q. "Can I use my money to buy a candy bar?"

(Your preschooler waving a $10 bill)

A. We both know that with that much money your child could buy ten candy bars, and you'll be tempted to say so. Don't be surprised if your child doesn't get it. Preschoolers don't think in abstract terms. To young children, all paper money is the same. Four quarters are preferable to a dollar bill because there are more of them (and they spin), and a nickel is better than a dime because it's bigger.

Simplify your tactics. Tell your kids that a $10 bill is much more than they need for one candy bar and that they should save it to buy other things. Then help them count out the exact change they'll need.

If the kids are still fuzzy about how much things cost, don't worry. At least they understand that money can be exchanged for other things, which is about as much as you can hope for at this age. They'll pick up the more abstract concepts when they learn about money in school.

Surviving With 'Tweens

By second grade, kids no longer prefer a nickel over a dime, and they can even make a stab at counting change. But they still have trouble taking in the big picture about money. Bonnie Meszaros of the Delaware Center for Economic Education learned a lesson or two from her own daughter, Morgan. When Morgan was 8 years old, her mom convinced her to put a $10 birthday gift into the bank by reminding her that she could draw it out again if she wanted to buy something. Would the bank give her the *same* $10 bill, Morgan asked. Her mother explained that she would get a $10 bill but not the same one because the bank had already used that to lend to other people. Morgan was appalled. In her mind, the purpose of a bank was to keep her money on a shelf until she was ready to take it out.

Similarly, one TV producer I know recalls that when she was a kid her grandparents gave her a collection of $2 bills. She decided to put them in the bank for safekeeping—and was devastated to find that the bank didn't keep the bills safe at all, put them into circulation. "I don't think my parents realized what I was thinking," she said. "At least, they didn't jump in and stop me."

Despite their misconceptions, children this age are eager to learn from you, so take advantage of the influence you still have. Amy Dacyczyn, the self-described "frugal zealot" who at one time published the newsletter *Tightwad Gazette*, a compendium of money-saving tips, noticed "spendthrift rumblings" in her daughter Jamie when she was about 7. So Amy began to take Jamie with her on her regular canvasses of yard sales. "It was a real eye-opener for her to see that she could get My Little Pony for 25 cents at a yard sale instead of $7 at a store," says Amy.

How to Spend a Buck

They're too big to sit in the shopping cart, and having them tag along grumpily behind you at the grocery store is like trying to shop with a ball and chain attached to each leg. But there are ways to get rid of your kids—nicely—that will benefit both them and you.

Send them to the cereal aisle with instructions to find a box of cereal that will be popular with your family, doesn't list sugar among its top ingredients and costs less than, say, $4. Tell them they can pocket the difference between your price limit and the actual price of the cereal. To challenge older children, show them how to look for the lowest unit price instead of the lowest price per package.

Have them choose three kinds of soft drinks (or some other product): A big-selling national brand, a less-popular national brand and the store brand. Note the prices per package and the unit prices. When you get home, pour the soft drinks into three unmarked glasses and try your own taste test. Which soft drink tastes best? Which is the best value?

While you're making your shopping list, let your children plan a special lunch for themselves and one or two of their friends. Have them stick to a budget—say, $10—and encourage them to use the weekly food advertising supplement as an aid. Then, while you do your shopping, send them off to do theirs and see if they can beat the budget without having to modify the menu.

Have your children help you clip grocery coupons and then track down the items at the store. Offer to match any savings you realize and let the kids put the money into their savings accounts.

Simply give them part of your list, with instructions on choosing the items you need. Your son takes frozen foods, your daughter takes dairy products, you take

LISTEN TO YOUR MOTHER

"How to count change" (from the question on page 89) was the first of what I had intended to be a list of ten tips for kids on how to feel comfortable about handling cash in public or buying something on their own. The idea was to ask grownups to contribute the best advice their own parents ever gave them on how to avoid losing their money or being cheated. But so many adults weighed in that the top ten became the lucky thirteen. Here are the rest, with compliments to contributors and their parents:

2. Always stuff your dollar bills deep in your pocket so they don't fall out when you reach in for a coin or bus token. Better yet, stuff them into a wallet or change purse, which you're less likely to pull out by mistake.

3. When ordering at a fast-food restaurant, round off the menu prices to estimate your total. That way you'll know you've been overcharged in case the clerk goofs and hits the Big Mac key twice.

4. Don't break the big bills. If your purchase comes to $7, pay with two ones and a five instead of a $10 bill. Once big bills are broken, you have a tendency to spend the money.

5. Spend the crummy bills and save the good ones for vending machines.

6. Always pay the pennies. If the price comes to $3.63 and you have a $5 bill and a handful of change, pay the three cents so that you don't get more pennies in change.

7. Ditto above, but with paper money. Suppose your purchase comes to $11 and you have a $20 bill and several ones. Give the clerk $21 so that you get a $10 bill in change. It's less cumbersome, and follows Tip no. 4 to save the larger bill.

8. If you have to use a big bill to pay for a small purchase, tell the clerk verbally—"Here's a twenty"—so there's no confusion. A good salesclerk should keep the bill out of the cash register until you get your change.

9. Clean out your pockets or purse each day and toss the coins into a savings jar. One man still follows this rule as an adult, and his spare change adds up to $40 to $60 a month, which he deposits in the bank or uses to treat himself to a nice dinner at a restaurant.

10. Don't take all your money to the movies or the mall. Take along only as much as you need to make your purchase. That way you don't risk leaving your life savings in your seat, or frittering it away at the candy counter. (And you won't have to worry about making change!)

11. Don't shove a pile of crumpled bills onto the counter and expect the salesclerk to sort them out. After the age of six or so, that stops being cute and starts becoming an annoyance to the clerk and the other people waiting in line—not to mention an invitation to be ripped off.

12. If you're out with your parents and want one of them to hold onto your money, make sure it's in a separate wallet. Loose bills and coins have a habit of getting mixed up with a parent's own funds, never to be sorted out.

13. Don't put money in your mouth, because you don't know where it's been. Actually, you do know where it's been, which is an even better reason not to put it in your mouth!

the middle of the store and you rendezvous at the meat counter.

The result: The kids learn valuable lessons in how to use a unit price tag, how to read ingredient labels, how to compare different brands, how to evaluate product advertising and how to stay within a budget. And *you* get your shopping done in peace (in a fraction of the time).

Once they've absorbed the basics at the local market, you can branch out. When his two sons, Craig and Lyle, were in elementary school back in the '70s, Ed Henry of Silver Spring, Md., gave them the responsibility of being "dad for a day." The Henrys lived in the New York City area at the time and the kids were always begging to be taken to an amusement park. So Ed would give the "designated dad" a budget and make him responsible for planning a family outing to the park of his choice. The kids would be up at dawn to push their red wagon to the ice house around the corner and buy ice for the cooler. In the car the designated dad would sit behind the driver and hand over the money at toll booths. At the park the kids would haggle over whether to eat or

IT MAY LOOK YUMMY. . .

The next time you see a commercial for a big, juicy, fast-food burger, ask your kids how the picture stacks up against the real McCoy. Then share with them a few fun facts about food commercials. For example, those juicy burgers are mostly raw, just seared for a few seconds on each side; the grill marks are added by hand, the sesame seeds are glued onto the bun one by one, and a piece of cardboard is slipped into the bun to keep it from getting soggy.

Other tricks of the food stylist's trade: Shortening, sugar and food coloring make ice cream that doesn't melt, liquid school glue makes cereal milk that looks creamy, and dishwashing liquid makes hot chocolate that looks bubbly (the marshmallows are styrofoam balls).

These and other behind-the-scenes glimpses into advertising aimed at children are included in a series of three half-hour videotapes created by Consumer Reports: *Buy Me That, Buy Me That Too* and *Buy Me That 3*. First shown on cable TV's HBO, *Buy Me That* and *Buy Me That 3* are available from Public Media Inc. (800-826-3456). *Buy Me That Too* is available from Ambrose Video (800-526-4663).

ride. (Craig always wanted to splurge on french fries, while Lyle hoarded his pennies for an extra turn on the coaster.) The kids were required to hold enough in reserve to pay the tolls on the way home but "once their money was spent, that was it," says Ed. With Craig in charge the day sometimes ended early, but Lyle often came home with money in his pocket, which he was allowed to keep.

Did the lessons stick? Lyle got his college degree in finance and works in the mortgage department of a commercial real estate firm. Craig produces music videos and picked up enough money sense along the way to run his own business.

Watching Television With a Critical Eye

By this age, kids are sophisticated enough to figure out when a commercial doesn't ring true in practice. When the oldest of my three children was 8, I took them to McDonald's to sample Mighty Wings, spicy chicken wings that McDonald's had been trumpeting in an advertising blitz. The 8-year-old observed that the real wings weren't nearly as juicy-looking as the televised version and the hot sauce wasn't as thick.

But ultimately you want to help them spot the hype before they're disappointed in a purchase. When your children see a commercial showing kids whooshing by on in-line skates or guiding a remote-control car around hairpin turns, ask them if they could do the same without practice. Kids naturally expect a toy to work exactly as they saw it perform on TV so it's important to teach them that they may need to be patient and learn to master a skill.

Before you spring for a much-wanted toy, take your children to the store and have them look at the coveted item in its box, where it isn't surrounded by a glitzy TV background and special effects.

Instead of rushing to be the first one on the block

to have a new toy, encourage your children to be patient and let someone else be the guinea pig. After your kids have had a crack at playing with the toy, they may find they can live without it after all. One youthful reader told *Zillions*, the consumer magazine for kids, about the dumbest purchase he had ever made: an expensive remote-control car that wound up eating batteries. If only he had waited, he discovered, he could have gotten the next generation car, with rechargeable battery packs.

Kids this age are old enough to understand the difference between fact and opinion, and you can use this as a talking point when you watch a commercial on TV. The next time you and your kids see the latest NBA hero quaffing a cold drink, ask the kids why they think he has chosen that particular form of refreshment:

CHILD'S PLAY

Talking with your children about money needn't be a chore. On the contrary, you can make a game of it. Even in today's high-tech world, some of the best teaching tools available to parents are low-tech board games. Here's a selection of classics and promising newcomers, all kid-tested by my panel of experts.

The Game of Life (Milton Bradley). A big hit among children of all ages because "it covers everything," in the words of one 11-year-old. "Everything" includes careers, college loans, mortgages, car insurance, dividends and taxes—an entire money-management course. Younger children may need some help reading the words, but they don't seem to have much trouble grasping the concepts.

Payday (Parker Brothers). A close second because "it's fun and funny." (One card reads, "Pay Tick Tock, Inc. We cleaned your clock.") The idea is to get from one payday to the next with money to spare. Kids love to take a chance when they land on the lottery square, but it's gratifying to hear them groan when they're instructed to pick up bills from the mailbox or pay a "monster charge"—with interest.

The Allowance Game (Lakeshore Learning Materials; 800-421-5354). Ranks up there with Payday because it's easy for younger children to understand and appreciate. As they make a circuit of the board, players are instructed to do things "that kids really do," such as play a video game or forget their homework. And the money denominations are manageable: The first player to save $20 is the winner.

Monopoly (Parker Brothers). Still popular, although from a child's standpoint this game's slower pace and longer playing time (does it *ever* end?) is a drawback. And compared with the other games, "you only do

---

- **Is it because** that's the absolute best-tasting drink on the market, or because the player happens to like it?
- **Did the soft-drink company** pay him to do the commercial?
- **Why would an advertiser pick** a TV or sports star to pitch its product?
- **Would your kids buy the drink** on the strength of a basketball player's say-so?
- **Is it possible that the player** can't stand the taste of the stuff?

Studies show that simply talking to your kids about ads can make a difference in how they regard commercials and how much they ask for. Children this age can also detect hype; by this time, they've probably bought or received as a gift something that

one thing," says a 10-year-old—buy and sell property. Parents can pick up the pace, and pique the interest of younger kids, by making a slight change in the rules: Let players start building houses and hotels as soon as all the properties are purchased, even if they don't own a monopoly.

Monopoly Junior (Parker Brothers). A welcome alternative to the senior version for both children and adults because you can actually finish a game in a reasonable amount of time. Instead of Boardwalk and Park Place, players buy Bumper Cars, Roller Coaster and other attractions at an amusement park, and charge each other admission instead of rent. The money denominations are smaller than in regular Monopoly, and the playing pieces are bigger—no little green houses to keep track of.

Presto Change-O (Educational Insights, 800-933-3277). At first blush the idea seems too simple: Follow the "Earn" and "Spend" directions on a circuit of the board and be the first to save $10. But there's a trick: Your stock of cash can never include more than one nickel, two dimes, three quarters, four $1 bills or one $5 bill, so, presto change-o, you're constantly rebalancing your accounts to make the right change. A 7-year-old found it "challenging"—and so did his mother.

Careers (Parker Brothers). This classic is tough to find, but you can buy it from www.eToys.com (my kids rescued an old but intact set from a neighbor's trash pile). Players choose their "success formula"—a combination of money, fame and happiness—and enter various occupations trying to collect the right number of dollars, stars and hearts. The game took a while to finish, but the kids enjoyed it enough to play again. "A little like Life," they concluded. Hint: Fame can be easier to achieve than fortune.

didn't measure up to its TV image. When *Zillions* publishes its annual ZAP awards (for "ZAP it off the air, please!") it is deluged with nominees. Among the recent winners, chosen by a panel of young readers: Flip 'n Dive Barbie, who, in the ad, does perfect front and back flips into a swimming pool and various other bodies of water. In real life, Barbie flopped. "All she did was sort of sit and fall," said one tester. In the ad, a computer-animated Hot Wheels Volcano Blowout erupts and sends Hot Wheels cars racing around a track. In real life, the volcano took lots of time to assemble and then fizzled: The mountain didn't breathe smoke, and the cars kept getting stuck. In the ad, Baby Tumbles Surprise! did perfect tumbles over and over again. The real surprise came when baby stumbled, over and over again. The doll tumbled only 25% of the time, said one tester, and even then "you had to push it hard."

Tricks With Allowances

By this time, your children are old enough to get an allowance (more, much more, on that subject in Chapter 8). If you give one, dole out a variety of small-denomination coins and bills. If the allowance is $2, for example, you might give a one-dollar bill and four quarters. This helps teach children money equivalents and also makes it easier for them to set aside money for specific purposes, such as saving or charitable giving.

Be on the lookout for unexpected openings to slip in a lesson that otherwise might fall on deaf ears—what author and parent Harold Moe calls "hot buttons." Moe recalls his own frustration in trying to get his son, Rolf, who was around 8 years old at the time, to save money. Then Rolf saw the original Star Wars movie and was hooked; he voluntarily saved his money to join the official fan club and was determined to become a Jedi knight. Moe saw his chance and leaped. "We talked about how Jedis have to save money for college, and the next day Rolf put on his

Jedi robe and opened a savings account." Years later, Moe observed with satisfaction that Rolf had several thousand dollars in the bank that otherwise wouldn't be there "just because we talked about the need for Jedi knights to go to college."

Rainy-Day Perk-Ups

Nothing tops old standbys such as Monopoly or The Game of Life for teaching kids how to handle money. If Monopoly seems daunting for younger kids, it's okay to bend the rules a bit to let players build houses and hotels even if they don't own all the properties of a single color. Or try Monopoly Junior, which older kids (and adults) will like, too, because you can play an entire game in about 45 minutes. You'll find a selection of my family's favorites on pages 76-77.

In addition to those, we recently tested a couple of new money-oriented board games and a classic:

■ **Moneywise Kids** (Aristoplay; 800-634-7738). In the "Bill Maker" version, players roll the dice, collect the appropriate amount (a six counts for $6 and so on down to one, which counts for $10) and exchange smaller bills for larger ones. The first to get a $100 bill

---

DEAR DR. TIGHTWAD

Q. When the Salvation Army kettles appear at holiday time, it's easy to teach kids the value of giving. What can we do for the rest of the year?

A. Charity begins at home. Kids will follow your lead. Even a simple act like contributing to the collection at church won't go unnoticed by your children.

If you have a favorite charity, don't just write a check and send it off. Talk with your children about what you're doing and why.

If you have neighbors who are elderly or ill, encourage your kids to offer their services to run errands, read, or just sit and talk.

Designate a special container for "found" money that kids pick up off the ground or under the sofa cushions. Then they can give the money to a charity or cause of their choosing.

Have the kids pack up their own clothes that don't fit and toys they no longer play with. Bring the children with you when you give away the old stuff.

FUN MONEY MATERIALS

Take advantage of rainy days and bedtime to slip your children some broccoli with their milk and cookies. Dozens of books, software programs, magazines, videos and Web sites teach kids about money and economic concepts in the context of fun. Here's a sampling:

Books for Younger Kids

- *Alexander, Who Used To Be Rich Last Sunday*, by Judith Viorst (Atheneum), about a boy whose money burns a hole in his pocket.
- *Arthur's Funny Money*, by Lillian Hoban (Harper Trophy), in which Arthur sets up a bike-washing business to earn money for a T-shirt.
- *The Berenstain Bears Get the Gimmies*, by Stan and Jan Berenstain (Random House), in which Brother and Sister Bear have the "galloping, greedy gimmies." Other money-oriented books in this series include *Trouble with Money, Mama's New Job, Meet Santa Bear*.
- *Eyewitness Books: Money*, by Joe Cribb (Alfred A. Knopf). An encyclopedic history of money, foreign currency and trading.
- *From Gold to Money*, by Ali Mitgutsch (Carolrhoda Books). Defines bartering, counterfeiting, minting and earning money.
- *Freckle Juice*, by Judy Blume (Yearling Books), in which Andrew uses five whole weeks of allowance to buy a secret freckle recipe and learns some valuable consumer lessons as a result.
- *The Go-Around Dollar*, by Barbara Johnston Adams (Simon & Schuster), in which a dollar bill travels from person to person. The book also explains where and how money is made.
- *The Peanut Butter and Jelly Game*, by Adam Eisenson (Good Advice Press). Young people learn the consequences of spending all their money the moment they get it.
- *If You Made a Million*, by David M. Schwartz

(Lothrop, Lee & Shepard), in which Marvelosissimo the Mathematical Magician shows what money looks like and demonstrates the concept of a million dollars.
- *Money, Money, Money*, by Nancy Winslow Parker (HarperCollins). A brightly illustrated exploration of the meaning of the art and symbols on U.S. paper currency.
- *The Monster Money Book*, by Loreen Leedy (Holiday House). Members of the Monster Club discuss money, managing and spending their dues and how to be a smart shopper.

Software for Younger Kids

- *The Coin Changer* (Heartsoft). Realistic graphics teach money-counting and time skills
- *Treasure MathStorm* (The Learning Company). Players learn math, time and money skills while they collect treasures, catch elves and melt the ice kingdom.
- *Dollarville* (Waypoint). The child learns basic money skills by helping Dollarville's citizens with their money problems.

Books for Older Kids

- *All the Money in the World*, by Bill Brittain (Harper Collins Juvenile Books), in which a boy gets his wish for just that, with disastrous consequences.
- *Coping with Money*, by Richard S. and Mary Price Lee (The Rosen Publishing Group). Advice on allowances, budgeting, investing and saving for college.
- *The Kid's Guide to Money*, by Steve Otfinoski (Scholastic). This illustrated guide discusses ways to earn, save, spend, share and invest money.

- *Smart Spending: A Young Consumer's Guide*, by Lois Schmitt (Atheneum). Explores budgeting, misleading advertising, consumer fraud, warranties and consumer complaints.
- *The Money-Book Store* catalog (National Center for Financial Education, P.O. Box 34070, San Diego, CA 92163; 619-232-8811) lists other financial games and books.

Software for Older Kids

- *Hot Dog Stand* (Sunburst Communications). Players manage money and run a business while operating a hot dog stand at eight computerized football games. This program is part of the *Survival Math* series.
- *The Oregon Trail* (MECC). Adventurers travel by covered wagon from Missouri to Oregon. They learn to make their money last the trip and shop for and buy supplies they need.
- *Whatsit Corp.* (Sunburst Communications). Would-be entrepreneurs run a small, one-product (whats-its) business for six months, making the same decisions that any business owner must make.

Videotapes

- *The Making of Money* (Bureau of Engraving and Printing; 202-874-3315). A history lesson on U.S. paper money and a fascinating look at how currency is engraved and printed.
- *The Money Story* (The U.S. Mint; 202-283-COIN). How coins came into use, a visit to the U.S. Mint and vignettes on kid coin collectors.
- *Piggy Banks to Money Markets* (Kid Vidz; 800-840-8004). Told through the eyes of kids who experience the pleasures and pitfalls of running their own businesses or otherwise earning money.

- *Money: Kids and Cash* (The Learning Channel & the American Bankers Association; 800-338-0626). A two-tape set that's organized in short segments: How prices are set, why people value gold, money in other countries.
- *Money: Bucks, Banks and Business.* (The Learning Channel & the American Bankers Association; 800-338-0626). A two-tape complement to *Money: Kids and Cash*.
- *Schoolhouse Rock: Money Rock* (Disney). Characters such as Lester the Investor and Tax Man Max teach money basics.
- *Time to Save* (Merrill Lynch). Travel through Savin' Dave's wacky world of saving to learn about money. Check with your local Merrill Lynch office or online at www.plan.ml.com/family for availability.

Magazines and Newsletters

- *Young Money* (800-214-8090). Covers careers, investing, money management and entrepreneurship.
- *Young Entrepreneur* (888-543-7929). Focuses on budding capitalists.

Web Sites

- *KidsBank.com.* Shows where money comes from and how a bank operates.
- *Taxi Interactive* (www.irs.gov/taxi). A lively site that teaches teens about taxes.
- *The Mad Money Room* (www.nbc.com/atthemax/money). A quiz for teens on earning and spending.
- *Moneyopolis* (www.moneyopolis.org). Math skills solve real-life financial problems.
- *She's on the Money!* (www.girlsinc.org/money), *Independent Means* (www.anincomeofherown.com) and *Girls Unlimited* (www.girlsunlimited.com). Focus on encouraging girls and young women to be financially independent.

wins. It's fast-paced action for short attention spans (expect to be begged to continue playing until your child wins), but only two at a time can play.

■ **Easy Money** (Milton Bradley). Before you start, you have to bundle the game money into color-coded wads of ten bills each. "Sounds boring?" the directions ask. "Make it fun by pretending it's real, and it's yours! Or get friends to join you—'group wadding' takes less time and can actually be fun." Actually, it's still boring, and our players grumbled throughout the task. Once you're playing you can pile up millions of dollars by landing on spaces named "Greed," Wall Street" and "Lottery." "You get a whole lot of money and it's so fun to hold it," gushed one player. Another added a dose of reality: "It doesn't teach the value of money because it doesn't seem like it's worth anything." And one tester had a request: "Package the money, please."

■ **Masterpiece** (Parker Brothers). This classic art auction game is not about money per se. But it does teach kids how to bid at auction to set a market price, and our testers had a great time doing it. They especially enjoyed palming off forgeries on unsuspecting players. And I liked the fact that, as a bonus, they learned the difference between a Rembrandt and a Van Gogh.

Then again, you don't need to buy a board game just to play around with money:

■ **All those catalogs** cluttering your den are freebies just waiting to impart a lesson or two. Give your children an imaginary budget of, say, $250 or $300 and let them choose an entire winter or summer wardrobe.
■ **If you decide** to order take-out food, make it your kids' responsibility. Present them with the menu, a price limit and instructions to plan a meal that satisfies the whole family and doesn't bust the budget.

Facing Down Peer Pressure

As your children move through their "tween" years—roughly age 8 through 12—they'll be influenced more by their peers and their peers' possessions. Now you'll hear the plaintive wail that death is the only imaginable alternative if they don't get those $120 sneakers or $80 jeans or whatever the latest overpriced fad happens to be. Steel yourself. It doesn't hurt to give in on small things, or even on a few big ones that are really important to your kids. But every family has its line in the sand, whether it's certain foods, Super Nintendo or a private phone, and it's worth digging in your heels. In fact, it may be more important for you to give your kids the satisfaction of listening to their wishes than to satisfy them. "Nobody ever died from not getting a Betsy Wetsy," said Eda LeShan, author of *What Makes You So Special?*, which counsels kids on how to deal with peer pressure.

What does hurt is for kids to feel they have to be like others in order to be worthwhile. Sympathize with their desire to fit in, and maybe even meet them halfway, but emphasize that it's okay, even desirable, to be different. Kids who don't learn to buck the crowd when they're young will have trouble saying no when they're teens.

DEAR DR. TIGHTWAD

Q. My 9-year-old daughter has trouble holding on to cash. Last week she was going to a movie with a friend after school, so I gave her a $10 bill. Apparently she accidentally pulled the money out of her pocket while she was at school and lost it, so her friend's mother had to pay for the movie. I paid her back, of course, but it was embarrassing. How can I make sure this doesn't happen again?

A. You probably can't. She is, after all, a kid, and kids are prone to bouts of carelessness and lapses in attention.

Your best bet to safeguard the cash is to lash it to one of your daughter's body parts—in a Velcro pouch around her wrist, for example, in a fanny pack, or in a wallet or one of those funky keychains that attach to her belt. That way she'll be less likely to pull it out when she reaches into her pocket for a tissue or a stick of gum.

In the future, consider having your daughter use her own allowance to pay for movies she sees with friends. Then if the money happens to disappear, it will be her loss and not yours.

Remember that the choices you make regarding such things as where you live and where you send your children to school can make a big difference in the amount of peer pressure on your kids, and in their, and your, ability to resist. Sending your kids to an expensive private school can end up costing far more than the tuition if you're constantly being pressured to keep up with the Jones kids' winter ski trips and summer camps. The easiest way to deal with such influences is to avoid them altogether by not sending your kids to the expensive private school in the first place.

Whatever lifestyle decisions you make, at some point you'll probably have to fight the battle of the latest fad. But if you've been talking to your kids about money-related issues all along and are willing to keep talking, you won't have to relinquish the field to their friends. Kids can accept differences among families if they understand their own family's philosophy and financial circumstances and if they feel they're getting a fair hearing.

KIDS' QUESTIONS

Q. "Can I have a new G.I Joe?"
(Your 8-year-old in the toy store while you shop for another child's birthday gift)
A. When kids are preschoolers and asking for small items such as a cookie at the grocery store, it's easy to keep the gimmies in check by granting them one request (see the preceding chapter). By the time they're 8 or 9 or 10, the stakes are higher, and so, presumably, are their financial resources. Tell them you're going to the toy store to buy someone else a gift, and if they want to tag along in hopes of getting something for themselves, they should bring their own money.

Q. "Can I have [fill in the blank]?"
(Asked by any child of any age about anything when all you want to do is get through your errand list)
A. Sometimes, a parent will agree to anything just to get out of a particular store or situation. No matter how flustered you are, "No" is always preferable to "Oh, all right" or even "We'll see." If your children detect any wavering at all, they will immediately assume it means yes. Tell your kids you are buying what's on your list and only what's on your list. If there's any reason at all why you shouldn't deny their request outright—maybe they've asked for a new folder for school or something similarly noble that they know you're a sucker for—at least be specific in telling them that "school supplies are for another trip," by which time their urge to buy may have passed.

Q. "Can I play ice hockey?"
(Or gymnastics, swimming, or any other sport that can't be played in your backyard and requires more than a ball and a pair of sneakers)

A. Put your kids' latest request in context with all the other things they do. Financial considerations aside, there's no reason to add yet another activity if their schedule is already fully booked. I propose a "rule of three": No more than three days a week per child of activities that require being chauffeured (so soccer practice twice a week counts as two, but piano lessons at school don't count). If there's no room in your kids' schedule for anything else, expensive or otherwise, the answer to their request should be obvious.

Suppose your child's request isn't out of the question—just expensive. Test her commitment by telling her she'll have to make choices: If she wants to swim two or three times a week, she'll have to give up gymnastics. If he really wants to try ice hockey, he'll start with used equipment.

Q. "Why do we have to buy my clothes at The Bargain Barrel? Why can't we shop at Chez Chic, where the other kids go?"
A. You can nip this classic confrontation in the bud if you're willing to make a deal with your kids. If your conscience and your wallet allow, tell them you'll buy an item or two from this season's "name" store, but not their whole wardrobe. So your son might choose the monogrammed shirt all the kids are wearing, but wear it over standard-issue jeans. With a limited amount to spend at the store of choice, he'll be inspired to shop harder for bargains or clearance sales (guided by you, of course).

Your kids will learn how to look cool on a budget, and you'll still have your pocketbook and your principles intact.

Q. "Why won't you buy me a new video-game system? All the other kids have one."

A. "If all the other kids jumped off the Empire State Building, would you jump, too?" will no doubt leap to your lips. But don't try to be too clever or you'll end up outsmarting yourself. Kids won't necessarily make the connection between jumping off buildings and buying video games (or if they do, they'll probably choose to ignore it).

Say what you mean, which, I hope, is that "because everyone has it" is the last reason you'd consider buying something. It's critical that your children understand that your family's values may not be the same as the Jones family's. Maybe you can't afford to keep up. Maybe you feel your children's current video-game system is in good enough shape and they don't need a new one (unless you're willing to let them buy it with their own money). Or maybe you just don't want to referee disputes between siblings about whose turn it is to play (in which case you might consider compromising on a couple of hand-held game systems).

In any case, the decision is up to you, not the Joneses. And whatever you decide, your kids will not be social outcasts, they will not die (*you* didn't when *you* tried the same ploy), and they will not stop loving you or move out.

That doesn't mean you should *never* buy your kids something all the other kids have. It just means you shouldn't buy them *everything* all the other kids have. Be discriminating, choosing those things your kids want most and—if you've done your job—least expect. The element of surprise is more than half the fun for both of you.

Q. "How come you always take my money to pay the pizza man or the baby sitter?"

A. Okay, maybe you don't always take their money. But tell your children the truth: Parents often borrow spare change from their kids because their kids are the only ones who ever seem to have any. It goes with being part of a family. If parents can learn to put up with little annoyances like kids who leave wet towels on the bathroom floor, kids can learn to put up with parents who raid their cash stash.

However, kids do have a right to be paid back in a timely fashion. Parents don't intentionally neglect to repay the money; it just slips their mind. Consider this a friendly reminder and an opportunity to clear your conscience. Before you go on to the next question, give your daughter the $5 you owe her.

Q. "[Insert name of brother or sister] always borrows money from me and never pays me back. What should I do?"

A. You could tell your child, "That'll teach you not to lend him/her money any more," but that's only part of the lesson to be learned. Brother or sister also needs to be taught the consequences of failing to repay a debt.

Try a little "tough love" by taking both siblings aside and explaining the meaning of the word "deadbeat." Then lay down the house rules about borrowing, which might go something like this: Henceforth, any loan of petty cash is expected to be repaid by allowance day, at the latest. If that doesn't happen, you'll deduct the money from the borrower's next allowance—plus interest—give it to the sibling, and tell him or her not to advance any more cash.

It may sound a little drastic, but the idea is to get the delinquent sibling to shape up. And you may never have to charge interest or cut off a kid's credit. When one parent outlined the house rules to his children, the $3 big brother had borrowed weeks before mysteriously turned up on little sister's dresser within hours.

I don't object in principle to siblings lending money to one another as long as neither the borrower nor the lender is being exploited.

Q. "I lost the $20 you gave me to rent a videotape. Can I have more money?"
A. The lost money was your child's responsibility, and you're under no obligation to make up the loss.

Having said that, I'm willing to make an exception if your child is sufficiently chastened. I once heard from a young woman who vividly recalled an incident from her youth, in which she lost the money her mother had given her to go to the grocery store. "I felt awful, and just having to go home and confess was worse than any punishment my mother could have inflicted." If your child has scoured the video store for the missing money and is obviously upset about the loss, go ahead and rent the tape yourself. If a child loses money by accident rather than by habit, there's no need to rub salt into the wounds.

That's especially true if you're partly at fault. Parents shouldn't get into the habit of peeling off $20 bills to give their children. Young children especially feel uncomfortable about carrying that much cash. Not only do they worry about losing it, but they also worry about losing the change—or being cheated by a dishonest sales clerk because they're little kids. Give your child an amount of money that more closely matches the purchase price. If you don't have anything smaller than a $20 bill, pay for the tape (or whatever) yourself.

Q. "I lost my library book and they're charging me $10. Will you pay it?"
A. In a situation as clear-cut as this one, not even your children should seriously expect you to come up with the cash. But make sure your kids understand that the fine won't go unpaid. If they don't have the money right away, they'll have to save it out of their allowance or do extra chores to earn it.

When kids lose money, they feel the impact immediately. When they lose something other than money, the financial consequences aren't always as direct. It can take time, and a little effort on your part, to get the point across. A couple of other situations:

■ Your son tries out for football but quits, carelessly leaving his uniform in his locker instead of turning it in. A month later you get a $150 bill for a lost uniform. Your son doesn't have $150, and it would take too long to work off a debt that size. The school wants its money now. Advance your son the cash, but deduct $5 a week from his allowance until the loan is repaid (or let him do extra chores to work off the debt more quickly).

■ For Christmas you bought your daughter the snazzy watch she'd had her eye on for months. By Easter the watch is history, and your daughter is pining for a replacement. Let her pine. If you're willing to consider buying a new watch (and there's no reason why you should), at least make her wait until next Christmas. Absence may make the watch grow less attractive, or your daughter more careful.

Q. "Why do you always make us turn off the lights when we leave the room?"
A. While it's true that you don't own the electric company (as many parents like to remind their children), kids, even teens, are often in the dark about household expenses.

Tell them you have to pay the power company for the electricity you use each month, just as you pay the gas company for heat, the telephone company, the cable TV company, the supermarket and so on down the line. Because there's only so much money to go around, you don't want to pay anyone more than you have to. That way you'll have more money left for other things the kids might enjoy—like going out for pizza on Saturday night. Now you're speaking their language!

Q. "Can I give all my money away to poor people?"
A. Admirable though it may be, the impulse of some children to give away all their money is as unrealistic as wanting to spend it all on toys for themselves. And other children can take unfair advantage of their generosity. Caught without exact change, one mom and dad sent their 8-year-old to school with a $5 bill to pay for a $2 lunch. When the girl's friends asked her for money, she didn't have the heart to say no, and ended up giving away all the change.

The trick is to bring kids down to earth without dashing their spirit. In the case above, Mom and Dad sat down with their daughter and explained that they needed the change from the $5 to help buy groceries for dinner, or pay for the next day's lunch, or buy school supplies—expenses that an 8-year-old could understand. A week or so later, they deliberately sent their daughter off to school with a $5 bill in her wallet and a reminder to bring home the change. She did. (If you fear that your kids are a softer touch, don't give them any extra cash that could end up in some other child's pocket.)

In order to grow up with a healthy attitude toward money, kids need to learn that it's a tool with lots of uses. Just as overspenders need to be prodded into saving money, overgivers need to have their charitable instincts channeled. Help them focus on a favorite cause that appeals to them, preferably one that's in your community so the kids can take their money there themselves or donate their outgrown toys and clothing.

Q. "There's a contest on TV, and the prize is a trip to Disney World. Can I enter so we can go?"
A. Your kids will likely not win any contest they enter, but hope springs eternal. Explain to your children that with a limited number of prizes and lots of entrants the odds are against them. But let them enter anyway. Losing is a fact of life best learned by experience (and your kids will be less inclined to buy lottery tickets when they grow up).

One woman recalls her own childhood experience with games of chance. "One day my dad decided he would teach me to play poker. Once I had mastered the game, he suggested that we play for pennies. With the innocence of youth (and, I must confess, a touch of greed), I quickly agreed. Dad proceeded to clean me out. I was shocked. He later gave me back the coins, along with a lecture on get-rich-quick schemes and the risks of gambling. But what I remember most vividly was the feeling in my stomach when Dad won all my pennies."

Some contests are more child-friendly than others. The best of them should be easy to enter, have better odds than one in a million, and award lots of prizes instead of one big one. Kids should be able to write in for a list of winners. For many children, losing isn't as much of a disappointment as not knowing who won. Here's an excerpt from a letter written by one 9-year-old to the television show "Ghostwriter:" "I entered the 'Ghostwriter' sweepstakes last year. After I sent it in I never heard from you again. I wasn't sure when you were going to pick the winners and I was upset." The letter-writer was rewarded with a personal response, and a Ghostwriter pen and poster.

If the contest requires your children to write or draw something, or otherwise expend some constructive effort, entering could be a worthwhile experience regardless of the outcome.

Q. "When I pay for something, how do I know they won't cheat me just 'cause I'm a kid?"
A. While it may make sense to respond "Always count your change," don't assume that children know how to do so. They may be frantically trying to subtract numbers in their head, unaware that there's a much easier way.

If they buy something that costs $3.63, for example, and they hand the clerk a $5 bill, tell them to count the change from the smallest denomination to the largest: two pennies to make 65 cents, then a dime to make 75 cents, a quarter to make $4, and a dollar bill to make $5.

This system isn't intuitive. One woman sheepishly confesses that she didn't figure it out until she was a teenager and got her first job working the cash register at a bakery. (For more tips on how to handle cash, see the list on page 73.)

Q. "The antenna on my new remote-control car is broken. What should I do?"
A. Now is not the time to say "I told you that car wouldn't last." If a toy has broken through no fault of theirs, children should do the same things you would do if you bought something that didn't work: Call the manufacturer's 800-number, if one is available, or take the item back (even if it means an extra trip to the store on your part).

Kids are consumers, too, and are entitled to the same remedies as grown-ups if they're dissatisfied with a product. But they don't know the ropes and often feel at the mercy of adults. So you'll have to give them some basic tips—for example, always save the sales receipt—and go with them to return the item until they build more confidence.

Q. "Why do athletes and movie stars get paid so much money?"
A. Even if it's true that celebrities are greedy, that doesn't do much to advance your child's knowledge of labor economics. It may be hard to accept the fact that sports stars earn more than teachers, but it isn't hard to explain.

It's just a simple matter of supply and demand for workers. There's a big demand on the part of team owners and fans for top players, but there's a very limited supply of Jordan-caliber players. So their salaries are bid up. There's also a demand for teachers, of course, but many more people are available to fill those positions, so school districts aren't forced to bid up their salaries as high (nor could they afford to).

Don't forget, though, that despite the glamor and the money, sports and movies are high-risk businesses. Team owners and movie producers expect superstars to more than pay for themselves by selling tickets. If a movie bombs, a star becomes a has-been. If a player is injured, his value plummets. Even if he stays healthy, he can be washed up by age 35.

In economic terms, players try to "maximize their income" before they're fully depreciated (used up) as an asset to their team. In other words, they try to make hay while the sun shines.

Why Is Money Green?

Kids think in concrete terms, so it's little wonder that many of the questions they ask about money involve hard currency and coins. "Why does all our money have to be green?" they want to know, or "Why is a nickel bigger than a dime?"

Grown-ups, of course, take money for granted and are generally clueless about its origins. "Because that's the way it's always been" is your natural response to your kids' questions.

And you're not far off the mark. In addition to being a medium of exchange (meaning that you can buy things with it), money is also a store of value (meaning that people are willing to hold on to it because they think it's worth something). To keep the public's confidence over the years, money has to be stable and reliable. That's why you won't see the Treasury changing the green in greenbacks to jade or teal, just because that happens to be the color du jour.

But 'fess up. Even grown-ups wonder from time to time why we call a dollar a "buck," or for that matter, who decided that the dollar would be the official currency of the U.S. In this chapter, which is comprised of kids' questions, you'll get a glimpse into the colorful past of U.S. coins and currency and the fascinating history of the language of money.

Chapter Seven

KIDS' QUESTIONS

Q. "Do we have to use coins as money, or could we use something else?"

A. People can use—and historically have used—almost anything as money, as long as it's recognized as valuable. Yap Islanders in the South Pacific used huge wheels carved of a special stone that was brought hundreds of miles over the open ocean. Native Americans used necklaces made of shells, which were called wampum; the darker the shell, the more valuable the necklace. Coins were finally settled on because the metal was valuable (many early U.S. coins were made of gold and silver), malleable (meaning it could be worked into different shapes and designs) and portable (it was easy to carry in your pocket).

Q. "Why is a nickel bigger than a dime if a dime is worth more?"

A. It goes back to when "major" U.S. coins—the dollar, half-dollar, quarter and dime—were made of silver. The half-dollar, quarter and dime were made in proportion to the dollar in size and weight. So the half-dollar was half the size of the dollar, the quarter was one-fourth as large as the dollar, and so on.

The nickel and the penny weren't made out of silver so their size didn't matter. They were considered minor coins—small change, you might say—and at one time could legally be used to pay only very small debts.

A nickel is only 25% nickel; the other 75% is copper. In fact, a nickel has far more copper than a copper penny (see the question above right).

There's no such coin as a penny; its official title is the cent. Penny is a colloquialism that goes back to the English word "pence." And there's no such coin as a nickel, either. Officially, it's a five-cent piece, or a half-dime.

Q. "Why is a penny made of copper?"

A. Actually, it isn't—or not much, anyway. A penny is only 2.5% copper; the other 97.5% is zinc. It used to be the other way around (95% copper and 5% zinc), but in the early 1980s the value of the copper in the coin was beginning to approach the penny's face value. So the U.S. Mint, the U.S. Treasury agency that makes coins, changed the composition of the cent.

Why wasn't the penny made of silver, like other coins? We don't know for sure, although probably because it wasn't considered a major coin. The first cents were minted in 1792 and they've been made of copper in some form ever since, except for the year 1943 during World War II, when copper was needed for the war effort. That year, pennies were made out of zinc-coated steel.

But pennies haven't always looked the same. They used to be bigger than today's version. The first "small cent," which is the size of the current coin, was minted in 1856. And today's Lincoln penny first appeared in 1909, when it was issued to commemorate the 100th year of the president's birth.

Q. "On the penny, why is Lincoln facing toward the right while presidents on other coins are facing left?"

A. It's not a political statement, it's just the way the artist happened to design the coin.

Q. "Why do some coins have ridges around the outside?"
A. In the old days, when coins were literally "worth their weight" in silver or gold, people sometimes cheated by filing the edges of the coins and saving the precious metal. The ridges—called reeds—were adopted to discourage filing and to foil counterfeiting. Nowadays reeded edges help sight-impaired people tell one coin from another. The penny and the dime are similar in size, for example, so the reeded edges on a dime make it easier to identify.

Q. "Is my silver dollar really made out of silver?"
A. Not unless your coin dates back to the 1930s. That's the last time a 90% silver dollar was minted. No silver dollars were issued between 1936 and 1970. The last two dollar coins— the Eisenhower dollar, minted from 1971 to 1978, and the Susan B. Anthony dollar (1979 to 1981)—are "sandwich coins" like the dime, quarter and half-dollar, made with a pure copper center, and coated with a mixture of copper and nickel.

Q. "Can I use one of my silver dollars to pay for an ice cream bar?"
A. You can—but the Good Humor vendor doesn't have to take it. All coins are legal tender, meaning they can be used to buy things or

"Money" comes from the Latin "moneta," meaning coin or mint. The Romans themselves "coined" that word from the temple of Juno Moneta, where Roman money was made. "Moneta" literally comes from the Latin word for warning; among other things, Juno, the queen of the gods, was also the goddess of warnings.
"Bank" comes from the Italian word "banca," meaning bench. Hundreds of years ago, businessmen met outside on benches to borrow money or to entrust their savings to someone to invest on their behalf.

pay debts. But the law doesn't require anyone to accept coins as payment. Every once in a while, for instance, you may hear about someone who thinks he or she has been unfairly ticketed for a traffic violation and pays the fine with a carload of pennies. But the joke's on the driver; the traffic court doesn't have to accept the coins.

Q. "Is it true that the government is going to issue a new dollar coin made out of gold?"
A. Congress is talking about issuing a new dollar coin that would be gold-colored and have smooth edges (to distinguish it from the quarter). But it wouldn't be made of gold. And it might not be made at all. Vending-machine operators and transit systems like the idea of replacing dollar bills with coins. The Chicago Transit Authority collects 325,000 bills a day and employs 20 workers just to straighten out dog-eared dollars. But Americans might not like the idea of carrying around more change and less currency.

Q. "How long do coins last?"
A. A coin in normal use can last 30 years. Coins are classified in three categories: "current," which are regular circulating coins; "uncurrent," which are worn but still recognizable and machine-countable; and "mutilated," which are unrecognizable, corroded, broken, bent, fused together or otherwise not machine-

countable. If you have coins in that last category you can send them to the U. S. Mint in Philadelphia, which will redeem them by the pound at close to face value (write to the U.S. Mint, Coin Redemption Branch, 101 N. Fifth St., Philadelphia, PA 19106). But you have to send no less than one pound of coins, separated by denomination. The Mint won't redeem individual coins.

Q. "How many new coins are made every year?"

A. Here's how they stack up on average: pennies, 14 billion; nickels, dimes and quarters, one to two billion each; half-dollars, between 30 and 40 million. There's no ceiling on the number of coins that can be struck; the Mint will produce whatever is demanded. The total value of coins in circulation is a little over $20 billion—compared with more than $455 billion in currency.

Sometimes the Mint has to produce more coins even though there seem to be plenty outstanding, because a certain number of coins are lost or taken out of circulation—like that jar of pennies sitting on your closet floor. At the end of 1990 the government conducted a coin census and figured there were 132 billion cents in circulation. Since then the Mint has produced billions more of the coins. Yet a few years ago there was actually a shortage of pennies, and the government had to appeal to Americans to get those cents out of their jars and back into circulation. (If you want to turn in your pennies to a bank, you may have to roll them first—a task that's tedious for parents

In the old days coins were valued for their precious metals—either gold or silver. Today they're valued for their electro-magnetic properties so they can be used in vending machines. That's why they're made of a copper–nickel alloy.

but is a fun way to occupy kids, especially if they're allowed keep the value of the coins they turn in.)

Q. "Who needs pennies, anyway? Why don't we just get rid of them?"

A. Congress has considered such a proposal, but it has never gone anywhere, mostly because of opposition from the states. For state revenue collectors, pennies are crucial when setting sales-tax rates; it's much easier to raise the sales tax by a penny than by a nickel. And if the rate is, say, 4% or 7%, pennies are critical to collecting the right amount of tax.

Q. "Who decides which person should appear on each coin?"

A. All those decisions are made by act of Congress and the Treasury Department. The Secretary of the Treasury has some discretionary power to change the design of coins, but has always left that up to Congress. If Congress isn't specific about how it wants a coin to look, the U.S. Mint can decide or, if there's time, even sponsor a design contest. The portrait of Thomas Jefferson on the nickel was chosen after a design competition among 390 artists in 1938.

Among current coins, the design of the Lincoln penny has been in circulation the longest, dating back to 1909, when it was introduced on the 100th anniversary of Lincoln's birth. Washington began appearing on the quarter in 1932, the 200th anniversary of his birth. In the case of Franklin D. Roosevelt (the dime) and John F. Kennedy (the half-dollar), it was each man's untimely death in office that prompted his almost immediate commemoration on U.S. coins.

Q. "If I find a really dirty old coin, is it worth a lot of money?"

A. Probably not. Remember, the average coin is in circulation for 30 years, so even if you find a penny that was issued 30 years ago (which sounds like ancient times to most kids) it isn't old by coin standards. On the other hand, you aren't likely to find a coin minted prior to 30 years ago, because most of those have been taken out of circulation by collectors. What you've probably found is a dirty coin made relatively recently that is worth its face value and nothing more.

But just in case: Don't clean the coin, especially if you can't read the date. If it really is old, you'll decrease it's value substantially if you polish it up. If you can't make out the date, have it examined by at least two different coin dealers. You can also get an opinion from the American Numismatic Association, 818 N. Cascade Ave., Colorado Springs, CO 80903-3279.

If the date is readable and it's older than 30 years, look up the coin in the *Guidebook of United States Coins,* the so-called "Red Book" that is published every year and is the bible of coin collectors. Remember, though, that just because a coin is old doesn't necessarily mean it's worth a lot. Age isn't the only thing that determines a coin's value; rarity, condition and demand are important, too. A worn Indian-head penny from the early 1900s might be worth $1. But a "proof" coin from the same era, distinguishable by its brilliant mirror-like surface and sharpness of detail, might fetch closer to $200.

The 1913 Liberty head nickel is worth around a half-million dollars. But don't bother rummaging around in your pockets or piggy bank. Only five of the coins were struck.

Q. "If I start collecting coins, will I be able to sell my collection for a lot of money some day?"

A. Don't count on it. When it comes to collecting, you should do it for love, not money—and that advice applies to coins, comic books, sports cards, dolls and all other collectibles. While it's possible to make money, the market for any collectible can be complex and fickle. In 1995 kids were searching their pockets for the so-called doubled-die cent, a coin with an imperfection that made certain features appear to have been struck twice. The first few coins discovered sold for more than $1,000, but as more turned up the price quickly dropped to less than $100.

On the other hand, collecting coins can be fun for kids because it doesn't take a lot of money to start buying coins that interest you—U.S. Civil War coins, worldwide coins with pictures of animals, or coins from a particular country, for example. You can even buy 2,000-year-old silver and copper coins for as little as $5 or $10 (for more information on coin collecting, write to the American Numismatic Association at the address at left).

Just don't expect that when you're 18 you'll be able to sell your collection for enough money to send yourself to Harvard. You might make the carfare—but not the tuition.

Q. "What do people mean when they say 'Do you think we're as rich as Fort Knox?' "

A. Fort Knox is a former Army base near Louisville, Ky. Back in the 1930s the U.S. government built a gold depository there to hold most of the gold that was owned by the government and which, at the time, backed up the value of the U.S. dollar. The outer wall of the depository was made of granite and lined with concrete, as a symbol of national security and the soundness of the dollar, which was "as good as gold."

The government's stock of gold is still stored at Fort Knox, and has been stable for quite a few years at around 150 million troy ounces (a troy ounce is slightly heavier than a regular ounce). The price of an ounce of gold has been around several hundred dollars for years, but the U.S. gold reserves are carried on the books at $42.22 per ounce.

Q. "Does the U.S. government ever spend its gold?"
A. Nope. The government does issue a gold coin. It's called the American Eagle, and it's intended for collectors and sold as an investment, not as legal tender. But, by law, the gold that goes into those coins must be newly mined in the U.S.

Q. "Do people still mine for gold?"
A. Sure. The U.S. produces around 11 million ounces a year, more than half of which comes from Nevada and California. Despite the legendary Forty-Niners and the Gold Rush of 1849, the biggest growth in the U.S. gold industry has come since 1980. Miners no longer use pans and picks. Chemical processes extract minute gold particles from the ore.

Even with the new gold supplies that are

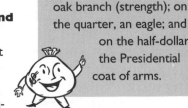

The **"heads" side** of a coin is called the obverse; the "tails" side is called the reverse. The Lincoln Memorial is pictured on the reverse of a penny; on a nickel it's Monticello, Thomas Jefferson's home in Virginia; on the dime, it's the torch (liberty), olive branch (peace) and oak branch (strength); on the quarter, an eagle; and on the half-dollar, the Presidential coat of arms.

mined each year, all the gold in the world would fill only half the Washington Monument.

Q. "Who thought of using a dollar as the main unit of U.S. money?"
A. It was adopted by the Continental Congress in 1785, although the first dollar wasn't actually issued until a few years later (it was a coin, not a bill).

Q. "How did they decide on the name 'dollar'?"
A. The word "dollar" actually dates back to 1518, when a large silver coin was minted in Bohemia in the valley (or "thal") of Joachim. Called the "Joachimsthaler," the coin spread across Europe, and its name was adapted to each country's language. In Dutch, for example, it was the "daalder," in Scandinavian the "daler" and in English the "dollar."

The Spanish peso, also called the Spanish milled dollar, was one of the principal coins in the early American colonies, along with traditional English money such as pounds and shillings. But once the U.S. declared its independence, the country gravitated toward the dollar, partly as a show of patriotism. The Mint Act of 1792 established the dollar as the official monetary unit of the U.S., and the first dollar coin was struck in 1794 (the federal government didn't print a paper dollar until 1862).

Q. "What are dollar bills made of?"
A. A secret formula that isn't really paper at all but a combination of cotton (75%) and linen

(25%). That explains why the bills can survive even when kids forget that their allowance is in the pocket of their jeans and throw them into the washing machine. In fact, the Bureau of Engraving and Printing—the U.S. Treasury agency that prints money—washes bills over and over to test their durability.

Q. "Why is money green?"
A. To be honest, the Treasury Department doesn't really know for sure, but can make a good guess.

Back in 1861 the federal government authorized the issuance of its own paper money. But it immediately faced a threat from counterfeiters. What was needed was an ink with a colored tint that would make the bills difficult to duplicate by the black-and-white photography of the time. Such an ink was developed and patented by a man named Tracy R. Edson. The ink had a green tint, which came to be called patent green.

When U.S. currency was last redesigned and made smaller in 1929, the green tint was continued because ink of that color was available in large quantities, and the color was highly resistant to chemical and physical changes. Besides, by that time Americans had come to trust their money as a strong, stable currency.

Q. "Why are dollar bills called 'greenbacks'?"
A. That nickname comes from the color of the ink and the fact that it's used only on the back of paper money. Look closely and you'll see that the front of each bill is printed in black ink. The Treasury seal and serial numbers are green, but that's a different ink that's added later.

Gold is stored in the form of bars that are a little smaller than building bricks but much heavier. Each gold bar weighs 400 troy ounces, or about 27.4 regular pounds.

Q. "Who decided which portraits would be on each bill?"
A. The current portraits, along with the design on the back of each bill, were chosen by a committee appointed by the Secretary of the Treasury in 1929.

Here's the lineup: George Washington on the one-dollar bill, with the Great Seal of the United States on the back; Thomas Jefferson on the two-dollar bill, with a picture of the signing of the Declaration of Independence on the back; Abraham Lincoln on the five, with the Lincoln Memorial on the back; Alexander Hamilton (the first Secretary of the Treasury) on the ten, with the U.S. Treasury building on the back; Andrew Jackson on the twenty, with the White House on the back; Ulysses S. Grant on the fifty, with the U.S. Capitol on the back; and Benjamin Franklin on the hundred, with Independence Hall on the back.

Until the currency redesign currently underway, the last significant change in the nation's paper money came in 1957, when the phrase "In God We Trust" was added.

Q. "Can the government change the color of paper money or put a different picture on it?"
A. It could, but don't hold your breath waiting for a blue suede bill with Elvis on the front and Graceland on the back!

By law, the design features on U.S. currency must have historical and idealistic significance, may not include the likeness of a living person and may not have sectarian significance (favoring one religion over another). The government could theoretically replace the current portraits of deceased American statesmen. But tradition and psychology would probably outweigh any popular trend. Part of the reason the dollar has endured in value, both here and around the world, is that its design hasn't changed much over the years. The government would be reluctant to shake that confidence.

The same is true of the color of money. In recent years red and blue fibers have been embedded in U.S. currency, but that was intended as an anti-counterfeiting measure rather than a fashion statement. It's true that other countries print their currencies in different colors, but Americans tend to regard those as "funny money."

The U.S. government prints more currency than other countries, and U.S. dollars are more often the target of counterfeiters. The Treasury wants U.S. notes to be uniform in appearance so that people feel compelled to look at the bills when they're paying for something or getting change, instead of just reaching for a bill of a different color or size. By paying closer attention, you'll be more likely to spot something fishy.

Q. "Why is the government redesigning our paper currency?"
A. The intent was more to foil counterfeiters than to make it look different. When you look at the new $100, $50 and $20 bills, the biggest change you'll notice in the new design is that

---

> **We've learned about the origin of the word "dollar,"** (see page 96) but the currencies of other nations often have interesting backgrounds. "Franc" comes from the Latin term "Francorum Rex," or "King of the Franks," an inscription that appeared on medieval French coins. Italy's "lira" comes from "libra," the Latin word for "pound." The "mark," used in Germany, means "to mark," or keep a tally. "Yen," the main unit of Japanese currency, is also the Japanese word for "circle." The theory is that money should "circulate."

---

the portraits are larger and slightly off-center. Over the next few years the $10 and $5 bills will be redesigned in a similar way (but the old bills will continue to be legal tender).

Q. "Has there ever been a woman's picture on American money?"
A. In addition to Susan B. Anthony, who appears on the dollar coins issued from 1979 to 1981, one other woman has appeared on U.S. currency—but not since 1896. Can you guess who that woman was?
a. Dolley Madison, President James Madison's wife, who saved valuable treasures when the British burned the White House during the War of 1812;
b. Martha Washington, George's wife; or
c. Clara Barton, who gained fame as a nurse during the Civil War and eventually founded the American Red Cross.

And the answer is . . . Martha Washington!

Q. "Who draws the pictures on U.S. money?"
A. U.S. currency is printed on presses using plates that are painstakingly engraved by hand by master engravers. There are fewer than twenty engravers in the country, and even in this age of computers they still work with hand tools similar to those used by Paul Revere. They're called letter engravers and picture engravers, and for each bill, one person does the signatures and all other letters, while another works on the pic-

tures and decorative scrollwork.

Q. "How much money does the government print every day?"

A. The Bureau of Engraving and Printing prints more than 35 million notes a day, with a face value of over $400 million, on its presses in Washington, D.C., and Fort Worth, Tex. Of the notes printed each year, 95% are used to replace bills already in circulation.

It costs a little less than four cents to print a bill of any denomination. Newly-printed bills break down approximately like this: ones, 45%; fives and tens, 12% each; twenties, 24%; fifties and hundreds, 4% each.

Q. "What's the biggest bill?"

A. The $100 bill is the largest in circulation right now. The government used to issue notes in denominations of $500, $1,000, $5,000 and $10,000, but they were discontinued after 1969 because there was little demand for them. The largest bill ever printed had a face value of $100,000, but it was exchanged among banks and was never circulated to the public.

Q. "How long does paper money last?"

A. That depends on the bill's denomination and how often it changes hands. For example, a $1 bill is handled most frequently and has the shortest average life—18 months. The average life span of other currency: $5 bill, two years; $10 bill, three years; $20 bill, four years; $50 bill, nine years; $100 bill, nine years.

> **In 1775,** the Continental Congress authorized the issuance of currency to help pay for the Revolutionary War. Paul Revere, a silversmith by trade, actually made some of the first plates for this so-called "continental currency." But the bills quickly lost their value, giving rise to the expression "not worth a continental."

Q. "What does the government do with worn-out money?"

A. It shreds the bills, then recycles or buries them. Each year the government destroys about $13 billion in worn-out currency.

Q. "What's that funny picture of a pyramid with an eye on top that's on the $1 bill?"

A. That's the reverse side of the Great Seal of the United States, which was adopted in 1782. At the base of the pyramid is the year 1776 in Roman numerals. The pyramid itself stands for permanence and strength, but it's unfinished, which signifies the future growth of the United States and the goal of perfection. The sunburst and the eye above the pyramid represent the overseeing eye of God.

The 13-letter motto, "Annuit Coeptis," means "He has favored our undertakings." Below the pyramid is the motto, "Novus Ordo Seclorum," which means "A new order of the ages" and stands for the new American era.

Even if they don't ask, you can impress your kids by telling them that the front of the Great Seal of the United States also appears on the back of the $1 bill. That's the picture of the American bald eagle behind the shield. The eagle holds in its right talon an olive branch that has 13 berries and 13 leaves. The olive branch stands for peace, and the number 13 always symbolizes the 13 original colonies. In its left talon, the eagle holds 13 arrows, representing war. The eagle's head is turned toward the olive branch, showing a desire for peace.

The top of the seal represents Congress, the head of the eagle the executive branch, and the nine tail feathers the judiciary branch of our government. The 13-letter motto, *E Pluribus Unum*, on the ribbon held in the eagle's beak means "Out of Many, One."

Q. "What does the Treasurer of the United States do?"

A. The Treasurer of the United States, whose signature sharp-eyed kids will spot on the front of U.S. currency, is the Treasury Department official in charge of the U.S. Mint and the Bureau of Engraving and Printing. The Treasurer is not to be confused with his or her boss, the Secretary of the Treasury, whose signature also appears on U.S. currency.

Q. "If I accidentally tear a dollar bill and tape it back together, can I use it?"

A. Yes. You can use the bill even if you don't tape it back together as long as you clearly have more than half of the note. You can also take it to your local bank and exchange it for a new bill. That's also true for bills that are dirty, defaced, limp or just plain worn out.

It's illegal to intentionally deface a bill by doodling on it, for example. But you're unlikely to be prosecuted unless you make a habit of drawing mustaches on George Washington. In that case, your artistry may come to the attention of the Secret Service, the agency charged with tracking down counterfeiters and protecting the nation's currency.

Like the word "dollar," lots of our words for money and other financial terms have their roots in other languages. A **"doubloon,"** the English word for a Spanish gold coin, comes from the Spanish word for double, because a doubloon was worth twice as much as a smaller coin called a pistole. **"Picayune,"** a word we use to mean trifling, or of little value, comes from the French word for a small copper coin. **"Dime"** comes from the Latin word *decimus*, meaning "tenth." When Thomas Jefferson proposed this unit of currency, he called it the "disme," a French term, because the coin would be one-tenth the value and size of the dollar.

Q. "If I only have a piece of a $1 bill, can I still use it?"

A. Not if it's less than half of the original note. In that case, your remnant is considered mutilated currency and isn't legal tender. If you want to exchange it for a new bill, you'll have to tell the Treasury Department how the money was damaged and provide evidence that the missing portion has been totally destroyed.

But if all you have is a small portion of a single bill, your chances of getting a replacement are slim. Each year the Treasury handles about 30,000 claims and redeems mutilated currency valued at over $30 million. But much of that is in the form of batches of bills that have been visibly damaged by fire, water, dirt, chemicals, explosives, rodents or insects. Nowadays, one of the biggest causes of mutilated money is microwave damage. When their money accidentally gets wet, people try to dry it in a microwave oven and end up turning their cash into ash!

All claims regarding mutilated currency are handled by the Department of the Treasury, Bureau of Engraving and Printing, OCS/BEPA, P.O. Box 37048, Washington, DC 20013.

Q. "How can I tell if a bill is counterfeit?"

A. Don't bother testing the ink to see if it smears. According to one bit of folk wisdom, a bill must be counterfeit if the ink rubs off. The truth is that genuine currency, when rubbed on paper, can leave ink smears, too. So the Secret Service doesn't recommend using the ink blot test to check out a suspect bill.

Instead, you should compare the suspect note with a genuine one of the same denomination and look for any differences in the characteristics of the paper or the quality of the printing. Genuine paper, for example, has tiny red and blue fibers embedded throughout. Counterfeiters often try to simulate those fibers by printing red and blue lines on their paper, but the lines are printed on the surface of the paper rather than embedded in it.

On a genuine bill, the overall printing is sharper and more distinct. Compare especially such features as the portraits, which should appear lifelike; the clarity of the sawtooth points of the Treasury seal; the serial numbers, which should be evenly spaced and printed in the same ink color as the Treasury seal; and the border, on which the fine lines should be clear and unbroken.

Before the federal government established an official U.S. currency, colonies, banks and even individuals issued their own money, which often wasn't worth the paper it was printed on. Even Benjamin Franklin got into the act, printing dollars on his own press for the colony of New Jersey. With typical Franklin bluntness, the motto on the bill read "Mind Your Business."

If you really believe you might have a counterfeit bill, the best thing to do is to put it in an envelope and take it to a bank or your local police department.

Q. "Can I see money actually being made?"

A. If you visit Washington, D.C., you can take a tour of the Bureau of Engraving and Printing. There's no charge for the tour, but in peak tourist seasons—spring vacation and during the summer—you need to pick up tour tickets in advance on the day of your visit (call 202-874-3188 for more information).

Two of the five U.S. Mints—in Denver and Philadelphia—are open for self-guided public tours. Contact the U.S. Mint Exhibits Office, 151 N. Independence Mall East, Philadelphia, PA, 19106; 215–408–0110 for more information.

Q. "Grandma told me I could use my birthday money for 'mad money.' Does that mean I have to get mad before I spend it?"

A. I presume most parents know that "mad money" is understood to be money you can blow on anything you want, but you probably don't know where the expression originated. And don't presume that your kids know what the phrase means—or, for that matter, that they understand any of the other money idioms and adages that litter our language.

We pay cash on the barrelhead, save for a

rainy day, and put in our two cents. Some expressions are intuitive, some have historical roots in everyday experience, and some we owe to Benjamin Franklin, whose *Poor Richard's Almanac* was rich in financial wisdom—"A penny saved is a penny earned," "Penny wise and pound foolish."

But your children won't necessarily understand any of these expressions unless you explain them. Then, if you come up totally blank and can't think of any other response to their questions, at least they'll know what you're talking about.

By the way, the expression "mad money" came into common use in the 1920s. It referred to money a young woman carried with her on a date so that she could pay for busfare home if she got "mad" at her escort for inappropriate behavior!

Part of the reason the dollar has endured in value, both here and around the world, is that its design hasn't changed much over the years.

Q. "How do people decide how many French francs or English pounds a dollar is worth?"

A. The value of a dollar can change every day, and it's decided in an open market by people who actually buy and sell money. In this way, the currency market is much like the stock market or even a flea market.

To understand how this works, it helps to think of money itself as the product that's being bought and sold. Suppose you're planning a trip to Paris. You'll have to pay for your hotel, your fancy French pastries, and your tickets on the Metro (the Paris subway), but in France they don't take dollars, they take francs. So before you leave home you'll have to buy francs for the trip from a bank or a money exchange. The bank gets its francs from traders all over the world who are linked by computer.

How many francs will a dollar buy? It all depends on how many francs the traders are willing to sell. If they are eager to get dollars—maybe because they want to buy American products, or because they just like the idea of owning dollars—they may be willing to make you an attractive offer of, say, six francs for a dollar. In that case, we say that the dollar is "strong."

But if they aren't very interested in buying dollars—maybe because they already have enough and don't want any more—they may offer you only four francs for your dollar. In that case, we say that the dollar is "weak"— and your trip just got more expensive, because you have to spend more dollars to get the francs you need.

Allowances: A Hands-On Experience

When it comes to money, topic A for discussion between parents and children is allowances. First, the kids want to know if they can have one. No sooner do they get one, or so it seems, than they want an advance. And before you know it they're lobbying for a raise.

It isn't only parents and children who lock horns on this issue. Parents often disagree with each other about such things as how much to give and whether kids who get an allowance should be required to do chores in return.

No single allowance system will work for every family. But any system will work if you follow two basic rules for success. One: Don't start giving an allowance until your children are old enough to manage it. Two: Keep the system simple so that *you* can manage it.

If you think that by denying your kids an allowance you'll be able to limit the amount of money they get their hands on, forget it. Studies show that kids who don't get allowances have access to about as much money as kids who do.

Since they're apparently going to get the money anyway, it's better to have them learn to manage it themselves than nickel and dime you to death. With an allowance, both of you will actually have more control over your children's finances—especially if you make it clear to the kids that the allowance isn't bonus cash, but will take the place of money you normally would have spent on such things as comic books, trading cards, art supplies, hair bows, or other kid-related expenses.

You don't need to give an allowance until your children are at least six years old. You don't want to rush things, and preschoolers generally don't understand the abstract idea of money anyway. Whether you give them 50 cents, $1 or $2, for example, they're not quite sure how much they have or how far it will go.

Once children start first grade they begin learning about money in school, so they'll know that if they get a $1 bill each week, that's equivalent in value to ten dimes or four quarters. They'll also have some idea of how much their dollar will buy. If your child is 9, 10 or even older and you don't already give an allowance, it's not too late. Some parents have even started their kids on an allowance when they became teenagers as a rite of passage to becoming more grown-up.

How Much Is Enough?

When setting an allowance, you should give enough so that your children can squander it, but not so much that you'll be upset when they do. Sit down with your children and decide what expenses their allowance will have to cover. You might expect an 11-year-old to pay for his or her own movie admissions, but that's probably too much to ask of a 6-year-old.

Don't underestimate a kid's cost of living. Take a lesson from Lamb Chop, the puppet on the perennially popular PBS show starring the late Shari Lewis and her animal friends. In one episode, the lovable lamb was negotiating for a raise in her penny-a-week allowance. "Do you buy anything?" asked Shari. Retorted Lamb Chop, "If I save it for 12 weeks, I can blow it on a pack of gum." Shari and Lamb Chop eventually settled on 7 cents a week, but if you're going to leave room for a pack of gum your children will need at least a quarter, not the nickel of your youth.

When you and your children settle on an allowance, be open and realistic about what you expect the money to cover. Besides movie tickets, you might want your 11-year-old to pick up the cost of snack foods and games at the video arcade but figure that basic expenses for clothing and school supplies are your responsibility. By the time your child is 15, however, it's reasonable to expect him or her to be kicking in for clothes, movie tickets and the French Club ski trip. It's a help to ask other parents how much they're giving. Ultimately, though, you can't let an "expert" or your neighbor down the street make your decision for you; you will have to go with your own instincts and values.

If you'd like some guidelines, however, I think first-graders need at least $1 a week to do any serious spending or saving; even $2 wouldn't be out of line. As children get older you can adjust that amount upward depending on how much of their own expenses you expect them to cover. One family decided to put their 12-year-old son and 10-year-old daughter on monthly allowances of $50 and $40 respectively— which sounds generous until you consider that out of that money the kids were expected to buy birthday gifts for friends, pay for their own movie tickets and other entertainment, and still set aside money for savings and charity.

Giving kids a weekly allowance that's equal to their age is another option, but that tends to over-compensate younger children. And it's too rich for most parents, judging from the figures on average weekly allowances nationwide. For 6-to-8-year-olds, the average is about $4.80 a week, according to the Nickelodeon/Yankelovich Youth monitor survey. That rises to $7 for kids 9 to 11 and $16.60 for 12- to 17-year-olds.

Instead, you might give a weekly allowance that's equal to half your children's age, so a 6-year-old would get $3 a week and a 10-year-old, $5. Or you might set up your own allowance schedule, starting at $1 a week at age 6 and increasing by $1 a week on each birthday. When your kids are 13, say, you could switch to a monthly allowance as a reward for good money-management skills.

Negotiating a Raise

To all kids who want a surefire strategy for convincing their parents they need a raise in their allowance, here's my advice: "Don't whine. No, your parents don't live in the dark ages. And, yes, they know how much things cost. They're the ones paying the household bills, remember? In fact, maybe they're reluctant to give you a raise because they can't afford to.

"Instead of complaining, take the initiative to make a list of your income and expenses (use the worksheet on pages 124 and 125). If you find you're saving zilch and you're squandering all your money on snacks and entertainment, you're not going to win sympathy—or extra cash—from your folks. Instead, try the needs-versus-wants exercise beginning on page 119; it may help you cut back on the unimportant stuff and save for the important things you want. Your parents may be so impressed by your initiative that they'll give you a token raise anyway.

"If you have bigger expenses—lunches, transportation, clothes—and are having trouble making ends meet, talk with your parents, or maybe take them on a shopping excursion to scope out the situation. Don't expect them to spring for the latest—and most expensive—wardrobe. You may have to compromise on less- expensive shoes if you really must have the latest in jeans. Maybe your parents will increase your clothing allowance if you're willing to accept more responsibility for buying your clothes."

One 11-year-old told me that when she wants a raise in her allowance, her parents make her come up with three good reasons why. Hint: "Because I need the money" doesn't count.

No Bailouts

Don't be surprised if your kids blow their whole wad on candy, trading cards and arcade games. Just bite your tongue and keep a firm grip on your wallet. You, of course, have the right to veto any purchase that's unhealthy, unsafe or in violation of your family's principles. Outside of that, though, you have to expect your kids to go a little wild, at least at first. You can only hope that they'll calm down once they realize that no more money is forthcoming to bail them out.

In my experience, kids will spend unlimited amounts of money as long as it's yours. When their cash is on the line, you may be surprised at just how tightfisted they can be. Child psychologist David Lustig relates the experience of one of his partners, who was accompanied to the store by his then, 8-year-old son. As they were leaving, the boy picked up a plastic toy and put it on the checkout counter. If he wanted it, he was told, he'd have to pay for it himself. Replied the boy: "You don't think I'd spend my money on that junk, do you?"

Linda Jessup is the founder of the Parent Encouragement Program, a parent support group that

---

DEAR DR. TIGHTWAD

Q. We're experiencing a problem with sibling rivalry. Ben, the older sibling, is 12 and starting to get interested in music, so he's buying CDs with some of his allowance money. His younger brother, Daniel, 8, always wants to play them. Ben has told Daniel to keep his mitts off, which we think is a little harsh. But they are Ben's CDs, and we're not sure that we should interfere.

A. Interfere, by all means. That's what parents are for. In this case, you need to contribute a little of the wisdom of Solomon.

The CDs do belong to Ben, so he's within his rights if he doesn't want his little brother pawing them with sticky fingers and possibly breaking them. But Ben needs to learn that along with the privilege of ownership goes the responsibility of being generous with what you own.

Tell Daniel that if he wants to listen to a CD, he can't just help himself but has to ask his brother. Tell Ben that if he doesn't want to hand over a CD to his little brother, he should at least be willing to play it for him.

As Daniel gets older, and the novelty of the new CDs wears off, they'll probably become less of a bone of contention.

teaches a practical approach to child-rearing. She and her husband, David, also developed a cradle-to-college system for teaching their own seven children how to manage money. A cornerstone of their plan was to stand firm and let the kids get out of their own tight corners. Imagine, for example, a situation in which a child is invited to a birthday party but has run through his allowance and doesn't have enough to buy a present (one of the expenses the allowance is supposed to cover). "We tend not to give loans," explained Linda, "so we would discuss his choices and the advantages and disadvantages of each." He could, for example, not go to the party because he doesn't have a gift. Or he could give something of his own that his friend likes. Or he could make a card and enclose a promise to buy the gift next week. He could give a gift of service and offer to help his friend clean his room or let him ride his bike. "We have also allowed kids to go without a gift and suffer any social consequences," said Linda. "But that problem has tended to correct itself."

Doing Good

Parents often ask me if they should force their children to save part of their allowance or give a portion to charity. It would be ideal if they were to show both forethought and thoughtfulness on their own with a little encouragement from you. But if saving and giving are important values you want to teach your kids, by all means, have them set aside a portion of their allowance for those purposes (and any others on which you put a premium). In the Jessup household, each child was expected to tithe 10% and put at least twice that amount into savings, just as their parents strove to.

One family requires their children to contribute 10% each to savings and to a charity of their choice. One year the kids decided to "adopt" a mother and her four children who had been deserted by their husband and father. "At Christmas, the gift-giving was

---

DEAR DR. TIGHTWAD

Q. Here's the situation: My daughter was teasing her older brother while he was doing his homework. He picked up the TV remote control and threw it at her. She heaved it back. But her aim was off and she broke our kitchen window, to the tune of an $80 repair job. My son says it's not his fault that his sister has rotten aim and that she should have to pay for the damage. What do you say?

A. Your daughter may have started the skirmish, but your son escalated hostilities when he threw the remote control. Once a projectile was involved, the conflict was out of control and there was no predicting the outcome. Both of them should share in paying reparations.

---

awesome; the kids used more than their allotted charity money to buy things for the family," says their proud dad. "On my son's Christmas card to us, he wrote that this year he had learned it was better to give than to receive" (see Chapter 9 for more tips on getting your kids to save money).

Work for Pay

One of the most controversial issues regarding allowances is whether you should expect kids to do chores in return. Child-development experts generally recommend that you not tie your children's allowance to chores. "If kids get the idea that the only reason they do what they're supposed to do at home is to get paid for it, you're going to develop a bunch of little mercenaries," said Martin Ford, a developmental psychologist and professor of education at George Mason University. "They won't develop the sense that they do things as part of their responsibility to the family."

Many parents apparently don't buy that reasoning. Perhaps the idea of simply handing money over to their children sounds too much like a free lunch. Or perhaps they can't figure out any other way to get little

Billy to make his bed. In any case, surveys consistently show that most kids who get allowances say they have to do chores in return.

After years of speaking with parents about this issue, I have concluded that there's an even more fundamental flaw in a system that's linked to chores: It can be an administrative nightmare for Mom and Dad. If Little Billy's income is dependent on work completed, you'll have to go to the trouble of coming up with a pay scale per chore and monitor which ones actually get done. If Little Billy makes his bed on only four days out of seven, do you give him his weekly dole? And what if one week he decides that he doesn't need any money, so he doesn't do any work? In my experience, many parents end up handing over the money even if their children don't do the work, so the system fails.

Consider Your Goals

To help you find a workable solution to the allowance-for-chores quandary, I offer this set of guidelines:

IF YOUR MAIN GOAL IS TO TEACH YOUR KIDS TO MANAGE MONEY, give them a basic allowance that isn't linked to chores but is tied instead to certain spending responsibilities. For example, you might require them to pay for their own video games, movie tickets, trading cards or other collectibles. It's the easiest system to manage, yet the allowance isn't just a handout; it's directly tied to financial "jobs" your kids are taking over from you. If you still want to teach them the value of working for pay, you can always let them earn extra cash for extra jobs such as raking leaves, washing the car or cleaning the garage.

How do you decide what expenses your kids should cover? It doesn't matter how much or how little they have to pay for as long as they have to pay for something. Their responsibilities should depend on their age and your expectations. Some parents give their children a relatively small allowance and consider it mad money. Others hand out a bigger amount, out of which older kids are expected to pay for such basics as school lunches or clothing. Either system can work if you follow a few general rules:

Start small, especially with younger children. Put them in charge of the single thing they most like to spend your money on, whether it's comic books, video arcade games, or popcorn at the movies.

One mother, who is an artist, often took her 7-year-old daughter, Roxanne, to museums, where the child loved to buy trinkets from the gift shop—with her mother's money. Mom finally told Roxanne that she would have to use her own allowance to buy souvenirs. As if by magic, Roxanne became more conscientious about bringing money with her—and the price of the souvenirs she purchased dropped drastically.

Anticipate conflicts. Suppose you expect your kids to pay for their own tickets when they go to the movies with friends. Then suppose your whole family goes to see a movie as a holiday treat. Who pays? One mom and dad decreed that on family outings parents would pay for the tickets—but the kids would have to buy their own popcorn.

In another case, a mother wanted to encourage

DEAR DR. TIGHTWAD

Q. I don't like the idea of just handing over an allowance to my kids, and I'd like to link the money with chores. Any suggestions on how to do this successfully?

A. Keep it simple. Try one of these strategies.

Choose-a-chore. Attach a value to household jobs and let your kids select the ones they want to do. This plan works best with kids who need or want money. If they don't, the work may not get done.

Point system. Invest in a big calendar or bulletin board and have your kids tally a point each time they do something helpful around the house. At the end of the week you can award, say, 10 cents a point. This plan works best for younger children who do fairly simple tasks that are roughly equal in value, such as making beds or setting the table.

Negative option. Put your kids' allowance—say, $5 a week—in quarters in a glass jar (or use dimes for a smaller amount). Each time your children don't respond to your request for help, take out a quarter. At the end of the week, they get to keep what's left.

her 9-year-old to read without going broke buying books for him. She agreed to pay for up to $5 worth of books when Sam brought home the monthly order form from his school book club. Above that, he was on his own.

IF YOU'RE SET ON MAKING CHORES THE QUID PRO QUO FOR GETTING AN ALLOWANCE, go ahead and do it. But to make the bookkeeping easier—and to make the connection between work and pay more direct—consider paying your kids as soon as a job is done to your satisfaction instead of waiting for a designated payday. Or consider putting your kids in charge of keeping track of chores completed. If they fall down on that job, their pocketbook takes a direct hit.

To avoid turning your children into little money-grubbers who refuse to do anything without being paid, expect them to do a couple of basic chores—making their beds, cleaning their rooms—gratis. If they ask how much you'll give them in return for making their bed every day, tell them what I tell my children—they'll earn your undying love and affection. You will ease the tension with a little humor and put a more positive spin on household tasks—which, you can remind your kids, everyone in the family (including you) pitches in to do without pay.

Two Families' Systems

Brent Neiser, of Denver, Colo., has always used a strict fee-for-service system with his two children. The Neisers didn't pay for certain "family" chores, such as doing the dishes or keeping one's room clean, but they put a price tag on jobs that a cleaning service or a neighborhood teenager might be hired to do: emptying the wastebaskets, cleaning the bathroom, raking the leaves, washing the car. It was the children's responsibility to keep a record of everything they had done and present their parents with an itemized bill by 9:30 each Sunday morning. Then they could immediately deduct 10% for their weekly tithe. The idea, said Neiser, was to give the children, both of whom were adopted at the ages of 8 and 6 from difficult backgrounds, a sense of family structure. But it had unexpected benefits. When little brother was old enough to take over the job of emptying wastebaskets, "he felt great," recalled Neiser. "He was getting to do something his big sister had done."

Carol McCracken adopted a different system when her son Matt was in seventh grade. Carol's story started out as a classic case of an allowance "system" that was too open-ended. Her son, Matt, got $5 a week, but had no fixed instructions about what the money was supposed to cover. He regarded it as extra cash that his mother gave him on top of everything else, so he would fritter it away, then come back and ask for more. "We were always arguing about money," said Carol.

Tired of bickering, she finally gave in to his requests by increasing his allowance to $50 every two weeks. That may sound like an awful lot, but $20 of the total was earmarked for school lunches. And the rest was specifically designated to pay for most of Matt's expenses aside from clothing: movies, other entertainment, snack food, fishing equipment ("an endless need," said his mother).

DEAR DR. TIGHTWAD

Q. My husband is always slipping our kids a couple of dollars to get them to practice their music lessons or sports. I don't like the idea, but he says it's not a lot of money and it will give them an incentive to work harder.

A. Your husband is probably wasting his money. If your kids like what they're doing, they don't need any other reward. If they don't like what they're doing, maybe they should be playing a different musical instrument or sport.

If you can't get your husband to change his tune, try getting him to change his system. Instead of simply paying off the kids in cash, suggest that he reward them with "music money": For every 15 minutes spent practicing, they earn, say, one dollar in music money. When they've accumulated 20 music dollars, they're entitled to a new CD or a trip to the movies.

Young sports enthusiasts often have their eye on a new tennis racket, soccer bag or baseball glove. In this case try "sports cents": For every 15 minutes of practice, you credit your athletes with 100 sports cents. Once they've accumulated enough cents to pay for the coveted piece of equipment, you agree to spring for it.

With the allowance tied to financial responsibilities, Matt learned quickly that he had to manage it carefully to make it last. (He tried cutting back on lunch, but his appetite for food turned out to be greater than his appetite for other stuff). When he discovered that he actually spent more during the summer, he began setting aside a portion each month toward a "summer fund." He used to have a bank savings account with nothing in it; now he's saving for a fishing trip to Montana, starting with money he earned over the summer by watering plants.

"I had said all this to him many times before, but it was my money instead of his so it just never worked," said his mom. "Now his savings have a purpose, and the best part is he came up with it, I didn't."

Which just goes to prove what I always say: Kids will spend unlimited amounts of money as long as it's yours. When it is suddenly their own cash that is on the line, it becomes a whole new ball game, and everybody wins.

DEAR DR. TIGHTWAD

Q: My son is 4. I know that's a little young to start an allowance, but I got tired of having him ask me to buy chewing gum. So I started giving him five quarters a week, one of which goes into his savings jar. The rest is his to spend. He has his eye on a pair of kids' rollerblades and he already had $17 in spare change in his bank, so I told him if he saved his four quarters for four Mondays he'd have enough to buy the skates. (I'm willing to kick in the difference).

So far it's been working. He's chosen to save his money instead of spend it, and when we went to an amusement park he didn't ask for any souvenirs once he realized he'd have to pay for them. But I'm wondering if this will continue once he has the skates and has less incentive to save.

A. Your son is a little young to be getting an allowance, but you're doing a number of things right: giving him quarters instead of dollar bills, which makes money more concrete and easier to understand, and setting a realistic savings goal—four weeks is about as long as a four-year-old can wait.

It will be an eye-opener for him when he has to surrender all his money for the skates, but that's a lesson, too. If he doesn't start saving again right away, don't worry. Just make sure he continues to use his own quarters to buy what he wants. Not having him bug you for gum any more will be an accomplishment in itself.

Getting the Jobs Done

If you don't pay your kids, how do you get them to do chores? You could simply try asking, especially if your kids are still young. Many parents anticipate doing battle on the chore front, but unless you and your kids are barely on speaking terms, they should respond to your request. After all, you are still the one in charge.

"If you project self-confidence in your relationship with your children, you won't have to rely that often on techniques to get them to do what you want," said John Rosemond, family psychologist and author. "Put your cards on the table, and walk away and let your child come to grips with the hand." Rosemond recalls an incident that occurred when his own daughter was a teenager and he asked her to wash the dinner dishes. She protested that she had too much homework, and he replied that she could fit in both. Again she refused. "I got up, looked at her and said, 'You know and I know that you're going to do the dishes, so there's no point in wasting any more time.' I walked out and she did the dishes."

Even if you're not a trained professional, this is worth trying at home. If it doesn't work, deal yourself a new hand. You might, for example, let your children have a say in choosing the jobs they have to do. That will probably cut down on the complaining and gives them a vested interest in doing the job correctly. After all, your purpose in requiring your children to do household jobs is to teach them responsibility and get help with some of the things you just don't have time to do. So why settle for mundane tasks that don't take much time anyway? Give them bigger jobs that are potentially more interesting—and more likely to get done:

SANTA'S HELPERS. Children as young as, say, 7 or 8 can wrap a stack of gifts or help trim a tree. What does it really matter if the paper is torn and the ribbon is more than just a little askew? Grandparents, aunts and uncles will love their gifts all the more. So what if one branch is sagging under the weight of 20 ornaments?

You can always move them after the kids are in bed.

KITCHEN AIDES. Put your kids in charge of planning and preparing dinner once a week or breakfast on Sundays. The next time you have to come up with four dozen chocolate chip cookies for the class Halloween party, let your children do the baking.

WATER BABIES. Put them in charge of watering the garden, washing the car or the (low) windows, hosing the deck—any outside job that requires water (preferably from a hose or sprinkler), especially when the weather is hot.

WARDROBE MASTERS. Make your kids responsible for at least sorting and putting away (and possibly even washing) their own clothes. Trust them to pack their own suitcases for family trips. (Just check to make sure they've brought underwear.)

PARTY PLANNERS. Anticipation is half the fun, so let them write the invitations, plan the games, put the treats in the goodie bags, make the poster for pin-the-nose-on-the-witch and help serve the food.

The point is to raise your parental expectations. Author and family counselor Eda LeShan tells of a friend who had to be out of town for a few days and put her 10-year-old in charge of taking telephone messages. "That's pretty sophisticated for a 10-year-old, but the child was very proud of being trusted to do it." One mother agreed to let her 11-year-old son take money from her purse for a comic book, only to find it was a special issue that cost $40. She kept the book until he worked off the debt—by helping her install drywall in his bedroom.

Routine Tasks

Children also feel more comfortable with what's expected of them when it is part of a daily routine. Chances are you already have a schedule for getting your kids to do their homework or get ready for bed, so you just have to make chores part of the drill. Making beds goes with brushing teeth in the morning, and clearing the table or taking out trash goes with doing homework at night.

Martin Ford of George Mason University is the father of two sons. When older son Jason turned 5, he received, along with gifts, one chore to do; another was added on each birthday. By age 7, he was responsible for making his bed, setting the dinner table and doing his homework. "It was a mark of maturity," said Ford, "and we made it a matter-of-fact expectation that he did the job." Ford figures it's just like the real world: "Some managers think you can't get workers to do anything unless you pay them," he said, but setting high standards and expecting them to be met works, too.

I Won't Do It

If your children flatly refuse, much as they might refuse to eat their peas at dinner, their behavior could be a symptom of a power struggle that you may be able to defuse by talking things out. (For example, you might say: "Just as everyone in the family is expected to sample at least three bites of all the food that's on the table, everyone is expected to pitch in and do his or her share of work.") If not, you may have to fall back on those few time-tested and well-chosen words: "Because I said so and I'm the

---

DEAR DR. TIGHTWAD

Q. I never liked the feeling of giving an allowance (it seems like welfare) and have found a much more interesting way to teach my 7-year-old about money. Instead of doling out a couple of bucks a week, I pay her a percentage of whatever money she can muster from gifts or handouts. That is, each week the Bank of Daddy pays her 5% on what she has accumulated, and she records the earnings in a pretty notebook that she picked out. She suggested that she open a bank account when she gets to $60.

A. You have developed a great system for encouraging your daughter to save, but you could use a bit more discipline on the earnings side. Letting her depend solely on gifts and handouts is too haphazard.

She sounds mature enough to handle an allowance, and it doesn't have to seem like welfare if you hand over responsibilities with the cash (as outlined in this chapter). You could also pay her for extra jobs she does around the house. Having a steady source of income could also stimulate her inclination to save. The Bank of Daddy may have to rethink that 5% interest rate.

DEAR DR. TIGHTWAD

Q: My 8-year-old son was bugging me to take him to the toy store so that he could use his birthday money to buy a remote-control car he had seen on sale for $30. When we got to the store, he discovered that the battery pack was extra—and it cost more than the car.

He bought it anyway, but it just about wiped out his money and he was in tears when we got out to the car. "Are you mad at me?" he asked. I assured him I wasn't. "Then don't tell me I learned a lesson," he replied.

A. Congratulations on your restraint. Your son did learn a lesson, but he didn't need you to rub it in.

Mommy/Daddy." That strategy works better with younger children than with adolescents, who may respond better to a deal. Simply tell them that until they make the beds/vacuum the floor/give the dog a bath, you will not take them to the soccer game/movies/shopping mall. Then stand firm. It shouldn't take more than one or two missed matinees for them to get the message.

Or, like the Jessups, you may be able to think of a more creative solution. By age 11, all of the Jessup children were expected to be jacks of all trades, able to do the laundry for the family, prepare a simple, well-balanced meal and do the marketing. Starting at age 5, each child was given a weekly job, which the child had a hand in choosing. For example, a child might go "into training" to learn how to vacuum, cook or make lunches. If the child chose vacuuming, "I'd ask what days I could count on having it taken care of, and I'd expect it to be done at that time," said Linda. If it wasn't, "I'd point out to the child that he or she chose the job and ask what the problem was." Sometimes the solution was as simple as a gentle reminder—one kid hung a sign from his own bedroom doorway to remind himself—or trading jobs with someone else.

But sometimes Mom had to take matters into her own hands. Once, when Linda was dissatisfied with the performance of her kitchen and trash crew, she prepared a sign, complete with vicious-looking flies, announcing that the kitchen was closed by order of the Jessup Health Department. When the kids arrived home after school, ravenous for snacks, Linda told them the kitchen was unsanitary and she wasn't willing to cook there. It proved to be a smart strategy: Four of the kids put together a team-cleaning effort and the kitchen was reopened.

One final piece of advice about chores: Things should get better. When your kids are 6 they'll leave their wet towels crumpled on the bathroom floor. When they're 13 they'll leave them crumpled in the closet. But by the time they're in college, they should have the presence of mind to hang them neatly—over the doorknob.

Needs and Wants

As children approach their teenage years, it's not unreasonable to expect them to manage their allowance on a monthly schedule—and not unusual for them to run out of money before payday. Even though they seem like irresponsible spendthrifts, your kids may simply be having trouble budgeting. It's often tough for kids (and grown-ups) to tell the difference between things they need and things they want and to set priorities. Here's an exercise that will help:

On a sheet of paper, have your kids write down their total monthly (or weekly) income from all sources—allowance, jobs, gifts. Then have them write down everything they are expected to buy with their money and what they would like to buy. Give them free rein to include everything from pencils to a Porsche.

A week or so later, pull out their paper again. Have the kids break the big list into two smaller ones: the boring stuff they have to buy—such as school supplies and lunches, toiletries and whatever else you've agreed on—and all the fun stuff they want. Tot up expenses in the have-to-buy column, compare it with total monthly income and see how much is left.

In another week or so, go back to the list. Now that your kids know they have, say, $10 a week to spend on the fun stuff, they can see that if they use the money to buy a CD every couple of weeks, they won't be able to afford the new jeans. If they must have the jeans, CDs will have to wait.

Seeing all this in writing and over the course of a few weeks somehow makes it easier to categorize the items on a wish list as must-have, can-wait or in-your-dreams. It may suggest other possibilities as well—a part-time job for your kids or even a bigger allowance. If none of this works, maybe your kids are irresponsible spendthrifts. Cut them back to a weekly allowance until they're more mature.

A Clothing Allowance That Works

By the time children reach their early teens, they ought to be on their own to buy birthday gifts or an occasional article of clothing for themselves. As noted in the preceding section, it may be time to see whether they can handle an allowance monthly rather than weekly. And by the time they're high school juniors or seniors, they could be managing a quarterly clothing budget.

Does that mean you can trust them not to buy a black leather jacket with lug nuts hanging from the collar? Not necessarily. But if you've done your job you should be able to trust them to buy the jacket on sale. When your kids begin begging for a clothing allowance, tell them you will consider it if they earn the privilege by passing a shopper's-ed course of your own creation.

Lesson one is taking inventory of every article of clothing they own, including underwear, socks and pajamas.

Lesson two is having them make a list of all the things they need, as well as things they want. Then tell them what you think is a reasonable allowance—the amount you'd typically spend on their clothes each season, for example.

With the help of catalogs, lesson three is letting them practice matching a new wardrobe with the available funds. With luck, they'll learn that 1) they can't possibly afford five silk shirts, or 2) they'll have to shop in cheaper catalogs. Both are valuable lessons.

Now your kids are ready for a dress rehearsal by going with you on a shopping trip. To make the task less overwhelming, limit your itinerary to, say, three stores. Add your own commentary along the way: How to spot a bargain at sales or off-price stores; how to select clothes that won't fall apart in the wash; how to choose items that are stylish but not faddish, so they'll last more than one season. Tell them what, if anything, you won't finance.

The final exam is an excursion on their own. Don't grade them on their choice of styles and colors—you'll have to live with those, within the limits you've set—but on how well they manage their money. It's okay to splurge on a silk shirt as long as they find a great deal on jeans or buy their quota of socks. If they shop smart, reward them with a seasonal allowance.

DEAR DR. TIGHTWAD

Q: I recently read an article written by a mother who had put her teenagers on a strict allowance of $5 a week. She admitted that the amount was artificially low, but she bragged about what a great exercise it was in self-discipline. What do you think of this as a treatment of children suffering from overconsumption?

A. It might work as shock therapy, but it's not a long-term cure.

Putting kids on a starvation budget is as bad as overindulging them. An allowance is supposed to teach them how to make responsible decisions about controlling their appetites for CDs and pizza. Rationing their income limits their ability to make decisions—and encourages them to pig out later.

Unless those kids are wearing rags or holding down jobs of their own, it's likely that Mom and Dad are still paying a big chunk of their expenses. Strict allowance aside, the kids might agree with Bart Simpson's rejoinder to Homer and Marge's typically lame attempt to persuade him to earn some money of his own: "Room and board are free, and Santa brings the rest."

I gave my son John his first clothing allowance when he was 16. We agreed on $200 for summer clothes, and he set off on his own. He bought shorts and several T-shirts from Old Navy and a collared dress shirt at Abercrombie & Fitch. Total cost: $140, and John carefully counted into my hand the $60 he hadn't spent. (Daughter Claire went along on that shopping expedition and was proud to have used her own money to buy a pair of warm-up pants on sale from Abercrombie.)

You can always tailor a clothing allowance to your own situation. Lest kids skimp on undies or go overboard on a leather jacket, some parents continue to buy the basics, such as underwear and coats, or dispense money in more manageable monthly chunks.

The idea is to teach your kids how to function in the marketplace, so that when they're legally able to shop with their own credit cards they'll show both good sense and good taste.

Good Grades, Good Pay

When it comes to rewarding kids for good behavior or good grades, let them know you're proud of them by giving them a hug, a word of encouragement or a special treat such as stickers or a later bedtime—anything but money. That way, the virtue of doing their homework or getting good grades becomes its own reward, and they learn the personal satisfaction that comes with a job well done.

Sometimes money can be too powerful a motivator for parents to resist. Frustrated by the lack of response when she asked her two new stepsons what was going on in school, one woman offered to pay the boys 25 cents, up to 50 cents a day, every time they reported something new they had learned. "That encouraged them to think back over their day; it got them using their minds," she said. When the boys kept forgetting to put on their seatbelts, she started a game: first one buckled up gets a quarter. "Boy, what a turnaround," she laughs.

Using money as an incentive can be appropriate if you give small amounts under the right circumstances. For example, reward your kids after the fact for behaving well at the supermarket instead of promising them money ahead of time if they don't throw a tantrum. It may seem like splitting hairs, but the former is more of a reward, while the latter is an out-and-out bribe.

Payment for grades is a particularly touchy issue. In their heart of hearts, parents suspect that they shouldn't be rewarding their kids' academic efforts with money. But they want their children to do well in school, and if coming across with some cash will do the trick, they figure it's a small price.

Again, pay the kids a compliment, pay the tuition at the college their good grades will get them into, but don't pay them money. Buying grades, or any other good behavior, distracts kids from the sense of accomplishment that should be their real reward. Besides, it can get expensive. And if you're trying to control your children's behavior with money you're doomed to failure, because eventually they'll earn their own.

I do know of cases in which parents have successfully used money as compensation for grades. One dad worked out a complex set of financial incentives that rewarded his 11-year-old son for improved grades, even if they weren't A's. A mom set aside time every week to go over school papers with her first-grader and paid him $1 for every 100%. But money seems to work best as a motivator when it's used in small amounts over limited periods of time; the longer you do it, the less effective it is. Your goal should be to wean kids from cash just as you eventually weaned them from treats when they learned to go to the potty.

Even in the situations noted above, factors other than money were at work. In the first case, the 11-year-old admitted that he was also influenced by a conscientious teacher who prodded him to do better. In the second case, Mom's interest and approval probably had as much of an effect on her son's performance as the money. Paying a compliment will buy better results than paying cash.

While promising a reward ahead of time is risky, a spontaneous blowout after the fact to celebrate a good report card is always a morale booster. Go ahead, treat your scholar to a banana split, or even dinner at the restaurant of his or her choice.

A MONEY RECORD FOR KIDS

Use this worksheet to keep track of your money. At the beginning of the month, start writing down the money you receive and the money you spend. At the end of the month, you'll see whether you came out even (you spent as much as you received), ahead (you spent less than you received and have money left over to add to your savings) or behind (you spent more than you received and might have had to borrow money from Mom and Dad to pay for something). You can do this for a whole year by making 12 copies of the worksheet (record the cost of using the copier at the library under Odds and Ends, below).

The worksheet may help you decide that you want to spend your money differently next month. Maybe you want to increase your income by asking for more odd jobs around the house. Perhaps you will spend less on snacks so you can save up for a new pair of skates.

But remember, just because something is listed on this worksheet doesn't mean you have to buy it—or that your parents will let you. Besides, they may expect you to use part of your allowance to buy school lunches. They may expect you to save some of your money and to give some of it to help other people or your place of worship. It's a good idea to write down those amounts first thing each month so you'll set them aside and not spend them on something else.

Month _____

WHERE MY MONEY COMES FROM

My allowance $ _____

Odd jobs _____

Babysitting, paper route and so on _____

Gifts _____

Money borrowed from my parent(s) (or someone else) _____

My Total Income $ _____

WHAT I SPEND MY MONEY ON

Money I owe my parent(s) (or someone else) _____

My savings (savings account or piggy bank) _____

The Parent Giveth, the Parent Taketh Away

When your kids misbehave, it's better to make the discipline fit the deed than to dock their allowance. If they fight about the TV, they don't watch anything. If they dawdle in doing homework or getting ready for bed, they don't play Nintendo.

My church or other charity (like Unicef)   _____

Gifts for my family and friends   _____

Lunch money   _____

Clothing I help pay for   _____

School supplies and fees (class parties, science projects and so on)   _____

Snacks (sodas, chips, candy, gum)   _____

Fun stuff I pay for

    Books, magazines and comics   _____

    Toys   _____

    Things I collect   _____

    Special stuff for my room (posters and so on)   _____

    Entrance fees (for the skating rink, rec center and so on)   _____

    Club dues & uniforms (Girls Scouts, 4-H)   _____

    Art and craft supplies (including taking pictures)   _____

    Holiday costumes (Halloween)   _____

    CDs, tapes and records   _____

    Video and computer games   _____

    Videotapes (bought or rented)   _____

    Movies   _____

    Other outings (amusement parks, museums, zoos and so on)   _____

    Souvenirs and postcards   _____

Odds and ends   _____

My Total Expenses $ _____

My Total Income $ _____

Minus My Total Expenses   − _____

Money Left Over $ _____

Still, monetary disincentives have been known to do the trick if you use them strategically. (Translation: Hit 'em where it hurts, but not too often.) When the Durney family moved to a new house with a laundry chute, the children got it into their heads that cleaning up their rooms meant tossing all items of clothing into the chute. Tired of fishing her kids' clean clothes out of the laundry bin, Peggy Durney told them each item of clean clothing would cost them 10 cents. That did the trick. Another mom fined her kids 25 cents for every wet towel or article of clothing found lying on the floor.

It would also be appropriate to make your kids pay if their carelessness causes damage that money can fix. When Lucas and Kendra Durney got into a friendly tussle while they were wearing their church clothes, Kendra's tights were ruined—and Lucas was responsible for replacing them. If the damage is more extensive—for example, your kids break a neighbor's window after being warned repeatedly not to play ball so close to the house—it's their responsibility to apologize and to offer to pay for at least part of the repair costs.

To discipline your children, try using some of the same strategies you'd use to get them to do chores, chief of which is the force of your own authority. If your kids pay attention to you in general and want your approval, just telling them what you expect of them—and indicating that you'll be disappointed in them if they don't deliver—can get them to do what you want.

That doesn't mean you should wield dictatorial power. Kids are more inclined to cooperate with you if you're open to them when they have a problem or complaint. But deep down parents know that their children are only as disciplined as they themselves are and that kids will push as far as they can. When parents draw the line, kids are stopped; when parents slide, so do kids. It's too exhausting to draw the line all the time, so you have to pick and choose your confrontations. To gain leverage, you may have to resort once in a while to techniques like time-out or grounding or the "if...then" gambit: "If you do 'X', then I'll be forced to respond by doing 'Y'."

Whatever you do, do it sparingly. Even good, effective tactics can lose their impact if they're overused. If you're basically insecure, your kids will sense that. Like the boy who cried wolf, you'll find that your attempts at taking charge will eventually lose their effect. You don't want to be forced into buying your kids' cooperation, and finding yourself in the position of the parent who lamented of her teenage son, "the only way I can control him is with money."

And Now, for Your Regularly Scheduled Allowance

If you lose track of when you've given your kids their allowance (and you suspect they're always trying to squeeze an extra week out of you) get into the habit of paying them on a regular schedule, preferably a quiet weekday—maybe even your own payday—instead of the hectic weekend. You might also consider Sunday night so the kids don't blow the money over the weekend. Same goes for giving kids a raise in their allowance. Agreeing in advance on an annual allowance review to take place on the child's birthday or the first day of school will save your child the trouble of nagging you, and save you the pain of having to listen.

In my own case (as described in Chapter 1) I decided to use a checkbook system in which I credit my kids' accounts with a monthly allowance. They write me checks as they need money, and earn interest on any balance they carry over to the next month.

Some families have come up with other creative and inexpensive solutions. One mom simply took scrap paper and made her two sons "coupon books," each with 52 dated coupons, one for every week of the year. Each coupon was good for a weekly allowance payment, and Mom agreed to pay the kids on demand for each coupon they turned in, even if they turned in more than one at a time. But each coupon could be used only once.

A Word of Encouragement

If you have tried allowance systems but have never been disciplined enough to make one stick, don't be too hard on yourself. You don't have to duplicate any system down to the last wonderfully organized detail. Just pick and choose the tips that will work best in your household. Instead of starting an allowance when his kids were age 6 or 7, for example, John Rosemond didn't bother with one until they were teenagers. Then, said Rosemond, "we used the allowance to represent the fact that we were going to give the kids expanded autonomy over their lives."

You wouldn't want to offer money as a reward all the time, but used judiciously, it can work. One family created an inventive system to encourage their daughter to practice the piano. For every half hour of toil, she earns one "piano dollar," funny money with Beethoven's visage subbed for George Washington's. When she accumulates 20 piano dollars, she's treated to a meal at the fast-food restaurant of her choice.

If you don't have the time or the discipline to construct an elaborate system, concentrate on whatever is most important to you, whether it's teaching your kids to manage an allowance, do chores or contribute to charity. If you do nothing else, at least talk to your children about money when the opportunity presents itself, such as when you're withdrawing cash from the bank machine or paying bills. Brent Neiser has walked his kids through their tax returns, taken them to rental property he owns and discussed the responsibilities of landlords and tenants, shown them his credit report, and talked about the virtues of prepaying a mortgage. Said Neiser, "I can't think of anything I wouldn't share with them."

KIDS' QUESTIONS

Q. "Jessie's getting 'lowance, so why can't I?"

A. Younger siblings catch on more quickly to everything (as you're already painfully aware), so sibling rivalry is the one exception to my rule about not giving preschoolers an allowance. If you're going to give your older child, say, $1 or $2 a week, go ahead and give younger brother or sister 50 cents. Chances are he or she won't understand how much that really is, so you might be able to get away with a quarter. The point is, give a token amount so he or she doesn't feel left out. And don't feel obliged to give anything unless your preschooler asks.

Q. "How come my friend Christopher's allowance is bigger than mine?"

A. Resist the temptation to tell your kids that Christopher's parents must have more money than you do. Your income shouldn't be the only factor, or even the main one, that determines your children's allowance.

Tell your kids up front that their allowance will be based on three things: how much you can afford to give, what you expect them to pay for, and how much money you think they can comfortably handle. If they bring up the subject again, you have a ready-made reply to rattle off.

In asking this question, your kids may be dancing around what's really on their mind. They may be fishing for a raise in their allowance. Or they may be trying to keep up with the Jones kids.

If you really can't afford to come up with more money, that can work to your advantage. What counts isn't the size of the weekly dole, but the experience kids get with making it last. If you have to limit your kids' income because your own is stretched, that's a lesson in real-world economics, and your kids will be better off for learning it. With more money to spare, Christopher's parents will have a tougher time teaching him the value of a dollar.

Q. "Can I have an advance on my allowance?"

A. Most times it's best to say no. Your kids are fervently hoping you'll forget about any money you've advanced them, so you'll need to keep meticulous records, or have a steel-trap memory, to keep from being rolled.

Besides, an allowance is supposed to help kids learn about deferred gratification. If you expect your children to save their own money to buy compact discs, it's self-defeating to advance a couple of weeks' worth of allowance so they can buy the hottest release today.

That being said, I know there will be times when some loan seems reasonable—especially if your kids don't ask too often and are generally responsible money managers. Rather than giving them an advance, however, simplify your bookkeeping by lending them the money for a specific purpose and a specific payback period. When one young man asked to borrow $250 from his parents to buy a bicycle, he also presented them with a list of extra chores and special jobs he could do to earn money to pay off the loan, and even offered to pay $50 interest. He earned $100 by painting his grandmother's porch, and made all the money over the course of one summer.

What you're trying to avoid is a permanent pattern of borrowing money that keeps your kids chronically in debt, and leaves you confused about exactly how much they owe.

Q. "If I don't spend all my lunch money, can I keep it and use it for something else?"

A. That may sound like a reasonable deal, but think about what you're getting yourself into. If your child habitually avoids the cafeteria, she doesn't need lunch money, which becomes a de facto raise in her allowance. If you think a raise is in order, give her one. If not, stop shelling out money for phantom lunches and keep packing those bologna sandwiches.

Lunch money appears to be a hot button among many parents. Here's a sampling of the mail I received in response to a column about older children paying for their own school lunches:

"I disagree that children should pay for their school lunches with their own allowance. Snacks, concert tickets and special 'trendy' clothing can certainly be financed through the allowance or the child's financial assets. But food, clothing and shelter are typical categories that are the traditional responsibility of parents."

"In your recent column you included lunch money in a child's allowance. This should never happen. I have too often seen middle and high school youngsters skipping lunch or just buying a snack in order to save money for other things they wanted."

"As a parent it is my duty to provide lunch. There is always lunch money in the designated drawer if my children decide they do not wish to pack their own lunch. They are expected to return any change to the drawer if they eat light. The kids do what they wish (within reason) with their allowance, but the lunch money does not belong to them."

If you're going to make older children responsible for managing their lunch money, you'll have to provide extra money over and above their discretionary income to cover the expense. If you suspect your kids aren't up to the challenge, or would starve themselves to buy a new pair of jeans, rethink your strategy: Dole out lunch money one day at a time, require kids to return any unspent cash, or bag the lunch money—and bag the lunch. (Note: An increasing number of school cafeterias are solving this problem by issuing student debit cards. Parents deposit a certain dollar amount in a school account, and students draw it down for lunch. The cards don't work in vending machines.)

Q. "Will you buy me that [fill in the blank] if I pay you back when we get home?"

A. Don't fall into this trap. As with advances on allowance, your kids are counting on you to forget about the debt. If you do cave in, at least hang on to the item you bought until the kids come across with the cash.

Q. "How much will you pay me to stay out of the way during your party tonight?"

A. Don't dignify this one with any answer. Rewarding your children for doing something good is tricky enough; paying them off for not doing something bad is simply blackmail.

Penny Wise: Kids & Saving

Chapter Nine

When Caitlin, the daughter of a friend of mine, was in first grade a few years ago, she forgot to return a library book at school. Told that she would have to pay a 10-cent fine, Caitlin sighed, "There goes my college fund."

That about sums up most young children's view of saving: clear that something good can come of it, but a little fuzzy about the details. Banks, for example, can be scary places for kids, who see their money swallowed up and are sometimes horrified to learn that if they deposit, say, a $10 bill, they won't get the same $10 bill back.

And let's face it: Saving in general can be a downer, especially for children, who crave instant gratification. If saving is spinach and spending dessert, which would your kids choose? To teach them that thrift is a virtue, you have to sugarcoat the vitamins.

Let kids savor their savings. As my 10-year-old son observed when he peeked over my shoulder while I was writing this chapter: "Saving can be dessert, too, if you save for something you want." Whether it's an action figure or toy car they want, let them spend the cash, even if the purchase cleans them out.

Reward their efforts. Save for America (425-746-0331), the nationwide school-based saving campaign in which more than 500,000 kids at more than 5,000 schools make bank deposits every week, rewards students with stickers. Frequent depositors qualify for bigger prizes such as cameras, books, compact discs—anything to keep them coming back.

"Kids in grades K through 3 get really excited,"

said a spokesperson for Save for America. "We think that if we can get them to stick with it for three years, they'll continue the habit."

At home, one of the most effective rewards is to match whatever kids put aside on their own. Even a dollar-for-dollar match isn't too generous.

Look at what happened to Greg Gonzalez. When he was was 7 years old, he signed up for a school saving program and started squirreling away $10 to $20 a week—money he got from doing jobs around the house and practicing the piano. By the time he was 10, he had more than $1,000. Not satisfied with the rate of interest he was earning in the bank, Greg withdrew most of the money and began diversifying into a mutual fund and stocks, even as he continued to replenish the money in his bank account. While some kids his age were frittering away their allowances on Big Macs and Mickey Mouse T-shirts, Greg was buying shares in McDonald's and the Walt Disney Co. While other kids were paying to see basketball games, he bought a piece of the Boston Celtics.

Despite their reputation as yuppie-puppies, today's kids, especially younger ones, aren't all unregenerate

DEAR DR. TIGHTWAD

Q. To get my 8-year-old interested in saving, I offered to match anything he put in the bank. But the deal was he couldn't spend the money on toys—he had to save for a major purchase down the road. Then he got the bright idea that he could put all his allowance away for five weeks, I'd match it, and he could get a new Nintendo game. I said no way. Since then, he's never put in a penny. I can't believe he won't take the match.

A. Would you take a 100% match for your retirement plan if your employer told you you could never stop working?

For an 8-year-old, a Nintendo game is a major purchase, and five weeks is an eternity. If you object on principle to video games, that's one thing. But setting up arbitrary rules on what your son can buy takes away his incentive to save.

Try this strategy. Tell your son that once he gets a minimum of $100 in his account, he can spend additional money on anything he wants (within reason). You can gradually raise the minimum balance, but as your son gets older, his goals will become larger and more expensive, his time frame longer and the match more attractive.

spendthrifts. Kids under 12 actually save around 30% of their income, about half in banks and half stashed away in drawers. That was the highest rate recorded for children in two decades and more than double what it was in the mid '80s, according to research by James McNeal of Texas A&M. Recent figures showed that 4 to 6 year-olds, who saved nearly 40% of their income, took top honors. The rate declined rapidly, to around 30% for kids ages 7 to 9, but then turned up again a little for children ages 10 to 12.

McNeal said the big jump in savings could simply reflect that parents are providing their kids with more money, or that parents are encouraging their kids to take more responsibility for managing money at an earlier age. But why speculate when we can ask an expert: Greg Gonzalez, what made you save? "I got excited about what the money would grow into and what I'd be able to do with it when I grew up." How would he advise parents to get their kids hooked on saving? "Make them excited about it too."

To raise a generation of super savers, give them a reason to save. To keep them interested, reward them for their efforts. To guarantee their success, devise a system that makes saving easy.

Eyes on the Prize

Kids today have more reasons to save than their predecessors did a generation or two ago: big-ticket items, such as designer clothing or video equipment and games, that their parents are reluctant to buy. If you are feeling in a generous mood the next time your son simply *must* have a pair of $120 sneakers, offer to pay a portion of the price if he picks up the rest of the tab. Such a deal is a win-win situation: You save money and get the psychological satisfaction of saying no to what you probably consider a ridiculous request; he learns to save money and gets the psychological benefit of hearing you say that two-letter word.

The younger the child, the smaller and more immediate the goal should be; it ought to be something—a toy car or a set of paints—that the child can reach within a few weeks. As young Caitlin showed in the example at the beginning of the chapter, "college," though certainly worthy, is a fuzzy concept in the faraway future.

One Family's Savings Goal

Older children can move on to bigger, more expensive goals. You can even make saving a family project. For the Coogans of Michigan (not their real name), the catalyst that got them into the thrifty frame of mind was a first-ever family vacation to Florida. Ray Coogan is disabled by a chronic illness. His wife, Trudy, is a hairdresser. Of the five Coogan children still living at home, four are teenagers with part-time jobs. They all decided to pool their money for the trip south to visit another Coogan child.

As organizer and chief cheerleader, Ray Coogan set a relatively low initial goal of $2,500. He figured meeting it would be such a morale booster that everyone would be encouraged to aim even higher and extend their stay in Florida. All working family members were given a savings goal and offered a bonus: For meeting their goal quickly or making an extra effort (by requesting extra work hours, for example), they would be rewarded with an additional $25 in spend-

---

DEAR DR. TIGHTWAD

Q. My 8-year-old daughter has her heart set on buying a laptop computer for kids that costs $100. I don't object to her buying it if she uses her own money, but I'm afraid it will take her too long to save that kind of cash and she'll end up discouraged. Should I try to talk her out of this?

A. You sound more discouraged than your daughter does. If she understands the terms and is willing to give it a try, let her go for it.

It is a big goal for a young child, but you could lend her a hand (without actually lending her any money) by breaking it up into more manageable chunks. For every $10 she saves, for example, you might offer a $1 match. Give her opportunities to do extra chores so she can earn the money more quickly.

If your daughter only makes it to $50 and then loses interest, she'll still have saved $50 to spend on something else. And that's not bad for a 8-year-old.

DEAR DR. TIGHTWAD

Q. My 10-year-old not only saves all his money, but he also keeps it in his room and counts it every night. He has over $200 and I want him to open a bank account, but he won't part with the cash. Am I raising a Scrooge?

A. Humbug. He's probably a typical 10-year-old who worries that if he puts his money in a bank he'll never see it again.

Try appealing to his hoarding instincts by pointing out that a sum that large needs safekeeping, and that banks will pay him for allowing them to take care of his money.

Don't insist that he put every cent in the bank. Let him keep $50 or so to spend on things he wants. Learning to spend money wisely is just as important as learning to save.

---

ing money for the trip.

Ray held weekly family meetings to track their progress. "It wouldn't have worked if we hadn't had him to spearhead the whole thing and light a fire under everyone," said Trudy. Within three months the Coogans had saved $4,000 and were on their way in a rented van. Next year, maybe they'll head west.

Play Numbers Games

If you really want to get older kids psyched up about saving, dazzle 'em with numbers—in particular, the magic of compound interest. (Interest, of course, is the money a bank will pay you for letting it use your money; compounding means that you also earn interest on the interest paid, which gives your savings an extra boost.) Kids are turned on by the idea that over time their money can grow. In one money-management course for high school students, the most popular chart in the workbook is the one that shows how fast an IRA will grow. To wit, if you put in $2,000 a year for nine years starting at age 22 and earn 9% on your money, your $18,000 will grow to $579,000 by the time you're 65. (By the way, 9% isn't an unreasonable rate of return. The Standard & Poor's 500-stock index has returned a tad over 10% annually, on average, since 1926).

For a dramatic illustration of the magic of compounding, Harold Moe, co-author with wife Sandy Moe of *Teach Your Child the Value of Money*, performs a trick that is guaranteed to knock the socks off everyone from young kids to adults. It works like this: Raid the penny jar or go to the bank and load up on pennies—say, $10 to $20 worth. Then take out a checkerboard and place one penny on the first square in the first row. Double the number of pennies in the second square, and continue doubling them until you reach the end of the first row, at which point you'll have 128 pennies. Then point to the remaining pennies and ask your audience to guess how many will be left after you've filled the checkerboard by doubling the amount of pennies on each square. After a suspenseful pause, announce triumphantly that there probably isn't enough money in the whole world to complete all 64 squares. (When my son saw this principle demonstrated on a kids' videotape about money, he was so bowled over that at first he refused to believe it was true.)

With older children, you can go on to more math legerdemain. The rule of 72, for example, states that dividing 72 by the interest rate you're earning tells you roughly how long it will take your money to double (and dividing 72 by the number of years in which you want to double your money will tell you how much interest you need to earn). If you're earning, say, 8%, your money will double in about nine years.

By the time your kids are in high school, they should be able to use the table on page 143, which shows how much a deposit of $10 a month will grow at various rates of interest over different periods of time. You can easily use the chart to calculate how quickly you can get rich with any monthly deposit.

A Spoonful of Sugar

No less a light than Sir John Templeton, the mutual fund pioneer and advocate of long-term saving, has observed that "learning to save is so important that parents should reward their kids for

---

DEAR DR. TIGHTWAD

Q. My 7-year-old has worn down and outgrown her bicycle. I don't mind buying her a new one, but I wonder if I should make her contribute to the cost or wait for her birthday, which is a few months away.

A. Go ahead and spring for the bike. You could have your daughter kick in a nominal amount, but a 7-year-old should have the pleasure of pedaling and her parents should have the pleasure of providing the wheels. Besides, leaving her to ride a bike that she has outgrown raises safety concerns. Just don't get carried away.

---

doing it." One of the most effective rewards you can offer is an incentive system in which you match all or part of your child's savings. This tactic works well with children of all ages, but especially teenagers who might be saving for a big-ticket item such as a car.

Rewards themselves don't have to break the bank. Sometimes a pat on the back is all it takes to push a child in the right direction. Consider the enthusiastic students of Bay Terrace School, P.S. 169, in Bayside, N.Y., which has a magnet program in business, finance and international trade. Many of the students participate in the school's saving program. What made them do it?

- **Hillary:** "It's a cool thing to do," said Hillary, who even advocated taking draconian measures if kids let their allowances burn a hole in their pockets: "Keep part of their allowance. When they ask for more money, don't give it to them."
- **Kenny:** "I never had a bank account before, and when I got the notice from school I said to my mom, 'Please let me have one.' Parents should tell their kids, 'What happens if your father loses his job and has to borrow money?' "
- **Rachel:** "I thought I would like to save for college, so I started the banking program and I usually put in $2 every week." But she might raid her account for some-

thing special—like one of the dolls from the Pleasant Company's American Girls Collection.

As in all other aspects of teaching kids about money, your attitude is critical. One of the biggest reasons kids don't participate in school saving programs is lack of interest on the part of parents. First National Bank of South Miami has sponsored Twiglet, a school bank that's run by students at David Fairchild Elementary in South Miami. In First National's experience, some children who are gung-ho about the program lose interest when their parents don't share their enthusiasm. "Either the kids don't get an allowance or the parents don't give them money to save," said a spokesperson.

Still, school banking programs, which were ubiquitous a generation or two ago and then all but disappeared, are making a comeback (see the box on page 139 for information).

Systems That Work

Key to the success of any saving regimen, whether for kids or adults, is getting into the habit of doing it regularly, and that means making it as painless as possible. Among younger children, banks often conjure up an image of a place that takes your money but doesn't give it back, so saving is best begun at home, where kids can keep an eye on their money and watch it grow. For the same reason, children will be frustrated to see their money swallowed up by a piggy bank that can be opened only by a well-aimed hammer. Better to make the money more accessible—in a jar or plastic bag, perhaps with a picture of whatever they're saving for attached as an incentive. One inventive 11-year-old kept each bill carefully displayed in a photo album (and even folded the bills around the edge of the page so that half appeared on one page and half on the next—a convenient way to double your money).

HELPING KIDS SAVE

In the school-based Save for America campaign, PTA volunteers collect the kids' coins at school once a week, and record the deposits on a computer. They then send the record of deposits electronically to a participating bank via the Internet (the actual money is still delivered in person to the bank). Save for America, under way in 45 states, has garnered more than $125 million. If you'd like to get your school in on the action, phone 425–746–0331 for more information, or ask your local banks if they have similar savings programs for schools.

I'm a big fan of fun savings banks for kids, and I do an annual survey of catalogs and stores to pick my favorites among collectible, mechanical and traditional banks (for a year-round selection, see eToys at www.etoys.com). Last year my sister bought my son a large, round metal bank painted like a baseball on the outside; open the hollow sphere in half, and the inside has a ballpark scene, with grandstand, spectators and a game in progress. The bank is one of Peter's favorites, and he has designated it as the repository of money he's saving for a Nintendo 64 video game system. He calls it his 64 Bank, and squirrels away the change from purchases he makes, as well as unclaimed coins he finds around the house. "You know what I like about my 64 Bank?" he asked out of the blue one day. "I like it when I think that I have $10 now, but in a year I could have $100 or $200."

If your children are disciplined enough to save a portion of their allowance on their own, congratulations! If not, don't be afraid to exert some parental pressure.

- **You can have them set aside** a portion for spending, a portion for saving and even a portion for long-term investing.
- **Keep the system simple** by having your kids save a flat 10% of their income.
- **Or you might choose** the spare-change method, which lets your kids spend their bills but encourages them to save their coins (which eventually can be put into rolls and taken to the bank).

Although they may grouse about it, your kids will appreciate any discipline you impose. When he was in fourth grade and getting an allowance of $1.50 a week, Jonathan Levy actually preferred that his parents hang on to the money and give it to him once a month instead of every week. "When you get it in bigger amounts it seems like you get more, and you don't spend it all at once on things like baseball cards like you sometimes do if you get it in small amounts," said Jonathan. "It's much easier to save that way."

When your kids want to hang out at the mall with their friends, suggest that instead of taking all their money with them, they take exactly what they need to play a couple of video games, get a snack, or buy a pair of jeans. What they don't have they won't spend.

How to Open a Bank Account

Eventually your kids will be old enough, or accumulate money enough, to be introduced to the fine points of a real bank account. Remember how it worked when you were a kid? You could walk up to the window, give the teller your deposit and have the amount stamped in your passbook, where it grew right before your eyes. Not anymore. Most banks have done away with passbooks, even for kids' accounts, and many have minimum-balance require-

---

A TAX TIP FOR CO-SIGNED ACCOUNTS

Make sure your child's social security number is used as the tax identification number on any account on which your name also appears as co-signer. That way, interest earned will be treated as your child's income for tax purposes.

Children can make up to $700 in investment income in 1999 without having to pay any taxes. Income between $700 and $1,400 will be taxed at the child's rate. But if your child is under 14, income above $1,400 will be taxed to him or her at your rate, even though the child is the principal owner of the account. That's the so-called kiddie tax, and it's intended to keep parents from ducking taxes by shifting income to their children. After your children reach 14, however, their income is taxable at their rate.

---

ments or impose stiff service charges on small balances that can add up to more than you make in interest and eventually deplete the account.

Jane Clark found that out when she opened an account for her son, Bennett, with about $300 in savings and birthday money. When Bennett's first monthly statement arrived, his mom was shocked to see that a $5 service charge had wiped out all the interest he had earned and then some. After several phone calls a bank official finally told her that the usual service charge on a small account should have been waived on a minor's account. Make sure your bank has a similar practice.

Bank policy on accounts for children varies among states, banks and even branches, depending on state law and banks' own preferences. As long as kids can sign their name, some banks will allow them to own accounts and make both deposits and with-

A BANK FOR YOUNG AMERICANS

Young Americans Bank (311 Steele St., Denver, CO 80206; 303-321-2265), which offers savings accounts, checking accounts, credit cards and loans, has mail-in customers from all 50 states and around a dozen foreign countries. The average savings customer is 9 years old and has a balance of around $480. Write or call for more information.

drawals. More commonly, however, you'll probably have to co-sign the account, and you control it; your child may not be able to make withdrawals without your signature.

One notable exception is Young Americans Bank in Denver, where all customers are under the age of 22. For kids under 18, Young Americans sets up joint accounts in the name of both parent and child, with two signatures required for all transactions. Parents actually need their children's authorization to make a withdrawal. The bank will also let you sign a release allowing your kids to make withdrawals on their own. Other financial institutions sometimes offer a similar option, so ask about it if you want your children to have more control over their own money.

After your children open an account at a bank, they may need your help in getting the money there. You may have to volunteer to be their personal banker, making deposits during school hours. Another option for older children is to grab a stack of deposit slips and let them make deposits by mail. They can give their cash to you, and you can write a check that they can send in with the slip. Nowadays some Internet-based money-management sites for kids let them open bank accounts online so they don't have to leave home.

No Withdrawals Allowed?

Once your children have put their money into the bank, should they be able to get it out— to buy those $120 sneakers, for example—or should they be required to keep it there for longer-

---

HOW YOUR MONEY WILL GROW

You can use this table to figure how much to save or invest to accumulate a specific amount by some future date. Say you and your daughter are planning for her to save $5,000 by the time she starts college six years from now. Assuming that she could earn 8% on her savings and investments, how much should she put away monthly?

Find the place in the table where six years intersects with 8%. Divide that number—926—into your goal of $5,000. The result tells you that your goal is 5.4 times the total generated by $10 monthly deposits. Your daughter will have to set aside $54 each month to reach the goal on time, assuming an 8% return.

YEAR	2%	3%	4%	5%	6%	7%	8%	9%	10%	11%	12%
1	$121	$122	$123	$123	$124	$125	$125	$126	$127	$127	$128
2	245	248	250	253	256	258	261	264	267	270	272
3	371	377	383	389	395	402	408	415	421	428	435
4	500	511	521	532	544	555	567	580	592	605	618
5	631	648	665	683	701	720	740	760	781	802	825
6	765	790	815	841	868	897	926	957	989	1,023	1,058
7	902	936	971	1,008	1,046	1,086	1,129	1,173	1,220	1,268	1,320
8	1042	1086	1133	1,182	1,234	1,289	1,348	1,409	1,474	1,543	1,615
9	1184	1241	1302	1,366	1,435	1,507	1,585	1,667	1,755	1,849	1,948
10	1329	1401	1477	1,559	1,647	1,741	1,842	1,950	2,066	2,190	2,323
15	2101	2275	2469	2,684	2,923	3,188	3,483	3,812	4,179	4,589	5,046
20	2953	3291	3680	4,128	4,644	5,240	5,929	6,729	7,657	8,736	9,991
25	3895	4471	5158	5,980	6,965	8,148	9,574	11,295	13,379	15,906	18,976
30	4935	5842	6964	8,357	10,095	12,271	15,003	18,445	22,793	28,302	35,299

term goals like that college education? That decision is up to you. For many children, being able to withdraw the money to pay for some short-term goal provides most of the impetus for saving in the first place. Just getting your kids to put money aside is a major victory, even if they end up spending it on something you personally wouldn't have bought. Or you may compromise by requiring your children to maintain a certain minimum balance above which they can make withdrawals.

But some families have a different philosophy. Linda and David Jessup believe their children shouldn't draw on savings for things like Christmas presents or sneakers. Instead, they might give their kids a stipend of $25 to buy Christmas gifts or require them to earn at least part of the money they need. When one of their daughters wanted to take over a paper route and needed a new bicycle, the family agreed to pay half the cost if she earned the rest. She did—and carted the papers around in a wagon in the meantime. "Savings aren't for whims or present expenses," explained Linda. "They're for your future."

Turn page for Kids' Questions→

KIDS' QUESTIONS

Q. "I have $35 in my piggy bank. Can I spend it all on a building set?"

A. Let your kids spend their money, even if you think they're blowing it all on one overpriced toy. If they have exercised the self-discipline to save in the first place, they deserve a reward.

Parents should certainly retain some veto power over how children dispose of their own money. You may not want them to have inline skates, for example, because you think they're too dangerous, or a video game system because you don't want them to be parked in front of the TV all day.

But price alone shouldn't be the deciding factor. Even if the coveted item is expensive relative to your kids' allowance, let them splurge as long as the purchase is otherwise suitable. Gazing upon the vast emptiness in their piggy bank will be a lesson in itself.

Q. "Why don't you just go to the bank machine and get some money?"

A. Control your impulse to point out that money doesn't grow on trees. That old chestnut may be colorful, but it's not very useful. Your children already think cash pops out of bank machines, and now you've really confused them.

Tell them instead that bank machines don't actually print money (which is what your kids

may think). Explain that the bank is like a big piggy bank: You get paid for working at your job and you deposit your paycheck into your bank account for safekeeping. When you get money from the bank machine you're actually taking money out of your own account. When the account is empty, it's empty.

Q. "How does a bank machine work?"

A. You don't have to be a technological wizard to take a stab at this one, even if it's only to assure your child there isn't a person inside the machine dealing out $10 bills. Here's all you need to know:

An ATM is like a computerized teller. You talk to the computer with your bank card, which tells the machine who you are. The machine then calls your bank to find out if you have enough money in your account to cover the amount of cash you're requesting. If so, the machine gives you the cash. If not, you're out of luck.

How does the cash actually get into the machine? It's loaded there by bank employees or outside security firms. Sometimes machines are "cashed up" several times a day because banks don't like to load them with large amounts. But over a long holiday weekend, for example, machines will hold more cash than normal.

Your Kid, the Investment Guru

Don't make the mistake of thinking that investing in the stock market is for adults only, sort of like an R-rated movie. On the contrary, it's more like PG-13. Children that age, or even younger, are able to understand how the market works, and, with a little parental guidance, become successful investors. Nicole Williams was only 9 years old and in the fourth grade when she noticed that she had earned a disappointing $11 on a $500 certificate of deposit. When the CD matured, she was champing at the bit to invest her money in a stock—preferably one that was about to split, so that she could get more shares. "Nicole is on her way; I just hope that I can keep up," said her mom, Rita.

Kids who own stock are in the minority among children, but they're a vocal and savvy group. I have interviewed a 12-year-old who publishes his own investment newsletter—and runs his father's individual retirement account—a teenage day-trader, and a junior high student who started to invest after playing a stock market simulation game as a class exercise.

In my experience, the children most likely to take an interest in stocks fall into three categories:

- **Kids who already have their own savings accounts** and start to notice that at today's rates their money isn't growing very fast.
- **Kids whose grandparents, parents, or friends invest** in the stock market.
- **Entrepreneurial kids who have earned** several hundred dollars or more at a job or business and have bigger plans for their money than a bank account.

Although they have a nodding acquaintance with Wall Street, children don't always understand its twists and turns—nor, if truth be told, do many adults. I'm bombarded with requests from parents and grandparents for material specially written to help children get started in the stock market.

The first thing parents and kids should understand is the principle of a market: Sellers ask a high price for their wares, buyers bid lower, and they reach an agreement somewhere in the middle. And that's it. No matter how complex they sound, no matter how sophisticated their computers, all markets are fundamentally the same, whether you're buying and selling stocks, baseball cards or foreign currency. And the goal of an investor is always the same, too: Buy low, sell high.

With that bit of knowledge in hand, you're ready to begin. If you have any budding investors around the house, hand them this book (after you've finished, of course). The following pages are written for all would-be Wall Street tycoons—such as Jonathan Hagelstein, for example. By the time he was 15 Jon was managing his own $10,000 portfolio, "more than his father and I had when we got married," said his mom, Ann. Jon built up a core of reliable blue-chip stocks, including AT&T, IBM and Bell Atlantic, and also owned some personal favorites, such as Topps and Reebok.

To support his investing habit, Jon earned $20 a week working at a health-food store and got an additional $5 to $10 in allowance and gift money. All of it went into a bank account from which he could make his own withdrawals without his parents' co-signatures. Not that he made many withdrawals for things other than investments. Jon saved most of what he got, and reinvested all his stock dividends in more shares.

All this started with ten shares of AT&T purchased for him by his father when Jon was 7. "This taught him how to make money by becoming the owner of a company," said his father, Robert. "He used to get angry at MCI commercials." For Jon, the real investment bug bit a little later, when he was 10 and wanted to collect Topps baseball card sets as an investment. "I told him he could invest in the cards or the company," said his dad. He chose the company. His shares split several times and turned out to be a "super investment."

Kids as Stock Pickers

Buying your children shares in a company is the best way to get them started in the market. Investing in only a few shares can be expensive as far as commissions go, although there are ways to minimize your costs (see the discussion beginning on page 161). But the lesson you're teaching is priceless and the options limitless. The beauty of it is, you don't even have to be an expert stock picker; you can let your kids do the choosing. Jon's strategy: "Look at which clothes kids are wearing in school, find out what recording labels they're listening to, what kind of CD players they have. When I go to the mall, I go to the toy stores and shoe stores and ask what's selling fastest."

When young people like Jon Hagelstein speak, even old pros like Peter Lynch listen. Lynch, the star money manager whose expertise at the helm of Fidelity Magellan helped make it the largest and most successful mutual fund in the country, observed in his book *One Up on Wall Street* that "the best place to look for the tenbagger (a stock that appreciates tenfold) is close to home—if not in the backyard then down at the shopping mall." When Lynch's three daughters came home from the mall raving about the Body Shop, a British company that specializes in soaps, skin-care products and perfumes, Lynch did some checking, and concluded that the company "would become a money machine" and bided his time to buy when the price was right.

I don't recommend that kids invest in penny stocks, so-called because they typically sell for less than $1 a share. Their low price makes them attractive to kids, but they're issued by companies that have a short or erratic earnings history, they aren't listed on any stock exchange and public surveillance is spotty. They're a gamble, not an investment.

How to Scout a Stock

Kids can be fickle customers, so there's no guarantee that the latest fad will be around long enough to make a success of the company that created it. If you're serious about getting your kids started in solid stocks with growth potential, you, and they, will have to do some research on the companies. And that's where many parents feel they are on shaky ground. 'Fess up—you may not even feel comfortable explaining to your kids what it means to invest in the stock market or helping them follow the price of a company's shares in the newspaper stock tables.

Relax. It isn't all that difficult, and you don't have to go it alone. This book can help, and so can a clever little volume called *Ump's Fwat, an Annual Report for Young People*, available through the Academy for Economic Education (125 NationsBank Center, Richmond, VA 23219). Ump, by the way, is a caveman, and the Mickey Mantle of his day in a primitive game called fwap that bears an uncanny resemblance to baseball. Fwatters toss rocks into the air and slug them with a club, or fwat. Ump's fwat was much coveted by the other fwatters, so he had an idea: Why not start a company to make and sell fwats? Thus might the first capitalist have been born.

Cave dwellers interested in investing in Ump's Fwat Co. didn't have access to all the information that you do when it comes to researching prospective stock picks.

You can get annual reports and other information for free by contacting the company directly.

A trip to your local library will probably turn up *Value Line Investment Survey* (or call 800-535-8760), which provides analyses of nearly 1,700 individual companies; gives historical data on prices, earnings and dividends; and assigns each stock a rating for timeliness and risk. Similar information is available from *Moody's Handbook of Common Stocks* and Standard & Poor's reports. One or

HOW TO READ THE STOCK LISTINGS

A A small "s" next to the listing means the stock was split or the company issued a stock dividend within the past year. This is your signal that the year's high and low prices have been adjusted to reflect the effect of the split.

B An "x" indicates that the stock has gone "ex-dividend." Investors who buy the stock now won't get the next dividend payment, which has been declared but not paid. Most listings stick the "x" next to the figure in the volume column.

C Sometimes a stock has been issued so recently that it doesn't have a full year's history on which to base its pricing. In such a case the 52-week high and low prices date from the beginning of trading and the stock gets a little "n" to the left of the listing.

D The dividend listed is the latest annual dividend paid by that stock.

E The yield is the stock's latest annual dividend expressed as a percentage of that day's price.

F The price/earnings ratio is the price of the stock divided by the earnings reported by the company for the latest four quarters.

G Prices—and price changes—are reported in 1/8-point increments. An eighth of a dollar is 0.125 cent.

	52 Weeks Hi	52 Weeks Lo	Stock	Sym	Div (D)	Yld % (E)	PE (F)	Vol 100s	Hi (G)	Lo (G)	Close (G)	Net Chg (G)
	28 3/8	12 1/8	ChileTel ADR	CTC	.39e	1.7	...	3019	22 15/16	22 1/2	22 15/16	+ 7/16
	14 15/16	4	ChinaEstrnAir	CEA		...	...	117	12 1/4	12 1/8	12 1/4	+ 1/4
	12 1/2	4 15/16	ChinaFund	CHN	.08e	.7	...	150	10 15/16	10 7/8	10 15/16	...
	13 15/16	3 1/16	ChinSAir ADS	ZNH		...	...	147	10 1/8	10 1/16	10 1/8	+ 1/8
	66 1/2	23	ChinaTelecm	CHL		...	...	256	61 3/4	61 1/4	61 3/4	– 13/16
	9 1/8	3 9/16	ChinaTire	TIR	.08	1.2	...	74	6 3/4	6 3/8	6 11/16	+ 1/4
	2 13/16	3/8	ChinaYuchai	CYD		...	...	153	1 5/8	1 1/2	1 5/8	...
	12 13/16	6 15/16	ChiquitaBrd	CQB	.20	2.8	dd	692	7 1/8	7	7 1/8	+ 1/8
▼	42 3/8	29 11/16	ChiquitaBrd pfA		2.88	9.9	...	16	29 1/4	29	29	– 11/16
	50 1/8	37	ChiquitaBrd pfB		3.75	9.6	...	9	39 7/16	39 1/4	39 1/4	– 3/16
	33 5/8	25 7/16	Chittnden	CHZ	.88	3.1	cc	213	29 1/4	28 5/8	28 11/16	– 9/16
	10 7/8	4 3/4	ChockFull	CHF		...	cc	53	10 3/8	10 3/8	10 3/8	...
	19 3/4	9 5/8	ChoiceHtl	CHH		...	19	321	17	16 3/4	17	...
	69	37 3/8 ♣	ChoicePoint	CPS		...	25	474	64 1/4	62 7/8	63 11/16	+ 1 1/2
	53 1/2	38 5/8	ChrisCrft	CCN	stk	...	93	1012	50 3/8	48 15/16	50	– 3/8
	18 1/2	11 7/8	Chromcrft	CRC		...	9	9	12 11/16	12 11/16	12 11/16	– 1/16
	76 3/8	54	Chubb	CB	1.28	2.2	14	8773	59	57 5/8	58 1/4	– 13/16
	50 3/16	27 1/16	Church&Dwt	CHD	.56f	1.2	24	2731	47 7/16	46 1/2	46 1/2	– 1/4
	3 1/8	1 1/8	Chyron	CHY		...	dd	128	1 3/8	1 1/4	1 1/4	– 1/16
	33 5/16	13 5/16	CIBER	CBR		...	29	1628	19 15/16	19 1/4	19 7/16	– 7/16
B — (x)	65	48 3/8	Cilcorp Inc	CER	2.46	3.8	39	1904	64 11/16	64 1/2	64 5/8	+ 7/16
A — (s)	26 1/2	8 67/128	CincBell	CSN	.40	2.2	19	14449	19	18	18 1/2	– 1/2
	26 1/2	24 9/16	CincGE deb	JRL	2.07	8.3	...	13	24 15/16	24 11/16	24 13/16	+ 1/8
	78	68	CinnGE pfA		4.00	5.5	...	z50	72 5/8	71 3/4	72 5/8	– 3/8
	39 7/8	27 5/16	CINergyCp	CIN	1.80	5.8	14	9474	31 7/16	30 5/16	31 3/16	+ 13/16
	8	3 1/2	CirctCityCrmx	KMX		...	dd	3234	3 11/16	3 1/2	3 1/2	– 3/16
s	52 31/32	14 13/32	CircuitCity	CC	.07	.1	cc	17372	47	44 5/8	46 3/4	+ 7/8
	26 13/16	22 5/8	CiticpCap pfA		1.78	7.4	...	180	24 1/16	23 7/8	23 241/256	– 5/128
C — (n)	24 7/8	21 3/8	CitigpCap pfX		.68e	3.0	...	425	23	22 13/16	22 7/8	+ 1/16
s	51 3/4	19	Citigroup	C	.56	1.1	27	[illegible]				
	25 11/16	21	CitigpCap [illegible]									

Reprinted with permission of the *Wall Street Journal*
©1999 Dow Jones & Company, Inc.

the other is likely to repose on your library's shelves. (S&P information is also available online at www.personalwealth.com.)

Financial publications such as *Kiplinger's Personal Finance Magazine, Money, Smart Money, Forbes* and *Barron's* are invaluable and easy-to-use sources. And, of course, the Internet is a gold mine of information on investing.

In Ump's day, shareholders might have tracked the ups and downs of Ump's Fwat Co. by scanning the stock tables in *The Gnu Yerk Times* or *The Welp Strit Journal*. So can you. Don't be intimidated by what at first looks like endless gibberish. The tables are easy to interpret—and are much admired by math teachers for the practice they give kids in using fractions, decimals and percentages. For a detailed look at how to read and interpret the stock tables, see the illustration on page 149.

To Market, To Market

Forget price-earnings ratios and market capitalization. When kids learn about the stock market, they cut right to the chase: "How long does it take to sell a stock, and when do you get your money?" asks John, an eighth-grader in my daughter's class at St. Camillus School, in Silver Spring, Md.

When I interviewed these students as seventh-graders (see Chapter 2), investing was a weak link in their knowledge of personal finance. Some had a vague understanding of what it means to own stock, but that was about it. And no one knew what a dividend was.

Then, as part of their eighth-grade algebra class, the students began taking an hour or two a week to participate in SMG2000, the online version of the Stock Market Game. Sponsored by the Securities Industry Foundation for Economic Education (212-618-0519; www.smg2000.org), the school-based game gives teams ten weeks to turn a virtual $100,000 into a winning portfolio.

Teacher Glen Mayers had several objectives for his 15 charges: to give the kids a taste of "real world" math and to make sure they didn't repeat his own experience of finishing high school without ever hearing the words "stock market" (he passed up the stock purchase plan at Safeway, his first employer, because "I didn't have a clue"). He also wanted the kids to use the Internet "for more than just chatting."

That's a challenge in the game's ten-week format, which tends to encourage going for a quick profit rather than long-term investing. As an informal observer and occasional guest lecturer, my goals were to give the kids a longer-term perspective, make sure they at least learned how the market works, and teach them what a dividend is. I also wanted to see how well a school could fit the game—or any other financial curriculum—into a day that's already packed with so many demands on a teacher's time. (In this case, Mayers decided to try SMG2000 because an interested parent—me—told him about it. Hint to PTA groups or individuals who want to introduce financial education into local schools: Find an interested teacher and give him or her materials to work with. You can get a slew of curriculum references through the Jump$tart Coalition for Personal Financial Literacy, www.jumpstart-coalition.org.)

> ## WHAT ARE BLUE CHIPS?
>
> The term "blue chips" was introduced in 1904 to mean the stocks of the largest, most consistently profitable corporations. It comes from the blue chips used in poker—always the most valuable ones.

It took at least one class period for the students to become familiar with the software—how to find ticker symbols, enter trades, and look up company descriptions. The kids liked the *Washington Post* site (www.washingtonpost.com) because they were familiar with the newspaper and because the user-friendly business section gave capsule news reports on each company, plus a chart showing price trends over recent months.

Right off the bat it was clear that when it came to picking stocks, the kids had more fundamental concerns than technical analysis. They were surprised to find out, for example, that Old Navy, the popular clothing chain, is actually owned by Gap, and that some of their favorite companies—notably Hallmark and Mars—weren't publicly traded (one team mistakenly ended up with shares in Hallmark Capital, a bank holding company). When they sell stock, they wondered, to whom do they sell? What does it mean when you hear that the market went up or down? And who is Dow Jones, anyway?

Playing the game in the fall and hoping for a boost from seasonal sales, the kids bought Hershey (Halloween candy), Sony (video games for the holidays) and even Anheuser-Busch ("Seasonal depression may make people drink more," observed one young investor). But all three of the teams were too skittish to invest their entire $100,000 ("It's hard for them to grasp how much money that really is," said Mayers). And often members didn't buy anything because they couldn't agree on a stock (shades of adult investment clubs).

By the end of the game's third week, it was clear the seasonal strategy wouldn't pan out the way they had hoped; most of the stocks hadn't moved much one way or the other. Since the game lasts for only ten weeks, the kids were beginning to think they might have to try something else to get a big price bounce. "We're looking for stocks that are down," said Diane, whose group ended up buying Disney at a price way off its 52-week high.

As it turned out, the kids didn't get a big enough bounce. During the ten-week contest the market rose an impressive 14%, mostly on the strength of a run-up in tech stocks. The winning student team in Maryland, members of an economics class at Southern Garrett High School, hitched a ride on rocketing Internet stocks to build a portfolio worth nearly $300,000.

The best of the three teams at St. Camillus finished what to them was a disappointing 283rd out of nearly 400 student teams, with a profit of about $1,100. But even though their instincts to go with proven con-

---

START YOUR OWN CLUB

For information on starting an investment club, as well as basic information on investing in general, contact the National Association of Investors Corp. (P.O. Box 220, Royal Oak, MI 48068; 248–583–6242). The NAIC's $39 annual membership fee includes a subscription to Better Investing magazine; for an additional $89 a year ($125 for nonmembers), members can subscribe to the NAIC Advisory Service, which analyzes three individual stocks each month.

sumer-products companies rather than bet on the latest Internet high-flier probably cost them the contest, over time they stand a better chance of reaping impressive returns with fewer sleepless nights.

The kids' experience was instructive in other ways as well. "You can't predict the market," said Diane. "We should have used more of our money," said Allison. "Just because something new comes out doesn't mean people will buy it," said Andrea, whose team was disappointed in the performance of Volkswagen despite its new Beetle.

"I learned not to let other people manage my money," said Anthony, with a sidelong glance at his teammates. (A number of kids preferred Mayers's go-it-alone alternative, in which each student chose a single stock and tracked it with paper and pencil and the newspaper stock tables.) And they seemed to have absorbed a lesson Mayers was eager to teach: "If you start making your money work for you when you're young, you can be set for life."

For my part, I hope they understand that a dividend is a stockholder's cut of the profits a company earns.

A Family Investment Club

At home, some parents, and grandparents, have made investing a family affair. Betty Taylor of Kansas City, Kan., started an investment club that included four generations of her family, including her father, her three children and her grandchildren. "The youngest ones owned stock when they came into the world," said Taylor.

Each member of the club, grandkids included, could contribute. Only those 18 or older got to vote on which stocks the family would buy and sell, but the younger children had significant input, often based on their considerable intake of things like frozen yogurt. The family invested in TCBY when it was a fledgling firm, watched as the stock price rose with the popularity of frozen yogurt, and then bailed out when lots of other companies cut in on the craze and the stock price faltered. "It was a great way to teach the children that once a company has a niche, competitors come in," said Taylor.

She also taught the children to invest in a few good stocks instead of spreading their money over a lot of companies (the family's portfolio generally included eight to ten stocks) and how to handle a proxy vote: "We told them to vote for the management if they liked what the company was doing, and against it if they didn't." When kids were between 8 and 12 years old, they learned to look up a stock in *Value Line* or color a chart tracking a company's earnings for the last ten years. Taylor encouraged teenagers to read a company's annual report, especially the report for the preceding year "so they could see what the president's goals were and whether he met them." When one of her granddaughters returned from a school trip to Russia, Taylor sat her down and debriefed her on which American companies had established a presence there.

Mutual Funds Made Easy

Besides shares of common stock, Jon Hagelstein owned shares in mutual funds. Investing in a mutual fund isn't as direct as buying shares in an individual company, so the concept isn't as easily grasped, especially by younger children. And as a hands-on learning experience, it isn't as exciting as being part-owner of a specific company. But as an investment, it has certain advantages.

What you are doing is pooling your money with that of other investors. The fund's professional money managers take all that pooled cash and invest it in a portfolio of stocks (or bonds) that is designed to achieve a specific objective. Growth funds, for example, invest in companies that have the potential to grow (along with the price of their stock) but do not pay much in the way of dividends. Income funds concentrate more on bonds and other investments that pay interest, along with the stocks of companies that pay consistent dividends. Although growth funds are riskier than income funds, they are probably more appropriate for children, who have plenty of time to ride out the market's ups and downs.

Mutual funds can be ideal investments for small investors, and that includes kids, for these reasons:

Some funds still have relatively low minimum initial investments. Even better, many funds will lower their minimum investment requirement if you sign up for a automatic investment plan of as little as $25 per month. And some funds are actually designed to ap-

---

SCOUTING THE WINNERS

To find winning mutual funds among the thousands available, you can turn to several personal-finance and investment magazines that provide regular coverage of funds and rank their performance on an annual basis, and sometimes even monthly.

Among the most popular periodicals covering funds are *Kiplinger's Personal Finance Magazine, Money, Smart Money, Business Week, Forbes* and *Barron's*.

As with stocks, you can track daily price changes for mutual fund shares in the stock tables of your newspaper. The illustration on page 158 shows you what to look for.

Other publications, available in libraries and bookstores or directly from the publisher, provide comprehensive directories of funds. Among the most useful that also include performance information:

- **The Handbook for No-Load Fund Investors.** Excellent guidance on choosing a fund, plus performance data on approximately 2,000 funds. Updated annually (P.O. Box 318, Irvington, NY 10533; 800–262–4729).

- **Individual Investor's Guide to Low-Load Mutual Funds.** Comprehensive information on almost 900 no-load funds compiled by the American Association of Individual Investors; members get the book free. Includes risk ratings and portfolio holdings. Updated annually (625 N. Michigan Ave., Suite 1900, Chicago, IL 60611; 800-428-2244).

- **Directory of Mutual Funds.** Published by the Investment Company Institute, this directory contains data on thousands of funds. It is updated annually, but contains no performance information. (Investment Company Institute, 1401 H Street, N.W., Suite 1200, Washington, DC 20005).

- **Morningstar Mutual Funds.** Expert analyses of individual funds, updated every other week by Morningstar Inc. (225 W. Wacker Drive, Chicago, IL 60606, 800–735–0700).

- **Value Line Mutual Fund Survey,** a biweekly publication analyzing the performance of about 1,500 mutual funds.(Value Line Publishing; 220 East 42nd St., New York, NY 10017, 800–535–8760)

peal to young people (see the discussion on pages 157-161).

Once you're in, you can buy additional shares in small increments.

You can purchase no-load funds—funds that charge no up-front sales fee—through the mail directly from the fund management company.

Your money buys instant diversification that isn't otherwise available to small investors who don't have the money or the inclination to invest in a dozen or so individual stocks.

Best of all, kids have lots of time to recover when the market hits the skids. Over time, investing in growth stocks or in a growth-stock mutual fund, will give them a better return than any other investment. Going back to 1926, large-company stocks have had an average total return (increase, or appreciation, of share price plus dividends) of around 10% a year; the total return on small-company stocks has averaged around 12%. You can't argue with those numbers— that return beats all other financial assets.

To make that point with her stepchildren, financial planner Anne Lieberman of San Rafael, Cal., opened a mutual fund account for each of them as a Christmas gift when they were 19, 20 and 22. Lieberman chose a fund that had a minimum initial investment of $100 and allowed her to invest additional money in increments of $25. The fund did so well that her youngest stepdaughter started to feel frustrated with the extremely low yield she was earning on several thousand dollars she had been keeping in the bank. "We talked it over, and since she expected to need the money in the next few years, I told her to leave it in the bank and not risk it," said Lieberman. "But she now understands the concept of investing, which most people don't get till they are well into their thirties."

Lieberman's experience points out something else to remember about investing in the stock market —it's a risky business and you can lose big. But, once again, kids have time on their side. If they choose a fund with a proven past or a bright future, they stand to win—and win big.

A Mutual Admiration Society

Kid-focused mutual funds are still a small flicker in the firmament of funds. But judging by my mail they're attracting lots of attention from both parents and kids, and their niche is expanding.

About a half-dozen companies earmark one or more of their funds for kids by spelling out a distinctive investment philosophy, setting a low initial minimum for custodial accounts or providing educational materials for young shareholders. And their returns haven't been bad.

A marketing gimmick? Perhaps, but if so it's one of the better ones. "You want to expose people to good investing habits as early as possible, and this is one way to do it," said Sheldon Jacobs, publisher of *The No-Load Fund Investor*.

Almost by definition kids are investing for the long term. If you are investing on behalf of a child, focus less on single-year performance than on fund quality in general. Here's the lineup of kid-oriented funds:

Stein Roe Young Investor ($1,000 minimum for a custodial account, or $100 with an automatic investment plan of $50 per month; 800-338-2550). Started in 1994, the pioneer in kid-focused funds is committed to investing 65% of its portfolio in stocks that affect the lives of children and teenagers. But that's not a limiting factor, according to Erik Gustafson, who manages the fund with David Brady, because "about 99% of companies fit that description." Young Investor has owned stocks you would expect to find in such a portfolio—Coca-Cola, Disney and Procter & Gamble, for instance—and some you might not, such as Citigroup, Walgreen and Global TeleSystems Group, a European telecommunications company.

Young Investor has been so successful that Stein Roe started another fund, Growth Investor, with identical holdings but with a lower expense ratio for people who

HOW TO READ THE MUTUAL FUND LISTINGS

Most daily newspapers publish mutual fund tables in the business pages. Here's a guide to interpreting them.

NAV is net asset value per share, what a share of the fund is worth.

Buy price is what you pay per share of the mutual fund.

Net Chg. is the change in the fund's NAV that day from a day earlier.

NL in the pricing column means you don't pay a sales commission when you buy shares of the mutual fund; that is, there is no up-front sales load.

p next to the fund's name means that it charges a yearly 12b-1 fee to cover the mutual fund company's cost of marketing, sometimes including commissions to bro-kers. Funds may be listed as NL, even if they charge this fee.

r means that the mutual fund may charge you a redemption fee (or back-end load) when you sell. These fees may be perma-nent or temporary, as with a contingent deferred sales fee, which may start as high as 6% and decline gradually the longer you keep your shares. A fund can have a re-demption fee but still be called no-load.

t means that both p and r apply.

x and/or **e** stand respectively for ex-cash dividend and ex-capital gains distribution, meaning that the fund has just distributed income to current shareholders. That day's NAV will be reduced by the amount of the distribution per share.

YTD%ret is the year-to-date return.

NAV   Net Chg   YTD%ret

Name	NAV	Net Chg	YTD %ret
SmCap	11.30	+0.03	+17.3
USA Gbl	19.93	+0.22	+22.2
BldProLoan	14.48	+0.09	− 0.9
Burnhm p	36.94	+0.46	+13.8
CCB Funds:			
Equity	23.07	+0.12	+ 8.6
CDC MPT + Fds:			
AggEql r	10.16	+0.14	NS
CoreEql r	10.14	+0.14	NS
GlobIndl r	10.08	...	NS
CG Cap Mkt Fnds:			
BalInv	11.72x	+0.07	+ 5.2
EmgMkt	6.85	+0.12	+36.5
HighYld	7.34x	−0.07	+ 0.6
IntFx	7.89x	−0.01	− 0.5
IntlEq	12.50	+0.07	+ 9.1
IntlFx	8.06x	−0.07	− 7.6
LgGrw	25.38	+0.48	+12.4
LgVal	14.19	+0.05	+ 8.8
LTBnd	7.89x	+0.05	− 6.2
MtgBkd	7.84x	+0.01	+ 0.7
Muni	8.22x	+0.01	− 3.8
SmGrw	18.41	+0.08	+ 9.3
SmVal	10.78	−0.02	+ 1.2
CGM Funds:			
AmerTF	9.08	+0.04	− 4.0
~~nDv~~	23.58	+0.03	− 5.2
	9.44	+0.09	− 2.8
		~~n.03~~	− 4.0

Name	NAV	Net Chg	YTD %ret
Conseco Fund Group:			
20A p	16.24	+0.10	+26.9
AstAlcA p	12.69	+0.07	+ 9.6
ConvSecA p	13.13	+0.22	+21.3
EquityA p	14.29	+0.03	+14.3
EquityY	14.48	+0.03	+14.8
FixIncA p	9.86	+0.05	− 0.3
FixIncY	9.90	+0.05	+ 0.1
HiYldA p	9.95	+0.01	+ 4.7
HiYldB p	9.92	+0.01	+ 4.5
Copley	37.68	+0.55	+ 1.7
Cornerstone Funds:			
NYMun p	0.71	...	−10.9
Countrywide Funds:			
EqtyA	23.49	+0.38	+11.4
GroVal p	19.27	+0.16	+14.6
IntBd p	9.53	−0.06	− 2.6
IntGvtA p	10.38	+0.05	− 1.9
Oh TF A	11.57	+0.04	− 2.1
TF IntA p	10.79	+0.02	− 1.0
UtilityA	17.81	+0.36	+ 1.8
CuFd Adj	9.93	+0.01	+ 2.9
CuFdST	9.84	+0.01	+ 2.8
CutlerEl	15.54	+0.18	+ 5.1
CutlerValue	18.63	−0.02	+11.3
DLB Fund Group:			
Disc Gr	17.79	+0.19	+12.0
FixInc	10.27	+0.05	− 1.1
Growth	13.20	+0.21	+ 3.0
MicroCap	9.34	+0.02	+ 8.5
	1.94	−0.04	+ 0.4
	~~n.03~~	~~+10.7~~	

Name	NAV	Net Chg	YTD %ret
EmgMkt	14.14	+0.10	+48.4
FL Int r	13.06	+0.03	− 1.1
GlbGrth p	36.51	+0.41	+ 5.0
GnCA r	12.69	+0.06	− 3.4
GMBd t	13.55	+0.05	− 3.4
GNY t	19.17	+0.06	− 3.0
GNM p	14.22	+0.05	+ 1.3
GrInc	20.38	+0.21	+10.5
GthOp	10.69	+0.14	+10.7
HiYld	11.78	+0.03	+16.6
InShTv A	1.97	...	+ 1.9
InsMu t	17.29	+0.07	− 3.0
Interm r	13.47	+0.03	− 1.3
InterGr t	13.41	+0.11	+ 6.9
Intlindex r	14.45	+0.01	+ 8.7
IntlVal	17.45	...	+15.3
IT Inc	12.41	+0.06	+ 2.9
DBaGn	14.66	+0.05	+ 1.8
LTGrR	19.19	+0.14	+ 8.6
LTIncR	13.75	+0.06	+ 2.4
LTGrInR	18.07	+0.10	+ 4.0
LrgCoVl	24.53	+0.08	+ 6.6
MA Int r	13.25	+0.03	− 1.4
MidcpVl t	22.36	+0.11	+25.6
Mas Tx r	16.02	+0.06	− 3.0
MunBd r	11.71	+0.05	− 3.7
NJ Int r	13.51	+0.03	− 0.8
NJ Mun r	12.59	+0.05	− 2.6
NwLd r	47.78	+0.02	+16.0
NYIn t	10.68	+0.05	− 3.0
NY Tax r	14.69	+0.05	− 2.6
	~~n.~~	~~+.05~~	− 2.0

don't want Young Investor's educational materials: an "owner's manual" explaining the principles of investing, an activities book for kids ages 3 to 12, and Dollar Digest, a colorful quarterly newsletter.

USAA First Start Growth ($250, or $20 a month; 800-235-8377). One of the newest funds to be directed toward kids, First Start Growth's prospectus requires it to steer clear of alcohol, tobacco and gambling stocks. But manager Curt Rohrman can invest in any other companies that are familiar to kids. He has kept about 80% of his portfolio in large-company stocks, including America Online, the CVS drugstore chain and Clear Channel Communications, which Rohrman says "owns the radio stations kids listen to."

He manages other USAA funds, but Rohrman feels First Start is a different animal. With First Start, he has close contact with young shareholders. Their investment ideas appear in a monthly newsletter that is part of USAA's money-management program for kids. And Rohrman even peruses *Seventeen* magazine for stock tips (that's where he found Steve Madden, a company that makes trendy platform shoes).

American Express IDS New Dimensions ($500, or $50 a month; 5% load; 800-437-4332). Not strictly a kid-focused fund, New Dimensions already had a 30-year track record when American Express chose it as the flagship of its Kids, Parents and Money program. "We needed a long-term investment as the foundation, and we went with the fund that had performed well through thick and thin," said Jan Holman, vice-president of investment services for American Express.

Like Young Investor and First Start, New Dimensions leans toward big, well-known companies: Cisco Systems, Wal-Mart, General Electric, America Online and Microsoft have been major holdings. Manager Gordon Fines "doesn't go out and look for kid stuff," said Holman. "He looks for investment opportunities." New Dimensions comes with educational materials for kids, including a quarterly newsletter.

Invesco ($250, or $25 per month; 800-525-8085). As part of its Driving Into Your Financial Future (DIFF)

DEAR DR. TIGHTWAD

After reading your column about eighth-graders playing the stock-market game, I thought you'd get a kick out of my own eighth-grade experience, in 1958.

As part of a unit on the stock market, the teacher gave each of us a hypothetical $100 to invest at the beginning of the year. My parents gave me an actual $100 to invest, provided I researched my selection. I bought one share of Walt Disney and two shares of Desilu (which I later sold, investing the proceeds in more Disney stock).

Over the years, I bought 100 shares of Disney. With my total investment of $3,533, I now have 400 shares worth $40,272. I might have found a better return than 1,083% over the 40 years, but not as good a story!

program for kids, Invesco makes special low minimums available on custodial accounts in four diverse funds. The one most directly comparable to other funds in the kids' niche is Blue Chip Growth.

Invesco doesn't send educational materials to young shareholders directly. But in connection with DIFF, it presents seminars on investing to groups of children in the Denver area, where the company is headquartered (for information, call 800-255-6927).

Monetta. The seven Monetta funds have minimum initial investments of $250 for all accounts, not just those for kids. But participants in the youth-investing program, called Monetta Express, still get some special perks. If you open a custodial account and sign up for at least $25 per quarter to be invested automatically, you receive Steady Eddy, a plush bean-filled engine and the first of eight train cars in the Monetta Express (the other seven represent each of the company's funds). When children accumulate an additional $500 in contributions they get the next car in the train, and so on until they collect all seven. You have five years from the date of enrollment to earn the entire train; or a single contribution of $5,000, divided any way you like among Monetta's funds, will do it.

The program, which also includes stickers and other rewards, is intended to "teach kids at a young age to set a goal and save for it," said a Monetta spokesperson. But the company also hopes it will bulk up low-level custodial accounts.

Among Monetta's funds, the most comparable to others in the kids' niche is Large-Cap Equity. Monetta's is the only youth program that offers a money-market fund, Government Money Market (for information, call 800-666-3882).

Royce Giftshares. Strictly speaking, Giftshares (800-221-4268) doesn't fit this category: Its minimum initial investment ($2,500) is too high for most children, and it doesn't publish educational materials or focus on stocks of interest to kids. In fact, its emphasis on investing in small companies is a more risky strategy.

But Giftshares (and a similar fund, American Century Giftrust) is an option for parents and grandparents who want to attach strings to a financial gift. Your contribution is set up as a trust that lasts as long as you stipulate (a minimum of ten years or until the beneficiary reaches the age of majority, whichever is longer). If you're concerned about teenagers squandering college money, for example, you can arrange for the trust to pay their tuition directly, or limit kids' access to all or part of the assets until they're past college age.

Be aware, however, that donors' options are restricted as well. Once you've put money into the fund, you can't get it out.

Low-Cost Stock Investing

As the *Kiplinger's* expert on kids and money, I get a flood of questions about how to introduce kids to the stock market—not to mention a few pokes in the ribs and conspiratorial winks from friends who assume that my own three children must be off and running on Wall Street. "So, what do your kids invest in?" they ask (wink, poke). At one point my editor even suggested that I write a story titled "My kid, the investment guru."

Catchy, perhaps, but, regrettably, wrong. While as a writer I try to practice what I preach, as a parent I have mixed success. A couple of years ago when Charles Schwab ran a special deal allowing holders of custodial accounts to make one commission-free trade, each of my kids invested $150 in stocks of their choosing—PepsiCo, Walt Disney and Hershey Foods. Since then Schwab hasn't repeated its no-commission promotion, and the kids haven't bought more stock. But the seeds have been planted, and as the kids grow I hope their interest will, too, along with the size and diversity of their portfolios.

Choosing stocks suitable for children is the easy part—just ask kids themselves, who intuitively live by the Peter (Lynch) principle of investing in what they know. If your kids are still young, choose something you know.

When Mark Stephens of Raleigh, N.C., began investing for his son, Hugh, 4, he chose two local utility companies—Duke Energy and Public Service of North

---

DEAR DR. TIGHTWAD

Q. We bought stock in Wendy's for our 14-year-old son and 6-year-old daughter, and they contribute their own money to buy more shares. Lately, however, my son has been saving for a Boy Scout trip, so his sister's holdings are catching up with his. Should we make up the difference?

A. Keep up with your investments on your son's behalf, but don't worry about his own.

Part of learning to manage money is setting priorities, and your children have made choices that make sense for them. Your son is obviously a thrifty young man. Even if his stock account is growing more slowly right now, he'll have a great time on the Boy Scout trip. And he'll have the satisfaction of knowing that he paid for it himself.

Because your daughter is younger, she has fewer choices when it comes to parceling out her money. But when she gets older and wants to save for space camp or a ski trip, the family books will balance.

Carolina—because he could buy initial shares direct from the companies, bypassing a broker, for a minimum initial outlay of $250 each. "My strategy is to save pocket change, and whenever I get $100 I dump it into one of the companies," said Stephens. "I started to go with something like Wrigley or McDonald's, but I'm just not thrilled with those stocks, and at this stage Hugh doesn't care."

On the other hand, members of the Stock MarKids investment club in Washington, D.C., cared a lot, actually holding some of their meetings at McDonald's restaurants when they started their club a few years ago as 9- to 11-year-olds. "We tried to show them that investing is about what you purchase," said Pat Smith, whose daughter Shannon is a club member. That's why the club bought General Electric and Johnson & Johnson. But it also bought shares in Trusted Information Systems, a local high-tech firm, just so the children could attend a company's annual meeting.

Using a Broker

StockMarKids bought McDonald's through the company's McDirect stock purchase plan, although it took a while to come up with the $1,000 minimum initial investment. But for other purchases they've used a traditional discount broker because trade execution is faster and "we can specify a target price," said Smith.

Nowadays one of the speediest and cheapest ways to trade small lots of stock is online. Many online brokers require a minimum of $1,000 to $2,000 or more to set up an account, including custodial accounts. (Regardless of whether you or your kids are buying the stock, purchases for children under age 18 have to be made through a custodial account. All you have to do is fill out a form from the broker with the minor's name and social security number and the name of the custodian.)

But there are a few brokers will let you open custodial accounts with as little money as you want: DLJdirect (888-456-4355; www.dljdirect.com); Suretrade (800-909-6827; www.suretrade.com), and Web

Street (800-932-8723; www.webstreet.com).

If you prefer the security of dealing with a human being, the discount firm of Bidwell & Co. (800-547-6337) will charge a commission of $20 plus 8 cents per share for up to 1,000 shares. There's no minimum to set up a custodial account, and no minimum trade. If you already have a working relationship with a broker, you may be able to cut a deal setting up a custodial account for your child at less than the going commission. If you're buying a larger number of shares for yourself, ask if you can register some of them in the names of your children (you may have to pay a registration fee).

Straight to the Source

Sarah Todd of Lena, Ill., had never dealt with a broker, either online or in person, when she decided to buy shares of stock as Christmas gifts for her four children. "Part of my reasoning was that I couldn't remember the gifts I had given them for past Christmases, and this would be something they'd remember," said Todd. She set a limit of $500 per child, each of whom got to choose his or her own stock, which mom then purchased directly from the company ("It was convenient for me to do at 8 or 9 PM," said Todd). John, 20, chose Merck (minimum initial investment $350 for direct purchases); Ann, 16, picked Dayton-Hudson ($500 minimum); Carrie, 14, chose Fannie Mae (which has a special $100 minimum for custodial accounts); and Matthew, 12, Wal-Mart ($250 minimum).

Hundreds of companies let you make initial stock purchases directly without having to go through a broker, after which you can enroll in the company's dividend reinvestment plan (DRIP) and buy fractions of shares, sometimes in increments as low as $10 (for Fannie Mae custodial accounts and Bob Evans Farms, for example).

But be warned: Both McDonald's and Disney, two of the most popular kid-oriented stocks, have steep entrance requirements—$1,000 or ten shares plus a $15 setup fee in the case of Disney, and $1,000 or 25 shares plus a $5 fee for McDonald's. More typical minimums are $250—for PlayStation-maker Sony, for instance, which is a foreign company sold as an American depositary receipt (ADR)—to $500 for toymaker Mattel.

In fact, companies that let you make initial purchases directly have been criticized for raising their fees and charging more of them. In addition to its enrollment fee, Disney charges $5 plus three cents per share to buy additional shares (in minimum $100 increments).

Not every company with a direct-purchase plan charges high fees, and some charge none at all. As an alternative to Mattel, for instance, Hasbro lets you enroll in its plan with one share and no additional purchase fees. The same goes for Wendy's, an alternative to McDonald's. The long list of other companies with single-share enrollment and no fees for additional cash investments includes Coca-Cola, Exxon, Harley-Davidson, Intel, Johnson & Johnson and Kellogg.

DEAR DR. TIGHTWAD

Q. Our 10-year-old daughter will earn about $300 this year in dividends and interest. Does she have to file an income-tax return? If so, can she get away with filing a 1040EZ because she's a child?

A. The answer to your first question is easy: No, your daughter doesn't have to file a return. Since all her income was "unearned"—meaning it came from dividends and interest rather than a salary—she could make as much as $700 in 1999 without owing tax or having to file a return.

But the answer to your second question is not "EZ." Assuming your daughter's income did meet the filing threshold, the type of form has nothing to do with age. What counts, among other things, is the source and amount of income.

You can't use the 1040EZ if you have any income from dividends or capital gains, or more than $400 in interest income. In that case, your daughter would probably have to file Form 1040A. And if she also had income from capital gains, she'd have to file the 1040 long form and a Schedule D. You can always skip lines that don't apply.

A number of fee-friendly single-share companies even offer some kid-pleasing perks. Wrigley shareholders get a box of 20 free packs of gum during the holidays. Each fall 3M shareholders have the opportunity to pay $9.50 for a gift assortment Post-Its and other company products, and Anheuser-Busch gives 15% discounts on admission to its theme parks.

Most companies do charge fees if you want to sell your shares, and time is not necessarily of the essence. While some plans sell shares daily, others can take weeks to execute your transaction. If you anticipate needing money at a certain time, you can ask the plan to send you the physical stock certificates, which the company must put in the mail within 72 hours of your request, and then sell through any broker, advises Charles Carlson, editor of *DRIP Investor* newsletter (7412 Calumet Ave., Hammond, IN 46324) and author of *The Individual Investor Revolution*.

"If you're a trader, these plans aren't for you," said Carlson. "But if you want to teach kids early habits of saving regularly, and are interested in a specific company instead of a diversified mutual fund, direct investing is an especially good way to go." (For a detailed list of companies that let you make initial purchases directly, visit Netstock Direct, www.netstock.com, and its companion site, www.kidstock.com.)

Other Stock Options

Sometimes you can circumvent dollar minimums for initial purchases in company-direct plans by buying a single share through another source (that's the case for each of the companies owned by the Todd family, for instance). And hundreds of companies with single-share DRIPs don't give you the option of buying that first share directly (for a complete guide to DRIPs, see the Directory of Companies Offering Dividend Reinvestment Plans, $37.95 from Evergreen Enterprises, P.O. Box 763, Laurel, MD 20725-0763; 301-549-3939). In those cases, you'll have to bite the bullet and go through a broker, or use one of the broker-free services that spe-

---

INVESTING ON THE WEB

Here's a selection of Web sites where kids (and grown-ups) can learn more about stocks and investing:

MainXchange (www.mainXchange.com). Interactive investing game with prizes.

Investing for Kids (http://hyperion.advanced.org/3096). Excellent primer produced by and for kids.

Stock Market Game (www.smg2000.org). School-based game with virtual portfolios

Young Fools (www.fool.com/teens/FamilyCollection980325.htm). Teen site from the Motley Fool.

How to Teach Young People About Investing (www.better-investing.org/youth/how-to-teach.html). A virtual curriculum with lots of resources.

Edustock (www.library.advanced.org/3088/welcome/welcome.html). Free real-time stock market simulation with 20-minute delay.

Investing in Your Future (www.tqd.advanced.org/3298/entrance.html). Financial calculators to see how different investments will grow.

Online Math Applications! (www.tqjunior.advanced.org/4116/Investing/investin.html). Real-life math using investment vehicles.

---

cialize in making initial investments at low cost:

The Low Cost Investment Plan of the National Association of Investors Corp. (248-583-6242; www.better-investing.org). Members of the NAIC plan can purchase stock in any of about 160 companies for a one-time setup fee of $7 plus the price of the stock (and a fluctuation fee of $10 or more in case the price goes up before the stock is purchased). A $20 annual youth membership includes a year's subscription (five issues) to NAIC's *Young Money Matters* newsletter, a $5 coupon for a child's first stock purchase, and a $24 coupon for *Investing for Life*, the NAIC's youth investor's guide that normally costs $30 for members and $40 for nonmembers. Share orders are pooled, so it could take several weeks for your purchase to be executed.

Temper Enrollment Service (800-388-9993; www.drp.com). Formerly available only to subscribers of the *Moneypaper* or *Direct Investing* newsletters, this service is now open to anyone. Temper will enroll you in about 1,000 companies that offer DRIPs for the price of the stock plus a fee of $20 per company (subscribers pay $15 for selected companies) and a sliding commission that ranges from 50 cents for one share to five cents per share for 100 shares. Temper accepts enrollment until the 25th of each month and makes purchases at the beginning of the following month. *Moneypaper* also publishes a *Guide to Dividend Reinvestment Plans*.

First Share (800-683-0743; www.firstshare.com) takes a co-op approach to buying shares in more than 250 companies. The membership fee ($24 for the first year and $19 annually after that) entitles you to buy as little as one share from other First Share members. There's a service fee of $5 or $10, depending on the company requested, plus an additional $7.50 transaction fee to cover the seller's expenses.

One Share of Stock (888-777-6919; www.oneshare.com) specializes in selling single shares of stock in certificate form that can be framed. Although shares often festoon nursery walls (Disney is One Share's biggest seller), the kids who own them are registered owners of the stock and can participate in a company DRIP, if one is available, as long as they meet the plan requirements (in Disney's case, that would mean a minimum purchase of ten shares). You pay the share price plus a flat fee of $49—steep to get a certificate, but brokers often charge $15 or more for a certificate that comes creased in a business-size envelope. And you can get shares in companies that are hard to come by through sources other than a broker: Apple Computer, the Boston Celtics limited partnership, the Cleveland Indians, Microsoft, Pixar, Tootsie Roll, Topps, and Yahoo, for example.

You and your children should first decide on which companies you want to invest in and then compare share-purchase options based on convenience and cost-effectiveness. Remember that no matter what you pay to get your kids started as investors, you're buying more than a share of stock. When Pat Smith's daughter Shannon grumbled that her mom didn't let her watch enough TV, Pat asked if there was anything she had done right as a mother. Replied Shannon, "You taught me about the stock market."

A Word About Risk

Jon Hagelstein had some words of advice for would-be Wall Street tycoons: Leave your investments alone; if you buy and sell a lot, you'll be "murdered by commissions." And steel yourself to take a loss. "I was fully aware I could lose every single penny," he said.

Getting your kids to save at all is great; getting them to appreciate the risks and rewards of various kinds of investments is icing on the cake. Just like adults, they'll have different tolerances for risk and make different choices, depending on how much money they have and what they want to use it for. Here's a rundown on their options:

GARDEN-VARIETY BANK SAVINGS ACCOUNTS. Still the best place to stash money earned from paper routes or babysitting. Your kids won't get rich fast on the interest they earn, but bank accounts are convenient and the money is safe as long as it's insured by the Federal Deposit Insurance Corp. (FDIC) or the National Credit Union Administration.

BANK CERTIFICATES OF DEPOSIT. These pay a higher rate than a regular savings account, but in return your kids will have to promise not to touch their money for a certain period—most commonly six months, one year, 2½ years or five years. Also, CDs can require a minimum deposit of several hundred dollars. They're insured by the FDIC up to $100,000.

MONEY-MARKET MUTUAL FUNDS. Instead of investing in stocks, these mutual funds invest in the "money market," which is a collective name that describes all the different ways in which governments, banks and corporations borrow and lend money for short periods. The interest rate changes every day, but it's generally higher than on regular bank accounts, especially when rates are rising. And, unlike a CD, your kids can get their money whenever they want it, although they (or you, on their behalf) will have to transact business by mail or phone. Money-market funds aren't insured; however, they're regarded as one of the safest uninsured investments around. Minimum balance requirements can be steep, but there are always exceptions that allow investors in for as little as $100 or waive minimums altogether. For older kids with money and savvy, money-market funds can be an alternative to a bank savings account.

STOCKS AND STOCK MUTUAL FUNDS. Over time, they offer the greatest rewards and carry the greatest risks. When chosen well, they can be the best alternative for kids who are saving for a long-term goal.

THE INS AND OUTS OF CUSTODIAL ACCOUNTS

Minors can't own assets in their own name, so if you want to save or invest on behalf of your children—or if the kids want to do it on their own—you'll need to set up custodial accounts. These generally come in two varieties, depending on the law in your state: the Uniform Gifts to Minors Act (UGMA) or, more commonly, the Uniform Transfers to Minors Act (UTMA). Opening one is as easy as checking a box when you open a mutual fund or brokerage account. All you need to do is name the child as beneficiary and an adult (typically you) as custodian.

Custodians have a legal right to manage and invest a child's assets, and to spend them on anything they consider appropriate for the "use and benefit" of the child. That can include school tuition, summer camp, a personal computer, even clothing, as long as those expenditures don't take the place of a parent's legal support obligations. And under no circumstances may custodians spend a child's assets on themselves.

How will anyone know how you spend the money, you might ask. It may be that no one will. But it's the possibility of getting caught, along with the pricking of your conscience, that's expected to keep you in line. The larger the amount of money, the greater your incentive to stick to the letter of the law. A tax audit could trigger a review of the accounts—and the IRS would probably be inclined to look closely if a custodial account held a large balance one year and a significantly smaller one the next, or showed considerable activity. Using the money for your own purposes would make you liable for taxes on the earnings. In addition to facing tax consequences, you have a fiduciary responsibility to the child as custodian of the account. If you misuse the assets, your child could sue you to recover the funds.

Giving money or other assets to children results in a couple of tax breaks for you. You can give as many people as you wish annual gifts of $10,000 each without

Learning for Real

That's what the options look like on paper. How well can young people cope with them in real life? A few years ago, Victoria Collins, a financial planner in Irvine, Cal., and her husband, David, decided to give the five teenagers in their combined families a real-world course in money management. They gave each child $4,000, with instructions to increase the value of their stake by saving or investing it. Each year their kids were to report on their progress, and at the end of the fourth year the one who had earned the best return would get the grand prize: a trip for two around the world using

having to pay gift tax. If both spouses join in the gift, you can give away $20,000. That can be an attractive estate-planning tool for parents and grandparents who would like to distribute assets from their estate before they die. While such gifts can reduce the taxes on your estate, however, they have no immediate impact on your income tax. Donations to charities can be deducted on your tax return, but gifts to individuals cannot.

Nevertheless, you do gain certain income-tax advantages. In 1999 the first $700 of earnings from assets held in a child's name is tax-free (that figure will rise in the future with inflation). The second $700 is taxed at the child's rate, presumably 15%. For children under age 14, investment income above $1,400 is taxed at the parent's rate.

Custodial accounts have a couple of drawbacks. Assets given to a child belong to the child irrevocably. That means you can't get them back, but the child can get them as soon as he or she reaches the

legal age in your state. Fortunately, most states have raised that age to 21, or allow you to specify an age between 18 and 21 or even older, making it less likely that kids will squander the money on a sports car instead of paying their college tuition.

Assets held in your child's name can also affect your eligibility for college financial aid because schools usually expect a bigger contribution from a student's assets than from a parent's. But don't let financial aid eligibility alone determine whether you save in a child's name. Some parents prefer to set up an account in a child's name as a convenience. That way, they can keep college funds separate and make it easy for other family members to contribute to a college account. Parents going through a divorce may prefer that assets be held in a child's name (with a neutral third party as custodian) so they don't become a bone of contention. And grandparents sometimes prefer to give assets to their grandchildren rather than their grown children.

mom's and dad's frequent-flier miles.

Sisters Jennifer and Nicole pooled their money and entrusted it to a stockbroker friend who piled up hundreds of dollars in commissions and a stack of trade confirmation slips but lost all their money. Todd invested in stocks and mutual funds that went nowhere. Kim had big plans for her money, but ended up letting it sit in a money-market fund—and almost eked out a victory by default. The eventual winner, David Jr., showed up at family meetings with charts and graphs explaining his strategy of investing in growth mutual funds (but even he lost $500 on a hot stock tip from a friend).

In short, said Victoria, "They did all the things adults do. But I'd rather have them blow the money now than blow the money for the down payment on the house later."

KIDS' QUESTIONS

Q. "If I have a share of stock, does that mean I have to share it with someone?"

A. Not exactly. Owning a share of stock in a company means that you own a part of that company—a piece of the action, so to speak. As one of the owners, you're entitled to a share of the money your company makes after all its expenses are paid—its profits. If you're a shareholder in Nike, for example, you stand to profit each time someone buys a pair of Nike sneakers. If you're a stockholder in Toys 'R' Us, you stand to profit every time someone buys a toy at one of its stores.

Profits are paid out in the form of a dividend, which is like the interest you earn on a bank account. Banks promise to pay you a certain rate of interest. Dividends, on the other hand, aren't guaranteed. The size of a dividend all depends on how much money the company makes. Sometimes even a profitable company doesn't pay dividends. Instead, it puts all its profits back into the company so that it can grow even bigger (Microsoft is a good example of a company like this).

When you're a stockholder, you can make money in another way, too. If your company does well and its stock becomes more valuable, the price of your shares will go up. If you paid $15 for a share of stock, for example, it might go up to $20 or even higher.

On the other hand, your company may not make much money, or could even lose money. If that's the case, it may not pay a dividend, and the price of a share of stock could fall from, say, $15 to $10 or less. That's the risk of investing in the stock market.

Q. "Can kids buy stocks?"

A. Yes, they can. Minor children (usually children under the age of 18) can't own stock directly. But all you have to do is ask your parents to fill out a simple form to open a custodial account—which means their name appears on the account along with yours.

With their parents' help, children can buy shares in any of the thousands of companies whose stock is bought and sold on stock exchanges, such as the New York Stock Exchange (NYSE), the Nasdaq market or the American Stock Exchange (AMEX). Once you have opened an account with a stockbroker (a person who buys and sells stocks for customers), all you have to do is call your broker and tell him or her how many shares of which company you'd like to buy (or go online to do the same thing).

Q. "How much does stock cost?"

A. The price is set by the market, and it all depends on how much buyers and sellers think the stock is worth that day. Some stocks sell for less than $10 a share, others for more than $100 a share. If you're interested in buying stock in a particular company, you can check to see how much its stock has been selling for by looking up the company alphabetically in the stock tables section of any newspaper or online. Stock tables have lots of small type and look long and boring, but they're really pretty easy to use once you know what you're looking for. (For some instructions on reading the stock tables, see page 149.)

Q. "How do I sell a stock?"

A. The same way you buy one, only backwards. You call your broker and tell him or her to sell your shares (or you enter your sale with an online broker). You'll get the market price of the stock that day.

But you shouldn't get into the habit of selling stocks frequently. You'll have to pay a commission on each sale, just as you do when you buy a stock. And that could eat up any profits you might have made if the stock has gone up in price.

Q. "But what if the price of my stock goes down?"
A. That can be an even better reason not to sell. The price of your stock is almost guaranteed to fall at some time. Maybe your company will go through a period when business isn't so great. Sometimes the whole stock market goes down because people are less enthusiastic about holding stocks.

But the best way to make money in the stock market is to buy shares in good companies that have the potential to grow, and hold on to them. Over time the stock market tends to rise, with downward blips along the way. When a stock price drops, young investors should follow the same strategy as adults: Ask yourself if you still like the company and think its future looks good. If the answer is no, go ahead and sell your shares. If the answer is yes, hold on—and maybe even buy some more.

Remember the secret to making money in the stock market: Buy low, sell high. It may take a while for prices to rise again. But if anyone qualifies as a long-term investor who can ride out ups and downs in the market, it's a 12-year-old.

Q. "Who is Dow Jones? They talk about him on TV a lot."
A. Actually, your question should be "Who are Dow Jones?" "Dow" is Charles H. Dow and "Jones" is Edward D. Jones. In the 1880s they founded the newspaper that later became

the *Wall Street Journal.*

In 1896 Mr. Dow began calculating the average daily price of 12 stocks. By the 1920s, the editors of the *Wall Street Journal* were tracking the stock prices of 30 big industrial companies every day. The 30 stocks chosen are representative of the broad market and of American industry.

What the editors did was add up the 30 stock prices and divide by a number to get an average price (it gets complicated here because they didn't divide by 30, but you don't have to worry about that). The average price they came up with was called the Dow Jones industrial average (or Dow, for short). Looking at movements in the average was a way of measuring whether the stock market as a whole went up or down. A rising Dow means stock prices went up; a falling Dow means they went down.

The Dow Jones industrial average became so popular that even after all these years, it's reported every day in the news. It's done by computer now, but the procedures are the same as those Charles Dow developed over a century ago, and a number of companies, including Sears and General Motors, have remained in the average since the 1920s.

Q. "Wow! I just got a 3-D Mark McGwire baseball card! Is it going to be worth a lot of money some day?"
A. Don't get your hopes up too high when it comes to making money by investing in the collectibles market. Old baseball cards are valuable if there's interest in the players and if the cards are relatively rare and in mint condition. (That probably lets out most of your parents' cards if they flipped them, stuffed them in their pockets or wrapped rubber bands around them. So don't let your parents blame grandma for tossing them out.)

Nowadays, with millions of cards being produced (and carefully preserved by kids with an eye to making a killing in the market), it's less likely that prices will shoot up in the future. Even if some do, it's tough to predict which players will generate the most interest a generation from now.

Collect for love, not money. There's a market for just about anything you can collect—Barbie dolls, Hot Wheels cars, McDonald's Happy Meal toys—but markets are fickle. There's no guarantee you'll be able to sell your treasures at the time you want the money and for the price you think they're worth. Kids, especially, can be taken advantage of. There are success stories, of course—like the young man who got hooked on collecting comic books when he was 4 and at 18 sold his collection of 10,000 books for $6,000, enough to pay for his first three semesters of college.

But any money you eventually make should be an unexpected bonus; the real pleasure should come from the thrill of the chase that is part of building and enjoying a collection.

If you still harbor the hope that some day all that work will pay off, the best you can do is:

- Focus on items popular with kids between the ages of 10 and 17. That's the time in their lives people like you will try to recapture when they're 30; they won't remember much before the age of 8.

- Treat collections gently. Better still, if you have the space and the cash, buy duplicates of some items—one to play with and one to keep in its box. The container can easily double an item's value.

- Look for collectibles with tie-ins to movie or television characters or well-known personalities, whether it's Ronald McDonald or G.I. Joe. That's what makes an item memorable.

Of Lawnmowing & Milkshake Stands

When my son Peter was 10 years old, he had an idea for a summer business that would, as he put it, "make some major cash." Along with his friends, Mickey and T.J., he would set up a stand at the corner and sell milkshakes. I didn't want to burst his bubbling enthusiasm, but I wasn't quite sure how this scheme would shake out. Would there be enough traffic at the end of our cul-de-sac to generate any business? Just how did they plan to get the electric milkshake maker down to the curb? And how would they keep the milk cold and the ice cream frozen?

Not to worry, Mom, Peter patiently assured me. Since this would be a three-man operation, he would stay in the house making the shakes, Mickey would man the stand to make sure nobody took anything, and T.J. would shuttle back and forth delivering the drinks. And, of course, they'd do it on a Thursday afternoon, the busiest day of the week for the piano teacher up the street.

My initial misgivings were perhaps typical of many parents with entrepreneurial kids. You'd think we'd be happy to nurture our children's interest in the free enterprise system. After all, the extra cash would help free us from the enterprise of keeping the kids in clothes, cosmetics and video games. And the kids might even lay the foundation for their life's work. Business tycoon Warren Buffett bought stock at age 12, made enough money to pay taxes at 13 and bought a farm in Nebraska before finishing high school in Washington, D.C. Computer king Michael Dell started his empire in his college dorm. Nowadays especially, when jobs are constantly in flux and every member of the work force has to be a little entreprenurial just to keep pace, it's important for kids to know that working for yourself is an alternative to working for a company or joining a profession.

But instead of encouraging our kids' grand schemes, we're often tempted to find the flaws in them—perhaps because we're afraid that we'll end up spending lots of our time minding the kids' business. But as Peter reminded me, children can be satisfied with small successes that don't necessarily require much in the way of parental input.

Several days after our conversation, I got an excited phone call from my son while I was at work. On the spur of the moment he and his buddies had set up their stand at T.J.'s house (on a busy corner) and cleared $21—not bad for a few hours work, even after they had paid me back for the milk and ice cream they used. T.J.'s mom contributed a long extension cord so they could make the shakes outside, and they kept the milk and ice cream in a cooler. They charged $1 per drink (the $1.25 banana special wasn't a big seller), and netted a few extra dollars from customers who tipped them for their good service.

If they did it again, Peter decided, he would plow some of the money back into the business in the form of a bigger sign. I figure that as long as I don't rein him in, he could be well on the way to achieving his goal of being the second-richest man in the world—by a penny. "Bill Gates made Microsoft," Peter once told me. "You can't dump a legend."

The ABCs of Capitalism

Why are we parents sometimes reluctant to teach our kids entrepreneurial skills? Often because, unless we're in business ourselves, we don't feel comfortable in the role. If truth be told, many Americans would probably be hard-pressed to explain the economic system that makes their country tick (and some might even feel vaguely guilty about it). In a study of Russians and Americans to determine their attitudes toward free markets, Yale economist Robert Shiller and two Russian colleagues found that Americans actually showed less understanding about how markets work and more hostility toward price increases and other kinds of capitalistic behavior.

But peel away the layers of econo-speak and the system really is quite simple. In fact, scratch the surface of the average American and you'll find an itchy capitalist. With the possible exceptions of eating and breathing, nothing is more instinctual than making money.

Brownies Equal Economics

Consider, for example, that American institution, the fund-raiser—specifically, a fund-raiser undertaken a number of years ago by my son's nursery school. The school was a nonprofit cooperative run by the 30 families whose children attended. For several years demand for nursery school slots exceeded supply, so the school enjoyed a long waiting list and a modest budget surplus. One year, however, a new day-care center down the road siphoned off customers; as a result of the lower than expected revenue from tuition, the school faced a deficit of about $300.

How to close the budget gap? We couldn't cut expenses because most of our costs were fixed. Besides, our problem wasn't a bloated budget but a revenue shortfall. The quick and dirty expedient of a special mid-year assessment was dismissed; consumer resistance would be too great, and it would breach the informal contract agreed to in the fall when tuition rates were set. The idea of raising money through an auction or a book sale was more appealing but was rejected as not feasible. Our potential market—the 30 co-op families and members of the church at which the school was located—was too small. What we had to do, everyone agreed, was tap a larger market at the lowest possible cost.

Someone proposed a bake sale at a local shopping center, and that drew a flurry of interest. It had a number of advantages: a commodity product that everyone was familiar with and that wouldn't suffer for not having a brand name; ease of entry into the market (we could set up shop in front of Sears); no need for outside financing because parents would be investing the cost of materials (we'd bake the cookies).

Another parent suggested a 50-50 raffle. Once the idea was explained—the winner gets 50% of the take—we were quick to see the potential. A ticket allotment of, say, $20 per family would go over better than an assessment because people would have a chance to make a return on their investment. Besides, we could sell tickets at the bake sale.

Eventually the raffle idea had to be scrapped because of regulatory difficulties: The church whose name the nursery school bears frowned on gambling. But the bake sale was a go. The goal, of course, was to maximize profits—or, as our bake sale organizer put it, "The more we bake the more we make." But we also had to determine the market-clearing price of homemade brownies and pineapple upside-down cake. In pricing my own nut rolls, I rejected a cost-plus approach; how could I put a price on my grandmother's research and development? Instead, I opted for market-based pricing: I called my mother in Pennsylvania and asked how much nut rolls fetch in bake sales there. Sell them for $5.50, she told me, and not a penny less than $5. Allowing for the higher cost of living in Washington, I figured we could get $6 easy.

We did. We also got $4-plus for cakes and did a brisk business in a scrumptious chocolate-and-cream-cheese concoction called black-bottom cupcakes (25 cents each, five for $1). We rotated our stock from the back of the table to the front, ran specials on slow-moving items and after four hours liquidated what little re-

---

WHEN I GROW UP . . .

In a survey of 1,000 kids by Time Warner, the top five occupations cited by 8- to 12-year-old wannabes were teacher (13%), doctor (11%), lawyer (8%), police officer (6%) and firefighter (5%). Other choices included astronaut, Mc-Donald's manager and herbalist.

Also: 60% of kids wanted to start their own businesses; 38% of kids wanted to do the same kind of work as one of their parents; and 51% of kids wanted to work in their own hometowns.

mained of our inventory with a special close-out sale. ("You couldn't even buy a mix at these prices.") The black-bottom line: a profit of $263.50.

And that's the economy in a nut roll.

Are Entrepreneurs Born or Made?

Everyone seems to agree that there's an entrepreneurial "type"—glad-handing extroverts who are convinced they've built the better mousetrap and have no qualms about ringing doorbells and telling total strangers all about it at great length. No room here for shy, quiet kids who'd rather fiddle with computers or doodle in a sketchbook.

It's true that some personality traits can increase one's chances for success as an entrepreneur. It helps to be well-organized and dependable, and to enjoy your work, for example. But building high-tech mousetraps and talking a blue streak aren't necessarily on the list. While Linda Menzies was researching her book *A Teen's Guide to Business*, which she co-authored with Oren Jenkins and Rickell Fisher (Master Media), she talked to 13- and 14-year-old teens "who had done so much that they made me feel old at 21," said Menzies. "I thought they'd be geniuses who had invented something, but they were just teens who had a good idea."

Walk into an average classroom of 13-year-olds and ask them for ideas on how to earn money, and it's likely that half will say babysitting and the other half lawnmowing. Bonnie Drew, author with her husband, Noel, of *Fast Cash for Kids* (Career Press), breaks it down even further. "I go to a school to speak to the students, and maybe two of 30 kids in a class are real entrepreneurs, by which I mean interested since the age of 4 or 5. Five aren't motivated by money at all. But the others might be motivated to become entrepreneurs if they had a specific goal and you got them at the right time." The catalyst could be a long summer vacation when they're looking for something to fill the time, or a burning desire for a video game system that you're not willing to buy.

Super Ideas at School

Or it could be a school assignment like the one that inspired Ronni Cohen's fourth-graders at Burnett Elementary School in Wilmington, Del. Cohen instructed her class of entrepreneurs (defined by the kids as "people who take risks and make choices so their company can make a profit") to invent devices that make it easier to eat pasta, and come up with a marketing plan to sell them. On this day, Ian is showing off his Super Duper Spaghetti

---

DEAR DR. TIGHTWAD

Q. Last summer my daughter, Diana, who is 14 years old, wanted to go on a trip to Washington, D.C., with a church youth group. Both her mother and I gave our consent, but we felt it was important for her to earn part of the needed $650.

Diana had in the past done babysitting and occasional lawnmowing. However, these jobs weren't going to provide her with the needed money in the short amount of time she had before leaving. We encouraged her to be creative and think of ways she might earn the necessary money quickly.

After much thought, she hit upon the idea of selling baked goods. She enjoyed cooking and felt this would be something she could do. We encouraged her to scale down this idea to something more manageable, such as cooking only certain items. She decided on cookies.

Diana negotiated with us to contribute the ingredients as our contribution to her trip. She then went to her computer (another hobby of hers) and developed an order and price list, which she distributed at church, among family and neighbors, and at her mother's and my workplaces.

The orders started flowing in. The cost of the cookies was $3 to $5 per dozen, and she was able to earn over $900 in under four weeks. The business would have continued had she not gone on her trip and then started summer school.

She kept an account of what she spent on ingredients and her net profit would still have exceeded $700 had we not contributed the ingredients.

A. Diana deserves a pat on the back—and so do you for helping to channel your daughter's energy into a project that she could manage, and then taking a businesslike approach to your own contribution. You provided support without doing the actual work.

Scooper, a gizmo made of a tea strainer with a spoon attached at the other end (for eating spaghetti without losing the sauce). Using a hardhat, a clothespin and Legos, Courtney has created an elaborate pulley that hoists the spaghetti off the plate. All the kids rattle off the "factors of production" that they have used in building their inventions: "materials," such as tape, glue, rubber bands, string and empty soda bottles; "capital," or equipment that can be used again on other jobs, such as screwdrivers, scissors and staple guns; and, of course, "labor"—their own and that of various family members.

Each child has also done a marketing survey for his or her invention, measuring supply and demand at various prices and graphing the results to come up with a market-clearing price, the point at which supply meets demand. Eventually the kids vote Josh's creation—a fork attached to an electric screwdriver—as most marketable and launch into a discussion of how to drum up demand for it. "Have a catchy ad." "Decorate it." "Make a small one for little kids." "Think of other things it can do, like whip potatoes, roast marshmallows and dig holes to plant seeds."

Closer to Home

School programs can provide the spark, but it's up to parents and other adults to fan the flames. Parents, family members and other entrepreneurs have the most influence on a kid's decision to start a business, according to a survey of high school students attending a conference for teen entrepreneurs at the University of Pennsylvania's Wharton School. You don't need to be in business yourself; giving your child an opportunity to earn money around the house may be encouragement enough.

After all, kids get their first taste of the world of work by making their beds and picking up their toys. As they get a little older, they learn that their parents are willing to pay them to do more grown-up jobs, such as raking leaves or shoveling snow. One day it dawns on children that other people will pay them to rake *their* leaves and shovel their snow, and suddenly mom and dad have a fledgling entrepreneur on their hands.

Something as straightforward as a family yard sale presents all sorts of entrepreneurial possibilities. One family gave their teenage son the food concession at their regular yard sales. He sold coffee, soft drinks and popcorn, and made $25 or $30 in a couple of hours.

When Bonnie Drew's two sons were young, they helped organize family garage sales. On trash pick-up days, older son Jon would get up early and scavenge neighborhood cast-offs for old bikes and bike parts. Then he'd rebuild the bikes and sell them at garage sales of his own. Kids began bringing their bikes to him for spare parts and repairs, and by the time he was 14 he was running a business fixing small engines. Younger son Robby, a "totally different personality," would buy boxes of candy at a warehouse store and then resell it to neighborhood kids. A musician, he eventually organized his own band. Whatever children end up doing, the impetus comes from home. "That's where they get the confidence," said Drew.

"What Can I Do to Earn Money This Summer?"

Judging by the number of kids who ask me this question, summer employment for children too young to get a "real" job is high on the wish list of bored (and broke) kids, as well as parents trying to peel their offspring away from the TV. Some seem to think there's a magic formula for making a quick buck over the summer. Well, there is a formula, but it isn't magic: A little imagination to find a need, plus lots of elbow grease to fill it, equals less time on your hands and more money in your pocket.

For the 12-and-under crowd, earning money begins with tried-and-true tasks such as mowing lawns or babysitting. But enterprising kids can give these old standards a new spin. Instead of just mowing lawns,

---

> ## ENCOURAGING YOUNG ENTREPRENEURS
>
> Lots of programs are available at all grade levels for teachers who want to introduce kids to entrepreneurship. Ronni Cohen's project, described on pages 182-183, was part of "Choices and Changes," sponsored by the Delaware Center for Economic Education. Every state has its own such agency; to locate yours, write to the National Council on Economic Education (1140 Avenue of the Americas, New York, NY 10036; 212–730–7007).

kids could sign up clients for full-service yard work such as watering plants or hosing decks (anything that can be done outside with water is a hit with children). Add leaf-raking and snow-blowing, and a summer lawn service becomes a year-round venture. Instead of waiting around for babysitting jobs on Saturday night, kids could organize a daily dinnertime play group that gives harried parents an hour or two of free time. Or sign up all their friends who babysit and match them with people in need of sitters, so parents only have to make one phone call.

To keep up the kids' enthusiasm, keep their jobs manageable and fun. Primary-school children still think in concrete terms—money can be exchanged for things. So they get a kick out of selling stuff, any stuff—old toys, pictures they draw, cookies they bake, and, yes, even lemonade.

You may have to put in a little time helping them bake the cookies or choose sale items that they won't want back the next day. But you don't have to spend days constructing an elaborate stand or hours minding the store. The kids will be happy to sit by themselves at a card table in your front yard for an hour or two and make $5.

Middle-school children between the ages of 9 and 13 are perfect for the service economy. They're old enough to take on jobs with a certain amount of responsibility and young enough to be enthusiastic about it. Summer lends itself to lots of possibilities: Feeding the cat and taking in the mail for neighbors who are on vacation; washing cars; lugging trash cans out to the curb each week.

One enterprising 12-year-old offered his services as waiter, busboy and gofer to an aunt who was giving a dinner party. Seven hours later he went home with $25 in his pocket. Two 10-year-olds set up shop doing hair braids for 25 cents each. They also offered a tie-dying service for birthday parties.

Your children will be happiest and most productive if they do something that taps their special talents or interests. If they're good at computers, they could tutor other kids, or adults, who need help. One brother-sister team shared a job reading aloud to a handicapped child in the neighborhood. If they're artistically inclined, they could make and sell jewelry or refrigerator magnets. One young lady made more than $100 during her summer at the beach by selling necklaces she made out of colorful fishing lures.

Young kids don't have wheels, but they don't need to go too far afield. They can make funky fliers and target likely customers in the neighborhood—families

---

DEAR DR. TIGHTWAD

Q. What is your opinion on kids going into their own little summer business? We live in a tourist community and last summer my children made a lot of money selling Kool-Aid and angle worms (great combination, huh?). They each had over $150 before the Fourth of July. The idea is they learn to earn. I love giving my kids things, but we can't really afford a lot with a big family, and I know the kids are more careful with spending money when they earn it.

But friends of mine think I'm denying my kids the fun of being given gifts for no reason. My contention is that you don't have to buy your kids' love by getting them stuff

they only play with for a minute and then throw aside, but I still feel like a prude.

A. Kool-Aid and angle worms—I can't think of a better summertime treat.

Your kids are ingenious, not to mention rolling in dough.

Refusing to buy your kids toys and expensive clothes every time they walk into a store does not make you a prude. It makes you a good parent (and you can tell your friends I said so). Of course, it's always fun to surprise your kids with treats for no reason. But who says they have to be expensive? In my experience, all it takes is a Slurpee from 7-Eleven.

with young children who are in need of babysitters, or older people who'd appreciate having someone else haul their trash cans.

Success Stories

Now that you and your children are interested, you need to be inspired. I certainly was when I judged an essay contest, sponsored by the Stein Roe Young Investor mutual fund, in which fifth- sixth- and seventh-graders were asked to answer this question: "How would you save enough money to open your own company and what would it be?" What impressed me was the number of businesses that were already up and running:

Carrie Hobson of Mesa, Ariz., had used $80 from her savings to start Carrie's Creations, which sold hand-painted aprons and personalized ornaments during the holiday season.

Melissa Arseneau of San Luis Obispo, Cal., sold jams and jellies made with grapes from her aunt and uncle's vineyard.

Jenna Skophammer of Fort Dodge, Iowa, had already sold a greeting card design to Hallmark and has designs on a company of her own, to be called Skop's Scribbles and Colorful Cards.

Molly Eaton of Oshkosh, Wisc, had founded the Reflect-O-Light Co., which paints reflective house numbers on curbs—the very same thing her grandfather did to earn money back in 1947.

Getting Started

Lots of kids who babysit or mow lawns are already in business for themselves; they just don't realize it. Officially, their work becomes a business when they earn at least $400 a year, because that's when the self-employment tax kicks in. Unofficially it becomes a business when they begin to take it seriously, by giving it a name, making fliers, handing out business cards or generally being more professional and more formal about the way they run it.

PUTTING IT ON PAPER. In adult businesses, the first crucial step is to draw up a business plan, a blueprint of the business that describes in detail the product or service you're going to offer, your target market, advertising strategy, potential competitors and financial projections. For kids, of course, that has to be scaled down, and lots of kids may be turned off by the task.

But they'll stand a better chance of success if they at least ask themselves some basic questions about their business, such as what their business will do, whom it will serve, how much they'll charge, how much they'll have to pay in expenses and how they'll promote it. Their "business plan" can be as simple as a one-page worksheet with those headings (see the list of questions on page 193).

Older teens can be more detailed and more ambitious. Author Sarah Riehm (*The Teenage Entrepreneur's Guide*, Arco; out of print) recommends that they decide on a time period (will it be a summer or year-round job?), set up a work schedule, separate their costs into those that are fixed and those that are variable, establish prices and estimate how much business is expected each month.

Kids should think about who their competitors might be and set goals for the business that are specific, reasonable and measurable. For example, "I want to be the best lawn service in Center City" is good, but "I want to achieve 100% customer satisfaction with no refunds" is even better.

RAISING CASH. A service business won't require much in the way of start-up capital, which kids will probably be short on. If they do need to raise cash, encourage them to rustle it up themselves by doing extra jobs around the house or holding their own yard sale. You can help finance the venture, but it's more important for you to provide moral rather than financial support. Kids shouldn't expect their parents to be their main customers, provide unlimited free phone time or furnish raw materials gratis. If you're going to set up the table and provide the pitcher, the lemons, the sugar, the water and the cups, you're entitled to more than a free glass of lemonade.

SELLING THEMSELVES. One of the toughest steps for kids to take is the one that leads to that first door. Carrie Hobson "felt uncomfortable going door-to-door . . . so I marketed my products by setting up a booth at my local grocery store and at my all-star softball games."

Kids who offer a service should be prepared to encounter cynical adults who don't believe that young people are disciplined or dedicated enough to follow through on their promises. It wouldn't hurt if young entrepreneurs were to prepare a written biography with details of their school or work experience and references to contact. Being polite will win adults

---

BUSINESS IDEAS FOR KIDS

I've culled this list from the books recommended on page 195. Once your children have identified ideas of interest, they can use the questions on page 193 to choose endeavors that are appropriate for their age, ability and resources—including how involved you want to be.

The lesson here is to match your children's skills, hobbies or talents with money-making opportunities.

- ❑ Window washing
- ❑ Curb address painting
- ❑ Outdoor painting (outdoor furniture, fences, doghouses, porches, decks or storage sheds)
- ❑ Garage cleaning
- ❑ Lawnmowing
- ❑ Pool/driveway cleaning
- ❑ Housecleaning
- ❑ Carpet cleaning
- ❑ Plant watering
- ❑ Pet grooming
- ❑ House-sitting
- ❑ Picking up papers and mail for vacationing neighbors
- ❑ Pet and plant sitting

- ❑ Helping people move (packing, cleaning up)
- ❑ Golf caddie
- ❑ Bike repair
- ❑ Birthday clown
- ❑ Birthday party planning
- ❑ Tutoring
- ❑ Typing/word processing
- ❑ Buying and selling used books
- ❑ Sign making and painting
- ❑ Gift wrapping
- ❑ Errand service, including grocery and dry-cleaning delivery
- ❑ Messenger service
- ❑ Flier distributor
- ❑ Odd-jobs agency set up with other neighborhood kids

over, and so will dressing neatly. Even if you're selling a lawn service, don't show up in an old T-shirt and cut-offs. Instead wear a neat polo shirt or, better yet, a T-shirt imprinted with the name and logo of your business.

That kind of sight advertising also helps kids who would rather die than ring a doorbell. So does a not-so-silent partner to help spread the word. As noted earlier, shyness needn't keep kids from starting a business. At some point, however, they'll probably have to make direct contact with prospective customers. And when they do, Bonnie Drew has some advice on how to be a super salesperson: Use the same powers of persuasion you use on mom and dad when you're trying to get them to take you to the ice cream store or buy a new bike:

- **Tell them all the reasons they should buy** your product or service and how it will help them.
- **Tell them why they need your service right away.** Instead of asking them if they want you to lug their trash cans to the curb, tell them when you can start.
- **Don't give up if customers say no.** If they say they don't have time right now, ask if you can come back. If they say they don't need the service, ask if they know someone who does.

DEAR DR. TIGHTWAD

Q. I thought it was enterprising and educational when my son and his friend, both in second grade, decided to have a yard sale of old toys and split the proceeds. As it turned out, my son contributed all the toys, and his friend ended up buying them. That would have been okay—but then the friend showed up and asked for his share of the proceeds! I felt that wasn't fair to my son, but I didn't want to interfere because a deal is a deal.

A. It's a raw deal if the parties involved are confused about the terms. Don't be afraid to help straighten things out.

You could have volunteered to go over all the transactions and count out the money. If your son's friend was unhappy about being long on toys and short on cash, you could have asked your son if it would be all right for his friend to return some of his purchases. Or you might even have paid him a small "salary" for helping out at the sale. If kids are going to learn a lesson about money, it might as well be how not to cheat—or be cheated.

■ **If they say yes, do the job promptly,** courteously and thoroughly. And always say thank you.

Mistakes Kids Make

Kids will be kids, even if they're entrepreneurs. At a time in their lives when they're particularly self-absorbed, it's often tough for them to live by the principle that the customer is always right.

Not being professional enough in their attitude—by showing up late, acting rudely or speaking crudely—is perhaps the biggest mistake kids make, and it's the surest way of alienating skeptical adults. Here are some of kids' other foibles, with advice on how to correct them:

GETTING BORED. It's typical of kids to get excited about something, jump in with gusto and quickly burn out. If you recognize your children in this picture, encourage them to start their business as a short-term venture during summer vacation or over a holiday. With the end in sight, they can get out gracefully if they lose interest.

GETTING IN OVER THEIR HEADS. Here are the three biggies:

Underestimating the cost. A big problem even for adult entrepreneurs, being short of cash is best avoided by choosing a business in which your kids' biggest investment is their own effort. If they do need equipment—say, a computer to print fliers, or a lawn mower—they should use what they have or borrow what they can, instead of buying something new, shiny and expensive.

Underestimating time. For young children just starting out, ten hours a week is enough to devote to a business. Before they start, they should draw up a schedule to see when they can best fit in the time; working weekends and once or twice on weeknights is plenty. After all, they're still kids and they need time just to have fun.

Overestimating their strength. Children can be tempted to take on a job that's too physical—moving furniture, for example—or just plain unrealistic—mowing ten lawns in two days. Making the effort to think through a business plan, even a rudimentary one, can help here. So can the timely intervention of mom and dad.

MILKING THE BUSINESS. Many kids, after all, start businesses to make money, and they're tempted to spend everything, when it may be prudent to plow some money back into the business. Starting a lawn service by borrowing mom and dad's mower is fine, but if the business takes off, it's time for kids to consider investing in a machine of their own.

OVER- OR UNDERPRICING THEIR PRODUCTS OR SERVICES. Kids often don't have a good sense of what their costs will be or what their services are worth. As in the bake sale example that introduced this chapter, kids have a couple of options in setting prices. In the so-called cost-plus approach, they tot up the cost of any raw materials they might need, such as cleaning supplies for washing cars, add in how much they want to make and come up with a figure. In the market approach, they find out what competing businesses are charging and set their prices accordingly. Their competitors can be anyone from the kid down the street who's also mowing lawns to a professional lawn-care service. Sarah Riehm recommends that a kid-run business should charge 25% to 30% less than its professional competition. One rule of thumb for youngsters who make products is to charge twice the cost of their materials.

When *Zillions*, the consumer magazine for kids, asked hundreds of children what they had earned on summer jobs, the survey turned up a two-tier price system: one (lower) price for parents and another price for everyone else. To set their prices, kids asked other kids what they were charging or sought advice from their parents. Some enterprising youngsters visited customers in advance and set their prices based on the

QUESTIONS KIDS SHOULD ASK THEMSELVES

What will I do?   _____

When will I conduct my business?   _____

Summers only? Year-round?   _____

What will the name of my business be?   _____

Is there a need for my product or service?   _____

Who will my customers be?   _____

How far from home can I conduct my business?   _____

Who else is doing the same business in my
   neighborhood?   _____

How much are they charging?   _____

Can I do the job better than the other guys?   _____

How much will I charge?   _____

How much time will each job take?   _____

How much money do I want to make?   _____

What's my goal for my business?   _____

What do I need to know to do the job?   _____

What kind of equipment do I need to do the job
   and where can I get it?   _____

How much money do I need to start my business?   _____

What kind of help will I need from my parents?   _____

How much of their time will I need each week?   _____

Do I need to hire other people to help me?   _____

How will I let my customers know that I'm available?   _____

difficulty of the job. One babysitter ups her fee if the kids look wild. If they look "really bad," she might not take the job.

Kids can also ask potential customers how much they're willing to pay, or do some informal market research by surveying their parents and other adults. That can work to a child's advantage because adults often put a higher value on the service than the child does (see the question on page 199). If the price is too low, the kids can bargain, or turn down the job. (For a fun lesson in how not to set prices, rent the video *The Gravelberry Pie King*, in which Fred Flintstone becomes a pie tycoon by selling Wilma's famous gravelberry pies for a price that doesn't cover the cost of the ingredients.)

Should you pay your kids for doing some of these jobs? It depends. You shouldn't pay your 13-year-old to stay with younger siblings for an hour or so after school while you run errands. But you should expect to pay for a Saturday night job, since he or she could easily land a paying gig. You could, of course, negotiate for a family discount.

LACKING CONFIDENCE. Some kids are doomed to failure because they don't really believe they can succeed. Encourage them to set their sights high while engaging in some down-to-earth planning, and they stand a good chance of pulling it off.

Nuts, Bolts and Red Tape

Starting a business is, after all, an introduction to the real world, so it shouldn't be surprising that as entrepreneurs your kids will be introduced to regulation, taxes and the fine points of the law.

Red Tape

They will probably set up shop as a sole proprietor, which is the easiest way to start a business: You just do it. Federal and state child labor laws restrict the age at which kids can get a job, the kinds of work they can do and the hours they can work. Under federal law, for

---

MORE IDEAS AND ADVICE FOR KID BUSINESS

If you or your kids need more inspiration, a number of sources can help:

- Daryl Bernstein's *Better Than a Lemonade Stand* (Beyond Words Publishing) describes 51 businesses, with hints on which supplies and how much time you'll need, what to charge, how to advertise.
- Bonnie and Noel Drew's *Fast Cash for Kids* (Career Press) lists 101 money-making projects for children under 16, arranged by season of the year. Also includes age-appropriate tips on how to handle the financial end of the business.
- *A Teen's Guide to Business*, by Linda Menzies, Oren S. Jenkins and Rickell R. Fisher (Master Media Ltd.), offers anecdotes from successful teen entrepreneurs and includes a section on how to land a job working for someone else.
- *The Lemonade Stand: A Guide to Encouraging the Entrepreneur in Your Child* (Gateway Publishers) is Emmanuel Modu's comprehensive guide for parents that includes chapters on legal and tax issues, business ethics, and business concepts your kids should know.
- *Acorn Entrepreneurs: Visions of Young Enterprises* (Paradise Productions; 210-820-3060) is a video collection of eight entrepreneurs ages 9 to 17. They share their experiences—good and bad—of starting and operating their own businesses.

---

example, 14 is the minimum age for most nonfarm work. But the federal law applies to employer-employee relationships. So if the kids run their own business or are independent contractors who babysit or mow lawns on a part-time, irregular basis for lots of different customers, they're not covered by the law. There are specific legal exemptions for kids who deliver newspapers, perform in show business or work for parents in their solely owned nonfarm business. For more information, call the Department of Labor at 202–219–4907 and order its free publication, *A Handy Reference Guide to the Fair Labor Standards Act.*

Once kids have decided on a name for their business, they should register it with the county government through the county clerk's office. Registration is required if they're going to be doing business under a name other than their own; it's recommended if they'll be using their own name. In some cities, kids may also need to get a license to operate certain businesses; check with your local authorities.

It's possible that your kids will have to contend

with homeowners associations and local zoning ordinances, which may not allow them to run a business in a residential neighborhood, post signs on their lawn or store equipment in the yard. In reality, however, neighbors, who tend to be the most vigilant enforcers of zoning laws, aren't likely to object to the kinds of service-oriented businesses kids are likely to start.

If your children will be selling directly to the public goods or services that are subject to state or local sales tax, they'll be expected to collect the tax. That means applying for a sales tax permit. If they'll be selling to a store for resale to the public, they probably won't have to collect the tax but may have to apply for a wholesale exemption certificate.

Taxes

If your child has net business earnings of at least $400 a year, the federal tax law kicks into gear. Technically your son or daughter is expected to file three tax forms:

- **Form 1040,** the basic two-page tax return;
- **Schedule C,** to report the business income and any expenses;
- **Schedule SE,** to figure the social security tax on self-employment income. (There's one important exception to the self-employment tax rules: They don't apply to newspaper carriers under age 18.)

Although a child claimed as a dependent on the parents' tax return can't claim a personal exemption, he or she does get a standard deduction. That deduction is either $700 or, if greater, equal to the child's earned income up to $4,300. (Those are the 1999 figures; they may rise in the future with inflation.) That means there may be no income tax due on up to $4,300 of earnings from the business. But there's no standard deduction to offset the self-employment tax. That 15.3% levy starts with the first dollar of net self-employment earnings. On $500 of income, this tax would cost $76.50. Check with your local Small Business Administration office or chamber of commerce to

> ## ORGANIZATIONS THAT HELP
>
> ■ **The Center for Entrepreneurship** offers a variety of resources and educational opportunities for prospective entrepreneurs, including students. For more information, write or call the Center for Entrepreneurship (Wichita State University, 1845 N. Fairmount, Wichita, KS 67260-0147; 316–978–3000).
>
> ■ **Junior Achievement** works with schools and businesses to introduce students to practical economic concepts, business organization, management, production and marketing. For more information, write or call Junior Achievement (1 Education Way, Colorado Springs, CO 80906; 719–540–8000).
>
> ■ **KidsWay** publishes *Young Entrepreneur*, a bimonthly magazine (888-543-7929), and sponsors Young Entrepreneur day camps, which offers grants for low-income youngsters, in a number of states.

see if any state or local taxes are due. (If you have a sneaking suspicion that few children with such low incomes go through the hassle of registering a business, collecting sales tax or filing an income tax form, you have a lot of company.)

Points of Law

If your children's business employs other children, their working hours will have to be limited as required by child-labor laws. Under federal law, for example, children who are 14 and 15 can't work more than three hours on a schoolday or more than 18 hours during a schoolweek. Kids under 14 can't work at all, unless it's in an occupation that the law specifically exempts: acting or performing, delivering newspapers or making wreaths at home (the state of Maine requested that exemption back in the 1930s, when making pine wreaths was a major state industry).

Minors can enter into contracts, but they're not legally bound to fulfill them. This may put off some adults, who may be reluctant to do business with a minor. To reassure skeptical adults, parents could become a party to the contract (although this would also make you liable if the customer was dissatisfied with your child's product or service). The best solution is for your children not to back out of a contract.

Check to see whether your homeowners policy covers any business-related injuries, say, to customers or employees. Some policies have so-called business pursuits clauses that specifically exclude such injuries. Even if yours doesn't, make sure you're covered.

All in all, the red tape shouldn't be sticky enough to discourage kids from starting a business. Most children don't make big bucks, so the procedure is fairly simple and straightforward. "I did a little of my tax return and my mom did the rest," said one young entrepreneur. "I didn't look forward to it, but it wasn't horrible."

Why You Should Care

The whole issue of how much, or even whether, young people should work is a hot potato (for more on that debate, see Chapter 13). But if your kids are inclined in that direction, there's a lot to be said for having them be their own boss and set their own hours in a job they enjoy doing. And it will yield dividends to you. Kids may not pay attention when you talk about being dependable, but if they lose a customer because they show up late to do the lawn, they learn a lesson parents can't teach. In addition, they learn to converse with grown-ups, use the telephone and budget both their time and (you hope) their money.

Entrepreneurship has also proven to be an avenue for channeling the creativity and hustle of inner-city kids into productive ends. A number of organizations—including the National Foundation for Teaching Entrepreneurship, in New York City, and the University of Pennsylvania's Young Entrepreneurs at Wharton—teach business skills to at-risk youth to build their self-esteem. "A lot of these kids don't even believe they can start a business. But once they see it's a way of making money and getting praise from family and friends, they become excited and involved," said the director of Wharton's program.

Zakia Andrews, an alumna of that program, started her own business selling lingerie at house parties and took it with her when she went to college. When Michael Freeman started the program at the National Foundation for Teaching Entrepreneurship, he didn't even know what the word meant. With a $25 stake from the course, he went to New York's wholesale district and bought novelty items like nail clippers and pens, then resold them to people in his Bedford-Stuyvesant neighborhood. Later he graduated to selling calculators, and finally, to teaching future entrepreneurs.

For kids (and adults) of any age, running a business gives a glimpse of the real world and a look at a

---

DEAR DR. TIGHTWAD

Q. My husband and I are fortunate to live in a neighborhood where young people come to our door asking if they can mow our lawn or shovel our walks when it snows. But I'm never sure exactly how much to pay them. What's the etiquette in a situation like this?

A. Often it's my children who are the inspiration for answers in my column, but this time that honor goes to my mom.

After a big snowstorm last winter, a neighborhood boy showed up at Mom's door asking if he could shovel her driveway. They never discussed how much he would charge, but she intended to pay him $10. When she couldn't find anything less than a $20 bill around the house, she figured his efforts were worth the price and offered him the $20.

When she did, he hid his hand behind his back. "It's too much," he mumbled. Mom pressed him to take the money, telling him he had done a good job and she wanted him to have it. He eventually accepted the cash, and both of them were happy about the outcome.

But the episode points out a valuable lesson for kids who do odd jobs and the adults who hire them: While children should set a price on their work, they often don't, depending instead on the judgment of their employers. If you have a figure in mind, tell the kids ahead of time so you both know what to expect and can iron out any differences up front.

Don't take advantage of child labor, but don't lavishly overcompensate kids for the work they do, giving them an inflated idea of their value in the labor force. Quote a figure that you think is fair and see if that's acceptable. If not, there's nothing wrong with dickering a bit, or hiring someone else.

career option they might not otherwise have thought of—and one that will look increasingly attractive (just look at the boom in Internet startups). As traditional employers attempt to stay lean and mean, jobs have become more competitive and more vulnerable. Young people should be aware that they have the opportunity to make their own living and don't have to rely on someone else for a job.

Last but not least, dreaming up a business of your own can be just plain fun. In the Stein Roe essay contest, Thomas O'Donnell wrote that because he enjoys sports and music, he'd like to open a store called Rock 'n Jock, which would sell sports equipment and CDs. Jeremy Mosst would some day like to open an agency for outer-space travel. Gillian Spiegelberg wants to start Woof Away, a dog spa that would "offer a day or two of fun, exercise and relaxation for your pooch."

And Jay Longosz had perhaps the most fanciful idea: starting a company to make Christmas lights "that would not break or burn out so quickly."

Teens: The Early Years

When my oldest child was a freshman in high school, I figured I was still a couple of years away from the expense of prom season. Then I received a letter from the mothers club at my son's high school asking me to contribute $25 (or whatever my budget would allow) to help pay for the school-sponsored post-prom party. I was also told it's customary for freshman families to pony up for one of the party's grand prizes—that year a mountain bike.

The truth is, I really didn't mind ponying up. After all, it was for a good cause—keeping the kids entertained, and contained, at an alcohol-free party where they could have fun without losing control. I hope new freshman parents will do as much for my son when it comes his turn for the prom.

Unfortunately, parents don't always have such a positive influence at prom time. Even as I read the mothers club appeal, out of my other eye I was scanning a story titled "Prom Night Means Teen Independence, Buying Spree for Parents and Kids" in a marketing trade publication. The prom, is seems is the "quintessential teen event," for which teens are ready to "break away and buy, buy, buy." They shell out anywhere from $175 to $600, including the dress or tux, tickets, and other necessary extras such as corsages, hairdos and limo rentals.

Far from balking at the expense, parents apparently encourage it. "When it comes to 'dress-up,'" marketers were advised, "parents are a key target because they share in the fantasy and are willing to pay for it."

In fact, when the Geppetto Group, a New York market research firm, interviewed teens across the country, the kids said they sometimes feel parental pressure in reverse: "My mom's been talking to me about my prom since I've been in the eighth grade. If I don't go, it will be such a disappointment to her," said one teenager in Michigan.

As children enter their teen years, their expenditures escalate and the stakes get higher—in just a few years they'll be on their own, in one way or another. But what the prom article brought home to me was that even on this ultimate night of teen fantasy and freedom, parents still are a force in their children's lives and have the power to influence kids for good or ill.

An Unreal World

By the time children become teenagers, they're hemorrhaging cash; in recent years, kids between the ages of 12 and 19 spent more than $140 billion per year of their own and their parents' money. Yet they can still be notoriously ill-informed about how much it costs to live in the real world.

Kids are under two misconceptions: "They think they're going to make a lot more money than they will, and they think things cost less than they do," said Darlene Todd, who heads her own financial planning firm in Chicago and has worked with older high school students in association with the Illinois Council on Economic Education. Todd told of a young co-worker who got the financial shock of her life when she married. She had been living at home, paying for her car, clothes and telephone and thinking that she was supporting herself. She hadn't reckoned on the cost of rent, insurance or food.

In extreme cases, you could end up with every parent's nightmare: the classic underachiever. Peter Spevak of the Center for Applied Motivation describes the type: As a child, an underachiever would rather play video games than study for the math exam; as a young adult he's still at home, dabbling halfheartedly in college courses and hanging around with younger kids. He figures he's entitled to the same kind of house and middle-class circumstances his parents enjoy, but he never stops to think that his parents had to work to get them. Delayed gratification frustrates him, and he can't deal with frustration. Well-adjusted adults would handle the disappointment of not being able to vacation in Florida by making alternate plans or saving to take the trip next year. Underachievers, explained Spevak, would "sit there and whine."

The best prevention is early intervention. Darlene Todd gave her daughter Susan a dose of reality therapy when she was 18. The two of them scoured Chicago newspapers looking for apartments that Susan could rent for $500 to $600 a month. They started out with three bedrooms in mind and ended up looking at studios—that Susan could share with a friend.

What Teens Know— and Don't Know

Today's teenagers are hardly babes in the woods when it comes to things financial. They are, after all, children of the revolution that popularized personal finance in the 1980s, and they couldn't help being caught up in it, at least peripherally. Trouble is, the little they know is enough to make them dangerous.

Checking Accounts

Teens know, for example, that checking accounts exist, but they don't always know how to balance one. That old joke about not being overdrawn if you still have checks is sometimes painfully on the mark. Kathleen Hennessey, a faculty member at Texas Tech in Lubbock who has counseled students on financial matters, recalls one student who came to her in tears with a sheaf of checks. She feared the checks had bounced, but they were actually canceled checks that had been returned to her routinely by the bank.

DEAR DR. TIGHTWAD

Q. Do I understand correctly that any child who received capital gains on a mutual fund in 1999 must file a return, no matter what his or her total income was?

A. No, that's not correct. Filing requirements for children can be a bit confusing, so the rules are worth repeating.

For 1999, a child doesn't owe any taxes, and doesn't have to file a return, unless he or she had more than $700 in unearned income—meaning income from dividends and interest rather than wages. (The threshold may rise in the future.)

If a child had more than $700 in unearned income (for 1999), then he or she would have to file a return. If part of that income was in the form of a capital-gains distribution, the child would have to file the 1040 long form and a Schedule D.

Credit Cards

Teens know how to use a credit card to buy things, but they're not always clear on how they're supposed to pay the bill. They think plastic is just another form of currency and don't understand that using a card is like taking out a loan. So they're vulnerable to the experience of the Maryland teen who went off to college, ran up $600 in credit card debt, faithfully made the minimum monthly payment, then suddenly realized she was hardly making a dent in paying off the bill. Her parents eventually bailed her out.

Saving

Teens know that saving money is a worthwhile goal—especially to pay for the expensive college education their parents have been fretting about for years—but for many of them CD means compact disc instead of certificate of deposit. Recent surveys done by the American Savings Education Council and Merrill Lynch indicate that only about half of teens interviewed said that they save regularly. There was a growing minority (18% up from 12% a few years ago) that spent all their money—whether from allowances, jobs or gifts—as soon as they got their hands on it.

Planning for college actually provides a convenient opening for parents to introduce their kids to the fine points of budgeting, saving and even investing. Yet when parents come to her to discuss how to pay for college, "very few of them even bring their kids," said Bonnie Hepburn, a financial planner in Acton, Mass.

That's partly because they're naturally reluctant to discuss the family's financial situation with the kids—and partly because they often share their kids' casual attitudes toward budgeting, credit and saving. But now may be the last chance for the whole family to shape up before the kids graduate and go off on their own, either to manage a household and pay bills they didn't even know existed or to attend college, where credit cards are as easy to get as pizzas at midnight—and just as habit-forming.

On-the-Job Training

You don't want to disclose the details of your family's financial affairs to younger children, but teens are old enough to learn the nitty-gritty of household finances. You might as well make good on your oft-repeated threat to make them pay the bills and use your bill-paying chores as a learning opportunity for them to write a month's worth of checks. To make your point more dramatically, adopt the tactic of one father. He brought his teens into line by getting his pay in cash, sitting his family down with the stack of money and a pile of household bills, and asking the kids to parcel out the money to pay them. By the time his kids saw how little was left, they were talking about getting part-time jobs.

Holding down a job is one way for kids to get an introduction to Life 101. Your kids will find it easier to appreciate the cost of adding them to your auto-insurance policy if you can put it in terms of how many hamburgers they'd have to flip to cover the cost themselves.

Whether you want your child to work and for how many hours merits separate consideration (see Chapter 13). If you prefer that your kids concentrate on schoolwork and extracurricular activities rather than a job, that doesn't mean they have to miss out on

DEAR DR. TIGHTWAD

Q. We just found out that our 13-year-old son has signed up with a mail-order music club to get eight compact discs for one cent. Now he's obligated to buy six more, at a potential cost of more than $100. He doesn't have that kind of money. If he doesn't pay up, will we have to?

A. Neither you nor your son should have to pay. If you don't, however, I presume you'll return the "free" CDs. In general, minors (usually those under the age of 18) can disavow contracts like these, and their parents (or other legal guardians) can't be held responsible. Write to the music club and explain the situation. An official of one of the major CD clubs says that in the circumstances you describe you'd be let off the hook: "If the parent comes and says,'My son is a minor and he joined without my being aware of it,' we will cancel the membership and the obligation." Sometimes parents aren't aware that their kids are piling up debts until the dunning letters start arriving. Don't be intimidated by fancy legal stationery. Write back and explain that your child is a minor and the letters should stop. Lest kids learn the wrong lesson—that they can renege on a deal with impunity—consider imposing your own penalty, such as confiscating the CD player or charging a cancellation fee.

real-world experience. Simply holding family meetings to discuss such financial matters as which car to buy and how to pay for it, how to cope with an impending layoff or how much to spend on holiday gifts can give your kids an invaluable insight into the kinds decisions they will have to make someday. And there is an immediate payoff for you. By seeking their input, you short-circuit any grousing later on if you wind up with a minivan instead of a sports car or if the customary Christmas pile is somewhat smaller than usual.

By the time your children graduate from high school, it's certainly reasonable to expect them to be able to manage their own checking account (although you will probably have to co-sign for them to open one if they're under 18). But at Young Americans Bank in Denver, the average checking account holder is 16, has a balance of $400 and no illusions about the money lasting as long as the checks. Linda Childears, president of Young Americans, says that the bank's account holders are very responsible and have very few problems with their accounts.

Giving young kids a simple explanation of how checking accounts work can avoid big problems later. I once witnessed an exchange between a mother and her 8-year-old, who was begging her mom to register her for a gymnastics class. Mom explained that she wouldn't have enough money until Friday. "You can write a check," said the child. "It wouldn't matter," Mom replied. "There won't be any money in the account until your dad and I get paid on Friday." The child accepted this explanation without a fuss.

Lesson one for kids, which they often pick up on their own, is that a check is a substitute for cash. Lesson two, which doesn't always occur to them, is where the money ultimately comes from to make good on the check. Lesson three is watching you write checks and subtract their value from your bank account. If they've absorbed that by the time they leave home at 18, they may run out of checks, but they're less likely to run out of cash.

The Budget Bugaboo

What gives teens fits is budgeting. In fact, adults and teens both have such a distaste for its eat-your-spinach overtones that the word "budget" has all but disappeared from the lexicon of financial counselors. Instead the focus is on dessert, in the form of a "spending plan," that's more freewheeling and less constraining than a budget. Here's how:

RECORD EXPENSES. Encourage your teens to write down everything they spend for a month, not necessarily to cut back on their outgo but to get control of it. "It may change their behavior and it may not, but the next time they go out to buy fries and a Coke they'll remember that 60% of their money is going toward junk food," said Kathleen Lenover, a financial planner in Denver who teaches a high school course in personal finance. (To help them develop a basic spending plan, suggest that they use the record-keeping worksheet on pages 212-213.)

SET GOALS. You stand a better chance of getting your teens to change their behavior if you encourage them to set goals. Saving money because it's the right thing to do is too abstract, even for teens. They need something to work toward, whether it's a new CD system, a college education or a school ski trip.

MAKE GOALS TANGIBLE. Whatever goal your kids settle on, have them write it down, which seems to provide a psychological boost. "When we write down what we're passionate about, there seems to be some sort of power that helps us accomplish it," said Lenover. "Kids eat this up."

MAKE GOALS STRAIGHTFORWARD. Lenover emphasizes what she calls the 70-20-10 rule of money management—70% to spend, 20% to save for future big-ticket purchases and 10% for long-term investing. Actually, the numbers themselves can shift to suit your purposes. For example, you might choose a 33-33-33 plan for spending, short-term saving and long-term saving, or a simple 50-50 for spending and saving. The point is that when a spending plan is that cut-and-dried, it becomes more manageable and less off-putting. (To make it even less scary, for both you and your kids, read the introduction to investing in Chapter 10.)

DECIDE WHAT'S IMPORTANT. Teens also need help with setting priorities—deciding which things they really need and which they merely want. Maybe this sounds obvious to you, but with teens you can't belabor a point.

Have them draw up a list of needs and corresponding wants. For example, they need school clothes but they want a fringed leather jacket that will exhaust their entire clothing budget. They need shoes; they want a pair to match every outfit, plus a few extras. They need transportation to school; they want a new car—and they want you to buy it for them.

Run down the list with them and attach a realistic price tag to each item. Writing down the numbers will make them seem more real to your kids and will give you room to maneuver. If there's $300 in your clothing budget and the kids insist on new jeans, they'll have to forgo the jacket (or pay for it themselves). If you're willing to spend $100 on shoes, they'll have to decide on four pairs at $25 each or two pairs for $50.

Esther Berger, a first vice-president of Paine Webber in Beverly Hills, recalls that when her oldest son approached driving age, he assumed that being a child in residence at 90210 automatically entitled him to a car. "I'm from Cleveland," said Berger. "I told him he needed transportation, but whether he got a new car, a used car or a skateboard depended on how much he saved, which his father and I would match." Michael saved $5,000 on his own and bought a brand-new Ford Escort.

DEAR DR. TIGHTWAD

Q. Every year I spend hundreds of dollars to outfit my pre-teens and teens with clothes and other back-to-school paraphernalia. This time of year is getting to be as big a financial strain as the holidays.

A. My personal preference is that kids wear uniforms to school, which cuts down on both money spent on clothes and time spent bickering about styles. If that's not an option, try these suggestions on for size:

Set a budget. The easiest way not to overspend is to establish limits in advance and give your kids a say in parceling out the money. Suppose you want to spend $300 per child. Older kids can take an inventory of what they already have and peruse catalogs to see how far their money will go. You can work deals with them—an expensive

shirt in exchange for budget jeans, for example—but have an idea of what you're going to buy, and where you'll shop, before you leave home.

Spread out your spending. If your kids see a nice item that doesn't fit into the budget, file it away as a possible holiday present and kill two birds with one credit card charge.

Don't sweat the little things. If your child needs a lunch box and wants one with a picture of the latest TV hero, go ahead and buy the box of choice—it's a cheap thrill. So are new notebooks and pencils. Kids get a psychological lift out of starting the year with pristine notebooks and crayons that have points.

Recycle the old stuff. Use old notebooks for art projects and grocery lists, and store puzzle pieces in last year's lunch box.

Expanding the Allowance

Once children reach age 13, they get more of their money from jobs than from allowances, and the gap continues to widen as they get older. In a survey done by the National Endowment for Education, a little more than half of the respondents said they work, while a little over one-third receive allowances.

But some parents take a different tack. When Joan Boucher of Denver was housebound with her infant daughter, she read about an allowance scheme for teens that intrigued her. For years Boucher bided her time. Then, when her daughter reached 13, she sprang it. Instead of a token allowance, she and her husband offered their daughter the opportunity to manage a sum large enough to cover all her expenses, such as savings, lunches, clothes, gifts and dancing lessons (with the exception of medical care and any parties she might have, which mom wanted to keep under her control). Her daughter was "dazed and delighted," recalls Boucher. With mom and dad to help, she spent an entire summer monitoring her expenses. "It gives the parent and child something genuine and valid to talk about, instead of 'why aren't you combing your hair differently,'" said Boucher.

They eventually settled on an allowance of $50 a month, a princely sum at the time, which they reevaluated every summer and adjusted upward or downward depending on anticipated expenses for the coming year. After that, the plan "took off and flew," said Boucher. "We had zero problems with the rest of the teenage years." The arrangement stayed in effect till her daughter reached 18 and left for college. It was the object of much envy on the part of little brother, who couldn't wait till he was 13 and got the same privilege.

A system like this is a hands-on lesson in distinguishing between the fixed expenses that can't be avoided—lunch money, bus fare, basic clothing—and the discretionary ones that may have to wait for another day. One blessed side-effect: It can also snuff out many a potentially explosive parent-teen confrontation. Mom and dad can't be expected to pay for those rock-concert tickets if money for that kind of entertainment is already built into the allowance. "The child knows the rules because they've been discussed ahead of time, so it erases parent-child tensions," said Boucher.

Wouldn't a teenager be tempted to squander the money? Sure—but not often. "You just have to stiffen your spine," said Boucher. "Of course they made mistakes and ran out of money in a few weeks. But they went without and they learned their lesson."

Kids and Cars

When your children become teenagers, one expense you probably won't be able to avoid in some form is the cost of driving. That's not to say you should buy your kids a car. On the contrary, I'm convinced that families would be better off, financially and otherwise, if kids didn't own a car of their own—even if they paid for it themselves. Just putting your teens on the family auto insurance policy can easily double the premium. If your child owns a car of his or her own, the premium will be even higher. Besides, owning a car is a long-term financial commitment; your child will probably have to get a part-time job just to support it. One thirtysomething man recalls that when he owned a car as a teenager, the first thing he learned to do was change the oil by himself. If he needed or wanted parts that were beyond his budget, he'd ask for them as gifts—sort of like "All I want for Christmas is two new front tires."

Money isn't the only issue here; maturity is important, too. One family counselor has concluded that in his experience it's better for adolescents to have use of an extra family car than to have one of their own. "I have found that the nicest of adolescents become rigid, selfish, demanding and difficult when they discuss 'their' car versus the 'family' car," he said. Also, it's less awkward for kids to explain to their friends that they've been grounded or can't get use of the car if it's a case of family ownership.

WHERE YOUR MONEY'S COMING FROM, WHERE IT'S GOING

As a teen, you probably have a steadier stream of income—and more of it—than when you were a kid. Your regular expenses have probably expanded, too. So it's never too soon to start tracking where your money comes from and where it goes.

This worksheet will help you achieve your goals. Make one copy of it for each month of the year. By recording your income and expenses this month, you can identify where you'd like to make changes next month. Maybe you want to increase your income by asking for more odd jobs at home or by tak-

ing a part-time job. You could stop buying CDs or comics for a while to save money for your class ring or prom. Maybe you want to save more for college or give more to charity.

Remember, your parents will still expect to have some say about your choices. They may limit the hours you can work each week or not allow you to buy a car. They may expect you to save a percentage of your income for college or to pay for your share of the family's car-insurance bill. Fill in those regular "fixed expenses" first thing each month and set aside the necessary money.

Month _____

INCOME

Allowance $ _____

Odd jobs _____

My job or business _____

Gifts _____

Money I borrowed _____

Total Income $ _____

EXPENSES

Money I owe $ _____

Savings _____

College savings _____

Church or other charity _____

Gifts for family and friends _____

Car payments and/or insurance _____

Gas, oil, repairs, fees and taxes _____

Public transportation (bus, subway) _____

Lunch money _____

Eating out and snacks _____

Clothing and accessories _____

Personal care _____

School supplies and fees _____

Telephone bills that I pay for _____

Recreation and hobbies _____

Sporting equipment and fees _____

Entrance fees for the skating rink, _____

rec center, and so on _____

Club dues, uniforms and other expenses _____

Art and craft supplies _____

Things I collect _____

Stuff for my room (posters and such) _____

Books, magazines and library fines _____

Software _____

Electronic equipment _____

CDs, records and tapes _____

Video and computer games _____

Videotapes _____

Movies _____

Concerts _____

Other outings _____

Prom (or other party expenses) _____

Vacations, other special trips _____

Odds and ends _____

Total Expenses $ _____

Total Income $ _____

Minus Total Expenses   − _____

Money Left Over) $ _____

Life would be a lot simpler, and less expensive, if you could just add your child to your insurance policy. And there are ways to cut down the cost. For starters, don't assume that your existing policy will give you the best rate. Exact comparisons among policies are difficult. But nearly identical coverage can vary in cost by 50% or more, so merely switching your policy to another issuer can save you hundreds, even thousands, of dollars.

You may also be eligible for premium discounts if your child is an occasional driver (driving the car on your policy less than half the time); is a good student (in the top fifth of the class, on the honor roll or with an average of B or better); has completed a driver's ed course; or qualifies as a nonresident student (because he's at college or boarding school 100 or more miles from home without a car).

If possible you might want to try delaying the day your child gets a license. Not only will you save money by putting off an increase in your insurance premium, you'll also save yourself some worry. Among teen drivers, even an age difference of one year can make a dramatically positive difference in accident statistics. For example, teens age 16 are involved in crashes 34.7 times per million miles traveled by the group. That figure drops to 20.2 for 17-year-olds. One dad went so far as to pay his daughter $50 for every month she delayed getting her license. It wouldn't hurt for kids to make their own financial contribution for the privilege of driving a car—possibly at least a token amount toward insurance, and certainly the cost of the gas they use.

Give Them Credit?

I'm sometimes asked by parents if they should consider getting their teenagers a credit card of their own. As one dad said to me, "My feeling is that it will be easier for me not to have to hand her cash when she goes shopping, and safer for her not to carry money around. Besides, she can learn how to pay her bills while she's still at home and I'm there to oversee her. Doesn't this sound like a win-win-win situation? "

My response: No, no, no. On the contrary, you could end up a three-time loser.

It's true that some kids under 18 do get their own credit cards—2 percent of 12- to 15-year-olds and 7 percent of 16- and 17-year-olds told Teenage Research Unlimited that they have credit cards in their own name. Anecdotal evidence suggests that they are often private-label cards issued by retailers that cater to kids, such as clothing stores, or that kids' names have inadvertently found their way onto adult mailing lists.

But most card issuers don't solicit children under age 18 or even accept them as co-signers on a card with their parents. In general, minors can't be bound by a contract, so the card issuer has no way to collect from a child if payments are delinquent.

It's much more common for a child to be an "authorized user" of a card issued in the parent's name— meaning, in effect, that you hand your daughter your card and wave bye-bye as she heads for the mall.

That's the worst of all possible worlds. You have no control over her spending, yet you're ultimately responsible for her bills, even if you both agree that she will pay for her own purchases. "I hear complaints about this all the time," said one customer service representative who has worked in the collections department of a retail clothing chain. "We require a minimum payment of 10 percent of the balance, and if the child pays less than that, the difference is recorded as delinquent. Lots of kids don't understand that."

While there's something to be said for real-world experiences—and lots to be said for teaching teens about credit—there's no need to turn teenagers into debtors-in-training. Far better to make them pay as they go, with cash that they earn or receive in a fixed amount as an allowance. If they learn to manage money while they're at home, they'll be less likely to go crazy with credit when they're off at college (for much more on credit cards and college students, see Chapter 14).

THAT'S LIFE!

Consider a kid's-eye view of the world. Food appears on the table. There's always (well, almost always) another clean shirt in the closet. A car and driver chauffeur you from place to place. Flick a switch and the computer turns on. Flick another and you're watching Nickelodeon. Life is good. Life is cheap.

With so much taken care of for them, it's not surprising that children can't appreciate what it costs to keep a household running. It's little wonder that they can't understand why a new bike just doesn't fit into the family budget. To give them a glimpse into the real world (which might prove eye-opening for you, too), try playing the following version of "Let's pretend," suitable for children of about 10 years old and up:

"Let's pretend that you're 18 and on your own. You work full time at a fast-food restaurant making $6 an hour. That's $240 a week for 40 hours of work, or $960 a month—enough to buy quite a nice bike, right?

"But you won't actually take home $960, of course; after taxes, your pay will be more like $840. And, remember, you're on your own now, so you'll have to rent an apartment. [Check market rents in your local newspaper. For our purposes we'll use $400 a month.] You'll have to pay for electricity and heat—but let's give you a break and assume that utilities are included in the rent.

"Now you're down to $440, out of which you'll have to buy food. To keep things simple, figure that you'll spend about one-fourth of what we spend as a family of four, so your share is around $30 a week, or $120 a month. Remember, that's just groceries, not restaurant meals or pizzas!

"You'll want a phone to talk to your friends—and maybe, once in a while, your old mom and dad—so that's another $20 or so a month (not counting the installation fee of $30). Can't do without the cable? Subtract another $30 a month. (And you thought it came with the TV!)

"Let's see, now we're down to $270. You already have a car—after all, we're just pretending—but gasoline sets you back around $15 a week (we'll assume you learn how to change your own oil). There's also the not-so-small matter of car insurance, at $1,600-plus per year for someone who's still a teenager.

"That leaves you $137 a month, or $34 a week, for all the good stuff, like pizza, movies, clothes and CDs. You can forget the bicycle, unless you decide to ditch the car and pedal to work. On the other hand, you could get a higher paying job, which will require more education, so you may have to take out student loans. But that's life."

Of course, your own family income is almost certainly higher than $960 a month, but so are your expenses. Even if you don't share the details of your household finances, running through an exercise like this can give your kids a frame of reference—and silence the pleas for a bike.

Who's Left Holding the Bag?

Lending teenagers your credit card and sending them off happily to the mall to buy a new pair of jeans can open up a Pandora's box of trouble. Suppose that instead of buying the jeans, your daughter spends several hundred dollars on clothes and CDs, and you don't find out about the expenditure until you get the bill several weeks later. Do you have to pay the charges even though you didn't authorize them?

You sure do. In the eyes of the law, the fact that your daughter had your credit card was authorization enough. "If your child has your card, a store has the reasonable belief that it can approve almost any charges," said an official at the Federal Trade Commission. If your child were to take your card without your knowledge, you could take advantage of federal regulations to limit your liability to no more than $50 in charges. But to qualify, you would have to notify the issuer that the card had been stolen, which could lead to a criminal investigation of your child.

In a situation like this, pay the charges, but make your daughter reimburse you—and next time, keep your credit card and make her pay cash for the jeans.

Here's another innocent scenario that can turn into a nightmare for parents. In a moment of weakness or expediency—which might occur, for example, when you're trying to run through a long list of errands quickly—you give your son your personal identification number and have him make a withdrawal from the ATM. Later he borrows your card to make a withdrawal of his own, which you don't discover until you get your bank statement. Can you get the bank to credit the money back to your account?

Not in this case. You had disclosed your PIN to your son, so any transaction he makes is considered authorized and you're responsible for it. If your child were to get access to your card and PIN without your knowledge, you could limit your liability. But as in the case of credit cards, you would have to claim your card was stolen and be willing to let the bank prosecute your child. (Your initial impulse to give your child up to the legal authorities will probably pass.)

In general, kids can be trusted not to clean out your account. But occasionally you do hear a horror story, as in the case of a 14-year-old boy who withdrew $600 from his parents' account before they caught on when their checks began bouncing. The boy had withdrawn the money in small increments and treated his buddies to video games and pizza.

The parents blamed the incident partly on youthful thoughtlessness and partly on themselves for divulging their PIN without explaining the connection between an automated teller machine and their checking account. They didn't throttle their son, but they did exact a stiff penalty: He had to get a job to repay the $600, along with an additional $600 (which his parents used to start a savings account for him). He was also grounded for several months, giving him plenty of time to sit down with his folks and watch them pay the household bills.

Checking Accounts for Kids

It should be obvious by now that I believe in making teenagers operate on a pay-as-you-go basis. Just as children need to walk before they run, they need to learn to manage cash before they can manage credit. Giving your kids a seasonal clothing allowance several times a year, and helping them open their own checking account—especially when they get their first part-time job—will do more to develop their money management skills than giving them a credit card.

I often get questions from frustrated parents who have tried to open a checking account for a minor child and been turned down. My advice: Keep trying at some other financial institutions. Banks have no uniform policy when it comes to setting up checking accounts for minors. One major bank, for example, is willing to open checking accounts for teenagers 16 and older as long as they have one piece of identification, such as a driver's license or a school ID, and parental consent. Another major bank, however, won't open a checking account for anyone under 18.

What bothers banks is that, as with credit cards, minors can't legally be held to a contract. "What happens if a kid's check bounces?" asks one bank president.

But don't take no for an answer. If a bank says it won't open a checking account for a minor, ask if you can open a joint account with your child, which many banks will allow. One local bank, for example, requires that a parent sign the account agreement with kids as young as 16—but only the child's name appears on the check and only the child has to sign it.

Another good strategy is to make a personal visit with your child to your own bank, which may be willing to accommodate a good customer. A community-based bank or a credit union may also be receptive to your request.

The closest thing to a nationally available checking account for kids is offered by Young Americans Bank (303-321-2265), where the average checking-account holder is about 16. The minimum deposit to open an account is $57.50 ($7.50 for checks); the minimum to avoid service charges is $150.

The bank is willing to open accounts for customers throughout the country, although president Linda Childears cautions that out-of-state merchants may be reluctant to accept a check from a Denver bank (Young Americans issues an ATM card but not a debit card).

To cash any check, kids need some form of official ID. "First I had my state ID and now my driver's license," said Tiffany Hill, who got her account from the State Employees Credit Union in Michigan when she was 16. "I'll definitely be way ahead when I go to college," said Tiffany. "I feel I know where my money is going better than many adults."

If safety is an issue and you'd rather not have your kids carrying around lots of cash, a checking account with a debit card can help ease your concerns. Suzanne Boas, president of the Consumer Credit Counseling Service in Atlanta, put her daughter, Heidi, on a quarterly clothing allowance when she was 13, and co-signed a checking account for her. That allowed Heidi to sharpen her shopping skills—"The fad-buying stage lasted a year or so until she saw how much it was costing," said her mom—and get used to a debit card, which Boas believes "is a positive transition for 14-to-18-year-olds."

With prepaid cash cards, such as one available from Visa, you can load up the card with a cash value that can be drawn down at ATMs that bear the Visa logo. The card is protected by a personal identification number and can be replaced if it's lost, but there's no name or number on it, so it can't be used by a thief. And it can't be used at the checkout counter—a safeguard against impulse purchases (call 800-847-2399 for the nearest issuer).

Light at the End of the Tunnel

Teaching your kids good money-management skills will be for naught if, like the parents in the prom example that led this chapter, you're willing to buy into and finance all you kids' fantasies. (For advice on how to handle the prom issue in particular, see the question on page 222.) It's true that when your children reach their teen years, they—and you—will bear the full brunt of peer pressure. And they will want to buy things because their possessions will help them define who they'd like to be—a car for the man- or woman-about-town or a closetful of clothes for the glamour queen or hip king. Your job in meeting this irresistible force is to be, in a sense, the immovable object—not simply because you say no but because you give your children a reason to say no.

It can be tough to resist when your kids are trying to fit in. Remember, though, that being part of a group doesn't have to mean spending a lot of money. Depending on their interests, encourage your kids to play sports, try out for the school play, work on the school newspaper or join a service organization or church youth group.

Getting involved will not only keep them busy, but

it will also expose them to a broader group of kids for whom money may not matter as much. In addition, they'll learn to shine in their own right instead of merely being a reflection of their friends.

Finding a comfortable niche can be tough for teens, but it's not impossible. One twentysomething woman, the daughter of a teacher, recalls that when she was in high school she couldn't keep up with fellow students whose parents were wealthier. How did she cope? By throwing herself into music lessons. She performed a piano solo at her high school graduation, which conferred a status that money couldn't buy.

Don't sell your kids short. In a survey by the American Board of Family Practice, a healthy majority of teens said they would be willing to get jobs, buy fewer clothes and give up some allowance to help their families through a financial crunch. And even the worst shall pass. In its surveys of the youth market, The Zandl Group of New York City found that by the time kids reached age 18 or 19, they grew rather sober about money. Asked what they would do with a million dollars, boys talked about investing it and girls said they'd buy a house.

Turn page for Kids' Questions→

KIDS' QUESTIONS

Q. "I'd like to invite Andy/Andrea to the dance on Saturday night. Do I have to pay for both of us?"

A. Call me old-fashioned, but here's my first rule of dating etiquette: He or she who does the asking should pick up the tab. My second rule of dating etiquette: He or she who picks up the tab should do it with his or her own money.

In a dating situation, it's bad form to say, "I'd like to invite you to the movies on Saturday night, but I don't have any money so you'll have to pay." Kids (and adults) should wait till they have the money before issuing the invitation. Or they can go in a group where no one pairs off and everyone goes Dutch.

If your child is on the receiving end of the invitation, it wouldn't hurt to bring along extra cash—just in case his or her date hasn't read my rules of dating etiquette.

Q. "The French Club is going to Quebec for spring break. Can I go (and will you pay for it)?"

Q. "The French Club is going on a ski trip for spring break. Can I go (and will you pay for it)?"

A. If the trip in question is part of the academic curriculum, as in the first example, you should probably be more inclined to let your kids go. But you shouldn't feel obliged to pay the full freight. Any kind of class trip should include class fund-raising. Beyond that, your children will appreciate the experience more if they have to come up with some cash of their own, even if it's just in the form of spending money.

If the trip in question is purely social, as in the second case, there are less compelling rea-

sons to let your child go—and no reason at all to pay for it. Teenagers should expect to finance a trip like this from their allowance, savings and money they earn from a part-time job.

Q. "The prom is going to be really expensive. You're going to help me pay for it, aren't you?"

A. Despite my rules of dating etiquette (see the first question), I can be flexible on occasion, and the prom is one of those occasions. It's such a big event in a teenager's life, and such a big expense, that you can justify helping out. For instance, parents could certainly pay for the prom dress or tux, which, after all, counts as clothing (although kids who get a clothing allowance sometimes go it alone. One teen bought a dress two sizes too big on sale at Bloomingdale's for $35, and Mom paid for alterations).

But making kids responsible for the bulk of the bill puts an automatic limit on expenses that have a tendency to get out of hand. It can also inspire some creative alternatives. The pre-prom dinner moves from a splashy restaurant with attitude to a quieter one with atmosphere. The rented limo becomes expendable. One PTA sponsored a successful used-dress sale. "When my friends were shopping for a dress, they always had in mind whether they'd be able to wear it again," says one practical teen, who has worn her own prom dress several times.

I also hear via the teen grapevine that it's cool for a couple to split the cost of a major event like this one. One senior who invited a boy to her prom paid for the tickets, while he picked up the tab for dinner.

In my opinion, neither parents nor children should be laying out money for a hotel room, and that's a matter of principle as much as price. To discourage the practice, one high school moved its prom venue from the hotel scene altogether, and class officers chose a local dance club instead. Tickets were a reasonable $15 per person because the class covered much of the cost through fund-raisers.

Perhaps the best way to keep expenses under control is for parents to take an active role in prom planning. They can host at-home pre-prom dinners or after-prom parties and breakfasts (supervised, of course) and have no trouble attracting kids. "I had 50 willing guests in my house after the prom," says one parent. "In my circle of friends, parents were always a part of things, so it was expected," says her daughter. At many schools parents sponsor all-night parties, with movies in the auditorium, karaoke in the gym, and a breakfast buffet in the cafeteria. For as little as $10 per ticket, it's the best deal in town. In my experience, proms are exciting and memories pleasant, but the event is rarely socko enough to justify the kind of outlay that seems to be common nowadays. Parents have to keep their perspective lest kids expect more than one evening can deliver, and end up both disappointed and broke.

One of the highlights of my own prom career was a green linen gown that fit like a glove but cost only about $25 (a bargain even then), and a long white evening coat made by grandmother.

One of the sanest observations about proms that I've run across is a newspaper quote attributed to a 15-year-old shopping for a gown. "I'm only a sophomore," she said, "and $250 is too much to spend on a dress."

Q. "What do you mean you can't afford to send me to a college that costs $20,000 a year? Haven't you been saving the money?"
A. Maybe you have been saving money, but if you have other priorities you're not obliged to spend it all on college tuition. Even if you're willing to do that, your children should never take it for granted. Get them involved in college planning as soon as they become teenagers so they have an idea of how much you can afford and how much you expect them to contribute. Neither of you should be surprised later.

To Work or Not to Work?

A couple of years ago, when the son of a friend of mine turned 15, my friend made what she thought was an embarrassing confession. It seems that her son was bugging her to let him get a full-time job over the summer, but she wasn't crazy about the idea. "We go on lots of family outings during the summer, and this would really tie him down," my friend told me. "I don't want to give up that family time, and I don't think he really needs more money than the allowance he already gets. But I'm afraid I'm coddling him."

I reassured her that it sounded to me like she just didn't want her son to grow up too fast. After all, once her son was in college he'd probably have to work every summer to earn spending money for the school year. In my opinion, enjoying family time while all the family members are still in one place doesn't count as coddling.

I remember with gratitude that my own mother let me keep my summers free when I was in high school. One of my aunts frowned on such "coddling," and was always bugging Mom to make me get a job. But she held her ground, even though the extra money would have come in handy. "She'll have to start working soon enough," was Mom's rationale, "and once she starts she'll be working all her life." (Mom was right. I got my first job—working in a bakery for $1 an hour—the summer after I graduated from high school, and I've been working ever since.)

Don't get me wrong. I don't mean to say that teenagers shouldn't work. You probably figure it's about time for them to start pulling some weight when it comes to paying for clothes, cosmetics and compact discs, not to mention gasoline (and insurance) for the car they'll soon be driving. Besides, you don't want to discourage their ambition or enthusiasm.

The trouble is, while a paying job can help teenagers sharpen their skills in the workplace, it can also be a two-edged sword. A recent survey by Teenage Research Unlimited showed that a significant number of teenagers have part-time jobs, working an average of six hours per week. (Once they hit 16, nearly half of them are working.) Older teens earn more money per week than younger teens: 12- to 15-year-olds averaged $32 per week; 16- to 17-year-olds averaged $95 per week; and 18- to 19-year-olds averaged $151 per week. Any way you slice it, that's a significant amount of discretionary income for a group of kids with no fixed expenses. By encouraging kids to work, it's easy to create a generation of teenage werewolves, obsessed with feeding their ravenous spending appetites for even more clothes, cosmetics and CDs.

Barbara Johnson and Barbara Bellinger, both bank officers in Connecticut, have conducted seminars in money management for high school students. In one exercise, they asked kids to assume they worked 15 hours a week earning $5.50 an hour. Out of their pay, they had to cover transportation to and from work, entertainment, and food other than school lunches. The challenge: Work out a plan for buying a $700 stereo without charging it or laying it away. "Most of the kids opted for working more hours," said Johnson. "When we raised the question of how that would affect their homework, they said they hadn't thought about it." A few were willing to cut back their spending and save more money out of current income, in which case it would take them about six months to accumulate enough cash to buy the stereo. But that was rare; most kids wanted to buy it as quickly as possible.

The more hours kids put in on the job, the more likely they are to experience other not-so-desirable side-effects. That's especially true of teens who work more than 20 hours per week, the national average among high school seniors who work. "When kids work a lot, they disengage from school," said Laurence Steinberg, a professor of psychology at Temple University who has done extensive research about teenagers in the workplace. Grades begin to suffer, children have less contact with their parents (who also have less authority over the kids), and drug and alcohol use go up, possibly because of exposure to older adolescents and stress on the job. Further, there's some evidence that all the real-world lessons picked up on the job aren't necessarily positive. "Our research finds kids more likely to become cynical," said Steinberg. "Over time, they're more likely to agree with such sentiments as, 'People who work harder than they have to must be crazy.' "

Less is More

Does that mean you have to resign yourself to supporting your kids with precious little contribution from them? Do you have to put up with them lounging around the house in front of the TV? Absolutely not. For one thing, studies showing the negative effects of working, while thought-provoking, aren't the last word. It's not clear, for example, whether working long hours caused the lower grades and other ill-effects experienced by some students, or whether a lack of interest in school prompted the kids to work long hours in the first place. In fact, some research shows that working doesn't have an adverse effect on teens. It appears that getting a jump on a job, especially in senior year, gives students who don't go on to college a leg up in the labor market.

Steinberg himself found that teens who worked less than ten hours a week got better grades, on average, than kids who didn't work at all. And the kids said they learned other things as well: how the business world works, how to find and keep a job, how to manage both money and time, and how to get along with other people. Girls who worked had a greater sense of self-reliance.

HOW TO TAKE ADVANTAGE OF ROTH IRAS

As soon as kids have earned income from some type of job—mowing the neighbors' lawns, babysitting for the family down the street or delivering newspapers, for example—they can start saving for retirement by opening a Roth IRA. Don't laugh. With a Roth, not only do contributions enjoy tax-deferred growth, but the money is tax-free when it's withdrawn.

And if your kids need cash before retirement for expenses such as college, they can withdraw their contributions without paying a tax or a penalty. Suppose your 15-year-old daughter earned $2,000 at a summer job. If she contributed that amount to a Roth, it could grow to more than $140,000 of tax-free income (assuming 10% annualized growth) by the time she reaches age 59½.

Age isn't a factor in setting up a Roth. What matters is that your child has earned income; investment income doesn't count, nor does an allowance or sporadic payment for chores that kids typically do around the house. Delivering newspapers, babysitting or mowing lawns for other people does count as paid employment. With a job like babysitting, however, it's unlikely kids would have a W-2 form reporting their income, so they should at least keep a careful written journal or a contemporaneous log of jobs completed. If your kids are working for you on a regular basis—as in the case of a boy who was being paid by his parents for specific chores to help with the upkeep of their two-acre property—it's even more important to keep careful records.

Your child may contribute a maximum of $2,000 per year or 100% of earned income, whichever is less. But kids don't need the full $2,000 to get started. And you can't reasonably expect them to put in all their money, no matter how much it is, and have nothing left to spend. Here's where you come in. To fund the Roth, you can give children cash equal to what they earn up to the $2,000 annual limit. That way they can save money and still have some to spend.

The toughest thing about opening a Roth for a kid may be finding someone willing to take the money. Mutual fund companies and others can be reluctant to open an account for a child because they worry about being able to enforce a contract with a minor.

But that's not universally true. Here's a list of large mutual fund companies who have said they're willing to open Roths for kids: Baron (minimum investment $2,000; 800-992-2766); Dodge & Cox ($1,000; 800-621-3979); Invesco ($250; 800-525-8085); Janus ($500; 800-525-8983); Neuberger & Berman ($250; 800-877-9700); PBHG ($2,000; 800-433-0051); T. Rowe Price ($1,000; 800-638-5660); Strong ($250; 800-368-1030); Stein Roe ($500; 800-338-2550); USAA ($250; 800-531-8722) and Vanguard ($1,000; 800-635-1511.

While many companies are reluctant to open Roth IRAs for minors, they'll be happy to open an account when your child turns 18. And that's when most kids start making real money from summer, part-time or full-time jobs.

So what's a parent to do? Remember that just because your kids are old enough to work doesn't mean they're grown-up. They still need your guidance in landing a job, setting their hours and managing the money they earn. Have them start with a summer job since there's no conflict with school—which is, after all, their primary responsibility. And since small doses of work seem to yield the biggest benefits, limit their hours if they want to continue working during the school year, at least until both you and they are satisfied that they can balance the job with schoolwork, family time and extracurricular activities. Ten hours a week are sufficient for sophomores, or 15 for juniors and seniors—with the proviso that they cut back if grades suffer, or be allowed to work more if they seem able to handle it. That should be plenty of time for your kids to learn the virtues of showing up on time, getting along with co-workers and customers, and not loafing on the job.

You're trying to strike a balance, as did the family who wrote me the following letter: "Several years ago our daughter volunteered at our local library during the summer. When she returned to high school, she was given the opportunity to work at the library 20 hours a week. We thought it would interfere with her studies, so we settled on 10 hours. She worked there for four years, through her second year of college.

"She developed a love for reading and became a history teacher for three years. Now she's an archivist at the National Archives in Washington."

Volunteering: An Alternative

If you don't need the money and you're more interested in having your teens learn job skills such as leadership and responsibility, as well as how to take orders and work with people, you might look into volunteer positions—working at a hospital, a child-care facility or a museum, for instance. Kids are often given more responsibility in these positions than in paying jobs, and they get exposure to a variety of careers and to slices of life that they might not normally come in contact with. If you would otherwise ask your children to divide their earnings among college savings, discretionary spending and charitable giving, you might consider waiving the giving requirement if the kids are doing volunteer work. To encourage a son who wanted to be a doctor, one father offered to pay him what he would have earned flipping burgers if he volunteered at a hospital instead. The son volunteered throughout high school and eventually did enroll in medical school.

Don't underestimate the value of extracurricular activities. Stephen Hamilton, director of the Youth and Work Program at Cornell University, points out that even more than school itself, extracurriculars give students a taste of life in the outside world because they often involve working with a group of people to accomplish a goal or task. In extracurriculars, as in the workplace, teamwork can be so important that if you're late you let everyone down.

Extracurriculars can prove lucrative as well. A couple of years ago I interviewed Michelle Sippel, a high school student from Nebraska whose essay on financial literacy had won her an award from the National Endowment for Financial Education. During the summers Michelle worked for her father, a veterinarian.

WHAT THE LAW SAYS

Federal child-labor laws limit the number of hours a 14- or 15-year-old may work: No more than three hours on a school day or 18 hours in a school week; and no more than eight hours on a non-school day, or 40 hours in a non-school week. (Also, work may not begin before 7 AM nor end after 7 PM, except from June 1 through Labor Day, when evening hours are extended to 9 PM.) The law doesn't restrict working hours for children 16 and older.

To encourage teenagers to stay in school, there's been a movement for state legislation limiting 16- and 17-year-olds to 20 hours of work a week (excluding agriculture) when school is in session. A few states have already done that. But the National Child Labor Committee feels that's too dramatic a reduction in work time for older teens, according to executive director Jeffrey Newman. At a certain age, said Newman, there has to be a "reasonable opportunity" for kids to work, especially kids who are unhappy or unsuccessful in school.

But during the school year she had set herself the task of finding scholarship money for college, a job that required talking to school counselors, searching the Internet and combing through guidebooks. She set up a filing system so she knew which applications she had to submit each month. In the end, she amassed enough money to pay for her education—and then some. "Being involved in school activities helped me get scholarships," said Michelle. "I earned a lot more than most kids earn from a job."

Which Job is Best?

If your kids are dead set on getting a job, get them thinking about what kind of employment is best suited to their personality: working outdoors or in an office? being part of a team or on their own? juggling lots of balls or focusing on one task at a time? The nature of the job has as much influence on kids as the number of hours they spend doing it. Who are they working with? Is the job interesting? Is it stressful? How much responsibility do they have? Will they make independent decisions?

In Steinberg's studies, two jobs stood out as being most kid-friendly:

■ **Retail sales in a small business.** One teen who worked for a small, family-run florist spent most of her time working side by side with the owner and got a unique perspective on the whole operation. Instead of just ringing up sales, she became experienced in ordering flowers, taking inventory and setting prices.

■ **Babysitting.** Believe it or not, this job ranked high because sitters worked in relatively pleasant surroundings and were given a fair amount of responsibility for making decisions. In addition, babysitters tend to be independent contractors who can set their own work schedules and enjoy the benefits of self-employment.

It's probably unrealistic to expect most 16-year-olds to know what they want to do with their lives. In fact, most kids that age have big gaps in their knowledge of how much education and training is required for a certain career, and even how much they can expect to earn. So even if it's a low-paid (or unpaid) position, or is temporary summer employment, any job in a field that might turn into a future career—being a copykid at the local newspaper, working in the mail room of a bank or other major corporation, helping out in an animal hospital, even working in a local T-shirt shop—can be an invaluable investment in the future. Linda Menzies, who at age 19 started her own graphic-design business, began her working life at 16 as a graphic designer creating packaging for a man who invented kids' toys and other novelty items.

Teens should look for jobs that allow them to manage time, money or people, advises one career consultant, and add new responsibilities each summer by building on their past experience. Students who do well in summer jobs establish good work habits that can last a lifetime, and make contacts that could help them get a fulltime job in the future.

For kids who don't plan to go on to college, the best jobs are those that exist in a school setting, such as vocational/cooperative education programs, so kids get the idea that work and school are related. A recent survey showed that many of today's teens say they'd like to be-

DEAR DR. TIGHTWAD

Q. This year my son earned $1,351 working at a job and $465 in interest from a savings account. I know the standard deduction for single people is $4,300, so I thought he wouldn't owe any tax. But our accountant says taxes are owed. How can this be?

A. Your son's thrift threw a wrench into the works. Children who are claimed as dependents on their parents' return don't automatically get the full standard deduction. For 1999, their deduction is either $4,300 or the total of their income from a job, whichever is less. So your son's standard deduction is $1,351, precisely enough to wipe out the tax bill on his earnings. But the $465 in interest isn't protected. He'll owe $69 in tax.

come high-tech entrepreneurs. But there may be a big gap between their ambitions and the math and science skills they're learning at school.

Frank Linnehan, who's on the faculty of Drexel University in Philadelphia, has done research showing that some key predictors of success on the job—measured in terms of both job attendance and performance—are grades and attendance while students are still in school. Linnehan studied the "career academy" model—a nationwide program of schools-within-a-school in which high-risk kids get small-group attention in a specific field of study, such as business, law or environmental science. In Philadelphia, the focus of Linnehan's study, students in career academies were given the opportunity to work after school during their junior and senior years. But they weren't permitted to interview for a job unless they had attended class regularly and maintained good grades—making the point in students' minds that the best way to succeed in the world of work is to succeed in school.

Hamburger Heaven

So far, however, such programs aren't widespread. When push comes to shove, many kids are going to end up—you guessed it—flipping burgers. That kind of work doesn't rank high on the list of stimulating, meaningful jobs, but it does have the advantage of being readily available and not too far from home. And most parents would probably be proud if their kids could survive, and even thrive, in what's perceived as a pressure-cooker atmosphere. It's a teen milieu, and many kids apparently aren't being harmed by the experience. In one study of fast-food workers, 63% of the respondents said they expected to graduate from a four-year college, and 19% more planned to attend some college or graduate from a two-year program. Overall, 67% of all fast-food workers and 64% of younger employees said they enjoyed their jobs.

It's also true, however, that not all burger joints are alike. In one study, workers were more satisfied with management personnel in franchised stores owned by an individual or small corporation than in company-owned stores. Company policies do make a difference. For example, the owners of some McDonald's stores have offered wage bonuses to kids with good grades. In conjunction with Communities in Schools, the nation's largest dropout prevention organization, Burger King runs a network of Burger King Academies, where at-risk kids get personal attention from teachers and counselors. A spokesman for Grand Metropolitan, the British conglomerate that owns Burger King, said many store managers come up through the ranks. "This is not necessarily the place you go and stay for the rest of your life, but for many kids it's a first step."

How You Can Help

For parents, the lesson once again is to stay in touch with your kids' work life. On the job or not, they're still kids, and you're still their parents. Get the scoop on where they're working from other kids who are employed there, or "interview" the manager yourself and ask about policies on teen work schedules. Would your kids have to work a minimum number of hours a week? How many nights? Is the manager flexible enough to accommodate studying for a big exam, playing in a big game or appearing in the school play? If the answers aren't satisfactory, steer your teens to another employer. On the other hand, your kids should know that if something goes wrong on the job, they can come to you.

Barbara Johnson tells a personal anecdote about her son, who was in his twenties when he decided to settle down and attend a rigorous college, then announced that he had saved enough money to get an apartment off-campus for the spring semester. "But how will you keep the apartment over the summer?" his mother asked him. "I'll keep living there and get a

---

DEAR DR. TIGHTWAD

Q. Last year my teenage daughter earned about $2,000 at a summer job, and money was withheld from her salary for income taxes even though she didn't end up owing any tax. Is there any way we can avoid withholding this year so she won't have to file a tax return to get her refund?

A. Possibly. Summer workers can block withholding if they didn't owe any tax the previous year and don't expect to owe any in the current year. And children claimed as dependents on their parents' returns can earn up to $4,300 at a job in 1999 before any federal income tax is due.

The fly in the ointment probably isn't your daughter's summer wages, but her "unearned income"—interest she's earned on a bank account, or dividends paid by a mutual fund, for example. If your daughter's unearned income is $250 or less, the total of that and her wages can't exceed the same $4,300 threshold.

However, when her investment income exceeds $250, she can't dodge income-tax withholding if her total income will exceed $700.

Although some summer workers can avoid income-tax withholding, there's no way around the 7.65% social security tax.

---

job to pay the rent," he replied. "Then how will you save the money to pay for the apartment when school starts?" she countered. "I'll work during school," he replied. "But," she reminded him, "your primary responsibility is to get good grades so that you can achieve your goal of getting into grad school." As a result of that conversation, her son abandoned the idea of the apartment and started talking about being a resident adviser in a dorm. "At first I thought it would be good for him to have an apartment and be independent, but what he really needed was someone to say no," said Johnson. "Parents don't set up boundaries as often as they should or remind kids of all the other things they have to do."

How to Manage Part-Time Earnings

In a magazine article on teens who work, dozens of young people bared their souls—and their closets. One revealed a young man's back-to-school wardrobe: Two leather jackets, six sweaters, 12 pairs of jeans, four pairs of shoes, two belts and loads of shirts, including a half-dozen silk ones. One senior girl had 20 pairs of dress shoes, with a purse to match each one, plus ten pairs of sneakers.

And it's all financed by those jobs that are supposed to teach teens the value of a dollar. It would seem, ironically, that they've learned the lesson: A buck will buy stuff, and lots of bucks will buy even more. Teenagers have so much income for discretionary spending that they can often afford the designer clothes and electronic gizmos their parents can't.

How can parents give their kids a more realistic vision of the world? First of all, don't buy your kids' argument that it's their money so they can do what they want with it. Neither you nor they may be aware of this, but it actually isn't their money. As long as you're supporting your children, you're entitled to at least a portion of their income unless you give them, either by formal agreement or practice, the right to spend and manage their own earnings. (In a number of states, the amount you can take is regulated. For example, the "Coogan law" requires that a percentage of the wages earned by child performers be put in trust for them until they reach the age of majority.)

Most parents wouldn't go so far as to confiscate their kids' income, but there's nothing wrong with sitting your teens down before they start working to hash out an agreement on how to manage the money they'll be earning. When they were young and you were giving them an allowance, it was appropriate for you to require that they save some or give some to charity. Now that they have the opportunity to earn serious money, it's appropriate for you to have some say in how the money is spent or saved.

Decide up front, for example, what's a reasonable amount of pocket money for a 16-year-old. The rest should go into the bank, perhaps to pay for a car (or car insurance), big-ticket senior-year expenses, or even as a starter fund for longer-term investing. It wouldn't be unreasonable for kids to be socking away at least half their earnings.

Now's also a good time to talk to your kids about how much you can afford to spend on college, and how much you expect them to contribute. Is private school within your family's reach, or is a state school or community college more realistic? Will you expect them to earn their own spending money, or help pay tuition as well?

One father agreed to foot the entire bill for college, but required his daughter to save a big chunk of her earnings so that she'd be financially independent afterward, with money of her own to buy a car or put down a security deposit on an apartment.

Help your kids open a checking account so they can get used to managing their own money. One 20-something friend of mine who is determined to get out from under a mountain of credit card debt was justifiably proud of himself when he recently bought a new TV/VCR—and paid cash.

When your kids get their first job, take a few minutes to explain to them the difference between gross income and take-home pay. You'd be surprised at how many teenagers think that if they're being paid,

---

DEAR DR. TIGHTWAD

Q. Last summer my 15-year-old cousin washed dishes in a restaurant and got paid only $4.25 an hour. His father said that was because he was considered seasonal part-time. Now he wants to get an after-school job and is considering going back to the restaurant. Shouldn't he be paid the minimum wage?

A. He should—as long as he goes back to the same restaurant.

When Congress increased the federal minimum wage to $5.15 per hour, it also created a special "opportunity wage" (or youth subminimum wage), which applies to employees under 20 years old. Employers are permitted to pay teenagers $4.25 an hour for the first 90 calendar days after their initial hire. Once the 90 days are up, teenagers must be paid the current minimum wage.

It doesn't matter whether the employee works only part-time or goes back to school in the interim. If your cousin started his job July 1, for instance, he would have been entitled to the minimum wage after September 28, and he still will be if he returns to the same employer.

If he works for someone new, however, the clock will be reset. The new employer could pay him the youth wage for the first 90 days.

say, $6 an hour and work ten hours, they'll take home $60. It comes as a shock to them that kids have to pay taxes, too.

No matter how much your kids make, they should take full advantage of a Roth IRA to start saving for retirement. They can contribute an amount equal to the money they earn, up to a maximum of $2,000 a year. Just a single $2,000 contribution could grow to more than $140,000 of tax-free income (assuming 10% annualized growth) by the time kids reach age 59½. And if they need some of the cash in a few years—to help pay for college, for example—they can withdraw their contributions without paying a tax or a penalty.

In fact, the Roth is such a good deal for kids that you should offer to reimburse their contributions, so that even if they earned $2,000 and put the entire amount aside, they'd still be able to enjoy the fruits of their labor. (For more on Roth IRAs and other finances for kids, see page 228).

A Word About Taxes

One bit of real-world experience that goes along with holding a job is filing a tax return. Your children may not actually have to file but it's a good idea to do it anyway—and not just because they're good citizens.

Let's say, for example, that your 16-year-old son earned $2,000 at a summer job. If that's his only income for the year, he doesn't have to file. But filing is the only way he can get back money withheld from his paychecks (except for social security taxes, which aren't refundable).

A dependent child can earn up to $4,300 from a job before a return is required. (That's the 1999 figure; it will be $4,400 in 2000 and continue to rise in the future.) But if any investment income—even interest on a savings account—is thrown into the mix, the rules change.

Since you'll claim your son as a dependent on your tax return, he can't claim a personal exemption on his own. Although he does get a standard deduction, it may not be a full-powered one. His deduction is either $4,300 (the regular 1999 amount for single taxpayers) or, if less, the total of the pay from his job plus up to $250 in investment income. If he had more than $250 in investment income, the excess would be taxed in the 15% bracket.

Tips on Finding a Job

Unless you're willing to give your kids all the money they want, or unless they're satisfied with what you're willing to give, they'll probably have a job at some point during their high school years. Studies show that children who receive allowances when they're younger are even more likely to work when they're older.

For most kids, job hunting means keeping an eye out for stores with Help Wanted signs in the window, putting in an application and waiting to be called. But

---

DEAR DR. TIGHTWAD

Q. My wife and I were against our 16-year-old getting a job, preferring that he concentrate on his studies. However, he convinced us to allow him to work, with the understanding that half of the money would be saved for college.

First of all, this isn't happening. Second of all, the company he is working for has said it would like to hire him full-time at a salary of $40,000. He trouble-shoots computer problems. Our problem is, we don't know how to convince him to complete high school, let alone go to college. Any suggestions?

A. It's easy to see why your son is being blinded by dollar signs. But you have one thing working in your favor: Your son is still a minor, and you are still his parent. I would tell him that he isn't permitted to take a full-time job, and I would contact the company and ask that it work out some kind of part-time arrangement while your son is still in school.

Explain to your son that aside from the fact that he is too young to quit school, he should put the salary offer in perspective. The $40,000 that seems like a lot now will grow exponentially once he has both a high school diploma and a college degree.

If you and your son communicate well, your word should carry the day. If you don't, get help from someone he'll listen to, such as another family member, a guidance counselor, or someone in the computer field who can assure him that he will be even more salable after he graduates.

they can improve their chances of getting a job—and, in particular, getting a job they want—if they approach their search more professionally. They should start looking early, presuming that it will take a couple of months to land a job, and be creative in their search. Don't assume, for example, that want ads are just for adults. Watching the classifieds could turn up a position as part-time receptionist in a doctor's office during after-school hours.

Other job-hunting tips for kids:

Prepare a Resume

Kids don't always give themselves enough credit for leadership skills and organizational ability that can translate into success in the workplace. Making the honor roll, being editor of the school paper, directing the school play, babysitting or volunteering at a local hospital can all look impressive to employers (especially if most of the other kids they've interviewed haven't bothered to spell out their accomplishments).

Dress Appropriately

At a large corporation or small business, dress is conservative but not necessarily formal—jacket and slacks for a boy (a suit isn't necessary unless the company is super straitlaced), dress or skirt and blouse for a girl. If they're applying at a more laid-back operation such as a summer camp or amusement park, they can afford to be more casual but never sloppy—shirt (with collar) and trousers for boys, skirt or slacks and blouse for girls (never jeans for anyone).

Observe the Niceties of Interview Etiquette

In one seminar on job skills for teenagers, participants are put through an exercise in which they are interviewed for hypothetical jobs ranging from astronaut to chef. The kids "tend to be quite cavalier about it," the seminar director said. "They will saunter up and slouch down in a chair." What they really need to do is look the interviewer in the eye, shake hands, address him or her as Mr. or Ms., sit up straight, and not be afraid to make small talk or ask questions.

Chalk it up to inexperience. But kids can be a quick study. To encourage her students to speak up, one seminar leader suggested a list of questions they can ask an interviewer. As instructed, one girl, who was being interviewed for a position as assistant zookeeper, asked the chief zookeeper why the previous assistant had left. "Oh, there was a terrible accident," deadpanned the zookeeper. "He was killed by a bear." "Then I think you need better training and safety procedures," the "interviewee" shot back at the surprised counselor. "I'm not interested in working at your zoo."

How to Succeed in Business

Much has been made of the fact that U.S. schools don't adequately prepare teens to succeed in the job market. Sometimes the skills that are lacking are academic ones in reading, writing and math. But sometimes kids are handicapped by their unfamiliarity with the workplace and an inability to connect what they're learning in school with the jobs they will hold when they graduate. In that case, a part-time job can help, especially if the hours are manageable and the setting is conducive to learning.

In the best of all worlds, your kids will be as fortunate as Danielle Schneider, who started working as a camp counselor when she was 15 and held several jobs in retail sales before finding her "niche," working 12 hours a week at a family-owned clothing and accessories store. The owners, she said, were "really good" about scheduling her work hours around her school activities—she was a cheerleader, vice-president of the student council, a member of the debating team, and an actor in school plays.

Schneider found that she thrived on the busy schedule, and on the work itself: "I think I have a good sense of fashion, and I liked helping people pick out clothes." Her co-workers were "like a family," and the atmosphere was friendlier than in the big mall stores "where you are always selling, selling, selling." Sure, there were days when she'd rather have stayed home, but having to get up and go taught her "how to be responsible and budget my time, which you have to do when you go to college." If they could be as contented as she, said Schneider, "all kids should work."

Off to College & On Their Own (Sort of)

Chapter Fourteen

Once you have paid the first semester's tuition bill for your college freshman, you may be tempted to breathe a sigh of relief that you have a firm grip on college expenses. But brace yourself. You're about to face the ultimate college financial crisis: sending an 18-year-old away from home with a book full of blank checks and independent access to credit.

If you want to avoid a flurry of "send cash" e-mails, or that scary late-night phone call—"Help! I've fallen into credit card debt and I can't get out"—don't let your kids leave home without laying down a family financial-aid policy:

DOWNPLAY CREDIT CARDS. Kids over 18 don't need your permission to get them, but they need your advice on how to use them if they're to avoid the common student traps. Kids tend to equate credit cards with free money (in a recent survey of college students, fewer than half of those interviewed knew the interest rate on their cards). And you can't count on kids to reserve their cards for an emergency—for a student, that could be anything from a week-end ski trip to an order of pizza for the entire dorm floor on the night before midterms.

KEEP CASH KING. Kids should know how to write checks, save their ATM receipts and balance their checkbooks before they leave home. When I talk to parent groups, I often hear confessions from sheepish adults about how their own parents sent them off to college with a checkbook but no clue how to use it (see the letter on page 247).

If kids know how to manage a cash budget before they leave home, they'll be less likely to get into trouble with cash or credit when they're in college. And today's cash equivalents—such as prepaid cards, debit cards and college-based "smart" cards you can load with money to pay for on-campus expenses—can give students emergency protection without unlimited liability.

GET A HANDLE ON INCIDENTALS. Figure on $2,000 or so in spending money for two semesters away from home, although that can vary widely depending on such variables as transportation costs and meal plans. Ask your child's school for its recommendation.

If you think your student would be overwhelmed by managing, say, $1,000 for an entire semester, dole out the cash monthly and take care of as many expenses as you can in advance—by stocking up on shampoo, for example, or getting a flexible meal plan that pays for late-night pizza in the snack bar if your child skips dinner.

BE CLEAR FROM THE START ABOUT WHO'S GOING TO PAY FOR WHAT. It's reasonable to expect kids to use money from summer earnings or jobs during the school year to pay for their own entertainment and long-distance phone calls to people other than you. It's reasonable for you to pay for transportation home—but your kids should make reservations far enough in advance to get a discount fare.

ANTICIPATE SURPRISE OUTLAYS. Who's going to pay if your child wants to join a sorority or fraternity, or take up an expensive extracurricular activity such as kayaking or horseback riding? Better to wait at least until the second semester—if ever—before either of you makes that kind of financial commitment.

KNOW YOUR CHILD. Not every college student is a spendthrift. For every anecdote I've heard about a college grad working two jobs to pay off credit card debt, I can cite a success story about a kid who escaped debt-free. One young woman managed to live through a year of school in New York City on her summer savings, with a few hundred dollars to spare. "She's very frugal," explained her proud dad. "But then, she has frugal parents."

College Credit

In an ideal world, the best credit card deal for college students may be no credit card at all. Think of it: No interest rate, no annual fee, no late charges. Many young people have told me they steered clear of credit cards simply because their parents discouraged the use of plastic. (At the other extreme is the 20-something young woman who once told me her parents "used to throw credit cards at me" rather than spend time with her. "It really messed me up financially as an adult," she said.)

In the real world, however, once children reach 18 they can get credit cards of their own without a parent's signature—or even your knowledge. And studies show that two-thirds of college students have at least one credit card. More than half of those students received their first card during their first year in college, where card issuers solicit students aggressively, often by offering an assortment of perks: travel coupons for free airfare, discounts on long-distance calls, coupons for free video rentals, or trip giveaways.

To get a card, all college students usually have to do is prove that they're registered at a four-year school and don't have a bad credit history. If they have no credit history, which is highly likely, it won't count against them. Some cards stipulate that students have minimal income, but that requirement can generally be satisfied if the kids have a savings account, participate in a work-study program or get an allowance from home.

Student cards carry low credit limits—$500 to $1,000—but interest rates and annual fees are high. Students don't have the long, spotless credit records that low-cost card issuers usually demand. Because credit limits are low, issuers have relatively low loss exposure.

In return, they get a golden opportunity to attract new customers who will stay on with them as adults. For American Express, which has been soliciting college students for years, students "have become some of our best and most loyal customers," said a company spokesperson. They are also among the best credit risks. College students have a better-than-average payment record, possibly because they're responsible users of credit, possibly because credit limits are low—and possibly because mom and dad are willing to bail them out if necessary. "If a card issuer threatens to cause problems for a child, parents will sell the farm to come up with the money to pay off the bill," said one college official.

Credit Messes

For students, a credit card of their own can be a golden opportunity to get a head start on establishing a credit history. And the good news is that most students report that they are paying their monthly balances in full and on time. In one survey, by the Institute for Higher Education Policy and the Education Resources Institute, more than 80% of the students interviewed said they owed $1,000 or less. Their main reasons for using cards were to "build a credit history" and for "emergency purposes."

But among those students whose credit card balances averaged more than $1,000, half had four or more cards and only 18% paid their balances in full. These students reported using their credit cards "because they are convenient" and to "stretch buying power."

That kind of thinking could pave the way for kids to slide into a pit of red ink that could take years to climb out of. A number of colleges run programs for seniors or recent grads in which they deal with the first year of transition from college to the real world. While these programs are primarily career-related, credit overload ranks high on the list of topics with which students and grads need help. It's not unheard of for a student to tell of running up a $10,000 debt by going out on the town with friends, putting the tab on a credit card, collecting his or her friends' share in cash and then spending the money. When he or she hit the limit on one card, it was time to get another.

Kenneth Wilson [a pseudonym] knows the cycle. When he was a college student in California, and working as a part-time waiter, he applied for, and got, ten credit cards. He paid his American Express bill in full each month but usually made only the minimum monthly payment on the revolving accounts. Then he started using one card to pay off another. "It became so easy that I kind of lost the idea of the true value of a dollar," said Wilson. "I was just in my own little world."

When his debts hit $20,000 and he began to miss payments, he applied for a debt-consolidation loan from one of his card issuers but was turned down. Then he was laid off, and his house of cards collapsed. Faced with the prospect of coming up with more than $600 a month for three years just to pay off the principal, Wilson filed for bankruptcy at the age of 23. That's hardly an easy way out because a bankruptcy stays on your record for ten years and can affect your ability to get a job or to buy a car or a house. If he had it to do

---

DEAR DR. TIGHTWAD

Q. Since I can remain anonymous, I'd like to tell you an embarrassing story from my youth that usually gets a laugh at my expense.

Before I went to college, my father took me to the bank and opened a checking account with me. I went off to school and began writing checks.

Soon I starting getting overdraft notices. Upset, I called home and asked my father if he was having financial difficulties. No, he replied, and whatever made me ask? When I told him about the overdrafts, he asked me when I had written my last check and for how much. I told him I couldn't remember. Look at the check register, he said. I stared blankly at the phone and asked, "What check register?"

A. You're a good sport for taking the heat on this one, but your father should be in the hot seat, too.

Children aren't born knowing how to balance a checkbook or master any other financial skill; they have to be taught. Contrast your experience with that of a woman whose father helped her get her first American Express card and emphasized that she would have to pay her bill in full every month. She took the lesson so much to heart that she assumed the same was true for all credit cards, even those that allow a revolving balance, and her father never saw fit to correct her misconception. To this day she pays all her credit card bills in full.

over, Wilson would have stopped with two cards and never would have charged anything he couldn't pay off within two months. "People don't understand that 19% in interest adds up really quick," he said.

Wilson's case may be extreme, but it isn't unusual for college students to charge to the max and then make minimum payments with little hope of making headway. If you owe $500 on a credit card charging 18% interest and you make the minimum monthly payment of 2.5% (but no less than $10) it would take you seven years to pay off the debt.

That's a lesson Jerry Stebbins tries to get across at money-management seminars he gives for students at Washington & Jefferson College, in Washington, Pa., where Stebbins is assistant dean for student affairs. The seminars are something of a personal crusade for

DEAR DR. TIGHTWAD

Q. Can you help out with a big problem we're having with a big kid who should know better? Our son, the recent grad, is living with us supposedly until he can save enough money to get a place of his own. When he moved in he agreed to do certain chores to help pull his weight, but he always seems to be "forgetting" our agreement.

A. Deadweights are never too heavy to get the old heave-ho, even if they are family members.

You started off on the right foot right by setting some conditions before your son came home, but you tripped up by not following through. And if you haven't, why should he?

The best solution I've ever encountered to this common problem comes from a mom who found herself in a situation similar to yours, and drew up a written contract of rights and responsibilities to be signed by her

and her son. A few of the pertinent provisions:

1. Jim will live in his old room beginning February 1. He will have saved enough money to move out by November 1.

2. He will pay $100 a month for his room and $100 a month for food, beginning with his second monthly paycheck.

3. He will be responsible for purchasing and caring for his own clothing, doing his own laundry and sheets and towels, and purchasing items for his personal use.

4. He will pay for his long-distance calls.

5. He agrees to wash the car every Saturday.

8. He will alternate cooking and grocery shopping with Mom.

The only thing wrong with this contract is that Mom didn't think of it before Jim arrived on her doorstep. Put your terms in writing, up front (and maybe the kids will think twice about moving back in).

Stebbins, who, in his own college days, ran up a $13,000 credit card tab that took him 18 months of $700-plus payments to pay off ("I ate noodles for dinner every night and couldn't even afford a tux to be in a friend's wedding").

Keeping Kids Clean

To keep kids from getting hooked on easy credit, Stebbins recommends that parents provide kids with a credit card at the beginning of the school year, and then get it back. Also, it has been his experience that students with a card on their parents' account, rather than their own, "seem less likely to binge-spend."

In that case, for better or worse, students wouldn't begin compiling a credit history of their own, because the account wouldn't be in their name as either the primary borrower or as co-applicant. If you'd like your child to have that opportunity but still want to look over his or her shoulder, consider opening a joint account, with you as the primary account holder and your child as the co-signer. That way you'd get a copy of the monthly statement and could flag problems before they spin out of control.

If you want to give your kids the chance to manage on their own while you still sleep soundly at night, help them get a credit card that's secured by a bank deposit, meaning that kids put enough money into a savings account to equal the credit limit on the card. As one example, Young Americans Bank in Denver (303-321-2265; www.theyoungamericans.org), issues a MasterCard with an annual fee of $15 and an annual percentage rate of 15%. The initial credit limit is $100, and can rise to $200 after six months, but it won't go any higher than that. However, if kids secure the card by putting money in a savings account, the credit limit can go as high as the account balance. (For a listing of other banks that issue secured credit cards, see www.cardtrak.com.)

Secured cards carry several benefits: They usually have a lower interest rate and a lower annual fee than unsecured cards available to teenagers; they guarantee that money will be available to bail out your child if necessary; and they emphasize the point that credit doesn't come without a cost. In addition, "our approach to credit cards is totally different from any other bank," said YAB president Linda Childears. "We deglamourize them" by keeping the credit limit in check, requiring kids to go through a detailed educational process about credit—and encouraging them to pay their bill in full each month. "We want young people to know that credit cards can be a good money-management tool but a bad credit vehicle," said Childears.

That's a lesson parents should be delivering to their kids before they leave home, along with some other key commandments of credit:

Keep all receipts and check off each purchase when the bill comes.

Don't charge anything you can't pay for in full when you get the bill, except in emergencies, when you might allow yourself three months to repay.

Don't get into the habit of making only the minimum payment each month.

Don't charge pizzas and other perishable items that will be used up before you even get the bill.

Don't charge to the max. Some cardholders assume that if an issuer gives them a limit of $1,000, they must be capable of repaying it. What counts is your cash flow, not the bank's high opinion of you.

Remember that a credit report can come back to haunt you, even if your parents bail you out. Prospective employers and lenders sometimes consult credit reports, and a record of delinquent payments can be read as irresponsible behavior—and cost you a job or the house you want to buy.

Don't drag your parents down with you. If your parents have co-signed for a credit card or loan and you renege on the deal, they're left holding the bag. (Not realizing the potential consequences of their own irresponsible behavior, kids often assume that their parents will guarantee their debts and are shocked when mom and dad are reluctant to take on the risk.)

If you do get into trouble on your own, don't let

things slide. It's okay to ask mom and dad for a bailout, but it's also okay for mom and dad to exact a price instead of just handing over the cash. To pay off several thousand dollars in credit card debt, one young woman took out a "consolidation loan" from her parents. They charged her 8%, compared with the 18%-plus she was paying to her card issuers. Note: This will only work if you don't rack up any more charges while you're paying off the loan.

For a lecture on credit that doesn't come from mom and dad, your kids can listen to *Smart Credit Strategies for College Students*, an audiotape recorded by Gerri Detweiler, former director of Bankcard Holders of America (Good Advice Press; 800-255-0899).

Defusing Bombshells

While college kids and credit cards get lots of attention (to the point where a number of colleges are restricting solicitations by card issuers), the most sticky—and costly—money conflicts you and your college student face could come as an unexpected bombshell.

Take this question I once received from a reader: "We just found out our daughter is failing a course that she needs for her major, which means she'll have to take it again—costing us an extra $1,000. What's more, she'll have to keep taking the class until she gets at least a "C." Who should pay for this unanticipated expense, our daughter or us?"

In this case, I told the parents that making their daughter foot the bill wouldn't guarantee that she'd make the grade. If she was doing poorly in other subjects as well, she might be in over her head. If that were the case, there would be no point in throwing good money after bad, no matter whose money it was. They should consider having her withdraw for a semester, or transfer to a junior college, until she was better able to handle the challenge.

But if their daughter was otherwise doing well and seemed to be struggling with just one course, there was no need to turn up the pressure even more by making her pay the whole bill (although they could make it clear that a voluntary contribution would be appreciated, even if it was turned down). I suggested they even try to cut future losses by paying for a tutor to help get their daughter through the class on the next go-round. If she failed again, it could be time to switch majors.

About a year later, I heard again from the parents with the rest of the story. When they got their daughter's first-semester grades, they found that she was, in fact, doing poorly in several courses and was on academic probation. "We were so shocked and upset when the letter arrived that we walked out of the room and told her we would need time to recover before we could even talk about it. When we finally did discuss things a couple of days later, it was our daughter who was upset. She said she had thought the money was the big issue and it had never occurred to her that we would be disappointed in her.

"We told her we'd pay the $1,000 for retaking the course if she got her grade-point average up to 3.0. She did even better than that and now her GPA is 4.0. She's considering changing her major so she may not have to make up the failed course. But she knows she'll have to pay for graduate school."

In this case, while the failed course was the immediate financial crisis, there's a deeper moral: You can't depend on money to control your child's behavior, either as a reward or punishment. Timeout, grounding, loss of privileges and financial penalties all have their place. But when you get right down to it, parents really have very little leverage over children of any age except the kids' desire to meet your high standards and

A CREDIT CHECKUP

Be as concrete as possible when talking to your kids about credit. For example, use an online financial calculator to show them how long it will take to pay off a credit card balance at various payment levels and rates of interest. To impress your kids that both good and bad credit habits are an open book, get your own credit report and examine it with your children. To request a copy of your credit record, contact:

- **Equifax,** P.O. Box 105873, Atlanta, GA 30348; 800-711-5341; www.econsumer.equifax.com.
- **Experian** (TRW), P.O. Box 8030, Layton, UT 84041-8030; 800-643-1584; www.experian.com.
- **Trans Union,** P.O. Box 390, Springfield, PA 19064; 800-916-8800; www.transunion.com.

not risk disappointing you. If kids have a healthy fear of letting you down, you'll still have influence over them when they're teenagers—and beyond.

A Success Story

Getting your kids off to college with as little money angst as possible means starting when they're young to communicate with them about money in general, and taking care of as many details as possible when it's time for them to go.

When Lynda and John McConnell sent off each of their three children to Wake Forest University, "we literally took their expenses item by item," said Lynda, down to figuring out the price of a haircut and allocating contributions to charity. Then they put the kids on a monthly budget. If they ran out of money, they had to dip into summer earnings, which were otherwise saved or tithed.

The McConnells helped their children open checking accounts when they were high school seniors. They got the names of prospective roommates and contacted them ahead of time to decide who would bring such essentials as the popcorn popper, refrigerator and CD player. Once school started, the McConnells began making monthly deposits into each child's checking account. They kept the children on the family health- and auto-insurance policies and gave each child a calling card for phone calls home.

Still, there were glitches along the way. Daughter Beth ran over budget a number of times, mostly because of long-distance telephone calls to friends. Son Johnny discovered that while his hometown bank charged a low monthly fee for his checking account, it charged a lot for ATM transactions. Had he gone with the on-campus bank, he figured he could have saved about $60 over four years.

Those kinds of problems are easily resolved. If you don't think your kids are up to the challenge yet, you may be able to keep tabs on their spending from afar. A growing number of colleges have an arrangement similar to the University of Maryland's "Terrapin Express." Parents deposit a sum of money with the university, and students, using their ID cards as debit cards, draw on the account to buy meals and books and make other on-campus purchases. That means fewer checks to write, less cash to carry and more control over where money is spent.

To help keep long-distance phone bills in check, MCI's personal 800-service, for example, lets you set up your own 800-number for calls home. If your child is living off-campus, AT&T's free Call Manager service will separate your child's calls from his roommates' on each bill, according to separate dial-in codes, so there's no question of who called whom.

One thing the McConnell kids didn't have a problem with were credit cards; they never had any.

Giving & Getting With Grace & Gratitude

Money and gifts (and gifts of money) can make for some pretty tricky social situations, requiring the perfect balance of tact and common sense. Even if you get a grip on your own gift-giving impulses, what do you do about everyone else's? The dilemma begins at birth, as doting grandparents bring material offerings. It's aggravated throughout childhood by extravagant birthday celebrations. And it's altogether complicated in situations of divorce. But take heart; in the following two chapters you'll find some commonsensical—and diplomatic—solutions.

Holidays and Birthdays

Many parents feel overwhelmed by demands—from both kids and advertisers—during the holiday season. If you identify with that, consider that it's possible to cut back on holiday overload without your kids' even being aware of it.

You could, for example, give them as gifts what you would have bought anyway: a new backpack for school, ice-skating lessons, a family outing to the circus. Wrap everything in sight, on the theory that to a kid, all gift-wrapped boxes are treasures. The boxes don't have to be physically large, and the gifts inside don't have to be expensive. But opening them prolongs the kids' pleasure without increasing your expense. When my children were younger I even wrapped each Golden Book individually, although the kids eventually caught on to that gambit. In one family, parents who were planning a winter trip to Walt Disney World stuffed the tickets into their kids' Christmas stockings, along with guide-books and other Disney paraphernalia. Planning the trip kept the kids happily occupied long after the post-holiday blahs might ordinarily have set in.

If you're faced with an overabundance of gifts from generous relatives—especially for very young children, who quickly grow bored or enjoy the packaging more than the present—quietly put away some of gifts to be opened on rainy days later in the year. Or set up a col-lege savings fund with a bank or mutual fund and ask family members to contribute in lieu of buying presents.

If you want to make a clean break with commercial holidays past, take the money you would have spent on presents and spend it instead on a family getaway or some other nontraditional gift. Author and family counselor Eda LeShan recalls that when her daughter was around 8 years old, the child was part of a family conspiracy to surprise her grandparents by flying Aunt Lilly, one of their oldest friends, from California to New York for a visit. When Aunt Lilly, wrapped in tis-sue paper and a bow, appeared on the stairs, "it was a Christmas that all of us will remember more than any other," said LeShan.

One of the best gifts you can give your kids is time—presenting them with a certificate entitling them to an afternoon or evening of your undivided attention for an activity of their choosing.

DEAR DR. TIGHTWAD

Q. After my daughter handed me a 14-item Christmas wish list from Service Merchan-dise, I asked her to add up all the prices and see how much it was going to cost me. Seven items—and a total of $159.95 later—she decided to stop and restart her selec-tion in preference order.

This exercise helped her practice her math by adding currency. It also helped her to set realistic expectations about holiday wishing in terms of U.S. dollars.

A. Let's see. If seven items cost roughly $160, then each item on your daughter's list cost an average of about $23. At that rate, the whole list would have set you back $320.

That's not exactly peanuts, but things could have been a lot worse. You're fortu-nate in having a daughter who didn't go overboard in the first place, and got even thriftier as a result of your exercise.

DEAR DR. TIGHTWAD

Q. I can't wait to hear what you think about the new "gift registry" one of our big toy stores started over the holidays. Kids can pick the toys they want, and the list goes into the computer. The store said it was a convenience for parents and relatives who weren't sure what to buy.

A. I am all for making a parent's life easier, but not at the cost of removing whatever magic is left in the holiday season. It's one thing for a child to make a wish list and wait in agonizing anticipation to see what will materialize. It's quite another to put in your order and wait for Grandma to ante up. Besides, parents shouldn't need a gift registry to tell them what their children want. They can go straight to the source and ask the kids—and pass along the word to Aunt Martha.

In the end, the real test of a successful holiday isn't the number of gifts you buy or how much they cost, but how well-suited they are to your children and how well they wear. It's only natural for kids to play with the glamour gifts first—Nerf weapons, American Girls dolls, anything electronic. But if, on December 26, they ask you to try the new board game, and on February 13 they build the model rocket, and on July 23 they start the third book in the complete *Anne of Green Gables* series, then you'll know you didn't go overboard. (You'll find more guidelines on page 259.)

What About Wish Lists?

While wish lists often strike terror into the hearts of parents, I think they're a useful tool that can help the holidays run more smoothly. Here's why:

Lists are an outlet for some of the holiday "buy-me-that" pressure. Sometimes just writing down all the things they'd like to have is satisfaction enough for kids. A toy that a child really, really wants in October may be totally forgotten by December. It's been my experience that children frequently make—and misplace—a number of different lists before settling on the one that goes to Santa. Older kids will be more discriminating, but they'll still push the envelope in hopes of stuffing it with as much as they can. They'll expect you to say no, so don't disappoint them. If they don't get what they want, they're not going to pack up and leave home.

Lists give you an opportunity to teach your kids how to set priorities. Take those lengthy lists your children have been constructing and have them rank the top ten items. (Tell them that the shorter the list, the more likely that Santa will remember what's on it.) Holiday catalogs can be a big help with older kids, who can appreciate how much everything costs. Ask the children what they'd keep on their list if they had, say, $200 to spend. (Remember, though, that this is just an exercise!)

Lists are an organizing tool for your own holiday shopping. After all, you and other family members are going to be buying gifts for the kiddies anyway. You'll be less frantic and more focused, and get your shopping done more quickly, if you know what you're looking for.

One of the best bits of modern-day wisdom I ever heard on this point came from a great shopping-mall Santa who didn't bat an eyelash when one youngster handed him a list of 28 toys. Santa patiently reviewed the items and told the child he'd plug it into his com-

---

DEAR DR. TIGHTWAD

Q. My 13-year-old daughter hangs around with a group of about a dozen girls, and her popularity is hard on our pocketbook. It seems like we're always buying a birthday gift for someone, and CDs for 12 kids start to add up. With the holidays coming up, she'll want to buy a present for everyone. Am I the only one who thinks this has gotten out of hand?

A. I think that if this is the worst problem you have with your 13-year-old daughter, you're a lucky parent.

The holidays may be the most expensive time of year gift-wise, but they also present the cheapest solution. Instead of buying presents for everyone, your daughter and her friends could each pick a name and play "secret Santa" for that person, giving small tokens and doing favors as the recipient tries to guess who her benefactor is. It's less expensive—and more fun—than buying everyone gifts.

There's no getting around birthdays, however. In a group like this, if you buy for one member you have to buy for them all. You could set a price limit per gift—but why are you doing the buying in the first place? At 13, your daughter is old enough to take on this responsibility and use her own money. If she's in charge, she'll be inclined to be less extravagant and more creative, and outlays will tend to regulate themselves.

puter to see what came up as available. What he actually brought, said Santa, would depend on how much room he had in his sleigh.

At some point, of course, it's up to you to set a limit on how much stuff you buy. Here are some guidelines on when to call a halt:

- **You're embarrassed** to tell your friends how many presents you bought for your kids.
- **You can't find enough** hiding places for all the gifts.
- **You can't remember** what you hid.
- **In their zeal to open all the gifts,** your kids resemble sharks on a feeding frenzy.
- **In the middle of opening gifts,** your kids get bored and walk away.

It's tough to put a number on just what that point is, since every family has its own gift-giving tradition. Three gifts may be two too many for a toddler who can't appreciate them, or for an older child who's getting a new computer. But three gifts is probably too few if you like to surprise your family with inexpensive stocking-stuffers.

If you need a number as a guideline, consider that families annually spend more than $300 per child on toys, and a majority of them are bought during the holidays, according to the Toy Manufacturers Association, an industry group. I recommend starting with a nice round ten presents—three "big" ones and seven "smaller gifts"—and adjusting up or down depending on how much you want to spend.

What Role Does Santa Play?

Children find such pleasure in Santa that they're happy to engage in what the poet Samuel Taylor Coleridge called "the willing suspension of disbelief." That gives you lots of room to maneuver when your kids raise the subject of gift-giving:

- **"If you won't buy it for me, I'll ask Santa for it."** Tell them that you and Santa are a team. He's not about to go against a parent's wishes—and jeopardize his job—by bringing a child a gift that is too dangerous, too expensive or otherwise not in the cards.

■ **"It can't be sold out; Santa's elves make it."** If a toy is a blockbuster hit, even the elves can't always keep up with demand. Sometimes Santa has to supplement the elves' output with toys from toy companies (they're more than willing to help out because of all the great publicity), so when they're sold out, Santa is, too.

■ **"Why can't I put just one more thing on my list?"** Santa has to read so many lists that you're doing him a favor by keeping it short—and there's a better chance he'll remember what you asked for.

Don't back yourself into a corner by telling your children, "We can't get it for you, but maybe Santa will." If Santa is that generous, the kids will think that no request is too outlandish.

And some remarks strain even a child's credibility, as in, "If you don't behave, you'll get coal in your stocking." I suspect that there are precious few kids, no matter how mischievous, who actually suffer this dire fate. And no kid, no matter how mischievous, deserves it. A good friend of mine recalls vividly that when she was about 9 years old her parents put a small lump of coal (along with lots of real gifts) in her stocking as a joke. My friend failed to see the humor, and wondered what

---

DEAR DR. TIGHTWAD

Q. Our kids are great believers in Santa, but every year their questions get tougher. I don't have any trouble explaining how reindeer can fly (everyone knows it's magic). But what do I say when they ask why Santa doesn't bring as many presents to poor people as he does to them?

A. Tell them the truth—that you supplement Santa's largess with gifts of your own, something that poor parents can't always afford to do. Turn their concern into a positive by getting them to help you choose a toy to donate to a holiday collection drive.

her parents were really trying to tell her. More than two decades later, her mom acknowledged that it was kind of a stinky thing to do, and the incident now provokes much laughter in the family.

Plausible answers forthrightly given will keep Santa alive in your household. By the time your children are no longer willing to suspend their disbelief, they'll be old enough to grow quietly out of the Santa myth. But for their sake, and yours, don't rush them into reality.

Pre-Holiday Bonus?

When kids ask for extra money to spend on holiday gifts for family and friends, parents are often at a loss for a response. Should they hand over the extra cash, or let the children be disappointed? The answer is a straightforward "neither."

Handing kids money to buy you a gift isn't in the spirit of the season, and I suspect children know that. But that doesn't mean they have to come up empty-handed. Keep in mind that some of us get a bonus at the holidays if business is good and we've done our job well. If you think your children have done a good job of managing their money or keeping up with their chores, it might justify a spontaneous something extra in their pre-Christmas stocking.

If they're old enough to handle the money, you could increase their allowance year-round and turn over the responsibility for buying all gifts for birthdays and holidays. That way they'd have the wherewithal; they'd just have to be smarter about managing it.

If they're not old enough to take over all gift-buying responsibilities, you could spot them, say $5 per holiday gift; anything above that they'd have to cover themselves. When one mom tried this tactic, her daughter was suddenly overcome with economy. "You'd be surprised at what you can buy for $6.19," said her mother.

You might also give them advice along with (or instead of) the cash:

Make a list. What's good for Santa is even better for kids. Writing things down helps them get organized ahead of time, keep focused once they get to the store and stay within their budget.

Check it twice. Take the kids on a pre-shopping trip without cash in hand. Children tend to spend everything they have on the first thing they see. Scouting the stores in advance will help them find things they like and can afford, as well as learn how to tell the difference between something that's a bargain and something that's merely cheap.

Don't throw your catalogs away. Sit down with your kids and look through them. They're a great tool not only for finding gift ideas but also for giving your children a sense of how much things cost.

Make a push for kid-made gifts. Parents, grandparents and even siblings can be suckers for cards, decorations or crafts that are handmade or computer-generated.

Next year, start a holiday club. If the children begin putting aside gift money around Labor Day, they should have a tidy little fund to help them buy presents in December.

If the children are still short on cash, they could do extra chores to earn more money, or chip in with siblings to buy a joint gift. Emphasize that presents don't have to cost a lot. Instead of spending money, they could spend time and give a gift of service (this year I'm going to hint that I'd like one of my children to offer to put all our family photographs in order).

If your children have a multitude of friends (as in the question in the box on page 258), instead of buying gifts for everyone they could each draw a name and play Secret Santa for one child—a custom that kids never seem to tire of, no matter what their age.

Emphasize the Meaning

One parent wrote me about her daughter's swiftly approaching first communion. Mom was worried that her daughter would get so carried away by the money that she would receive that she'd forget the religious significance of the occasion.

I put this question to parents of different faiths whose children celebrated religious milestones and came up with a number of suggestions.

The most extreme was simply to ask family members not to give any financial gifts. Another suggestion was for the parents and child to agree to contribute any money to charity, perhaps using it to buy food baskets for poor families in their community. Still others thought the child could keep the money, but have her treat it as serious savings by putting most of it in the bank or in her college fund.

If everyone else in the family will be giving financial gifts, you should give one that has religious significance, such as a prayer book or Bible. Children take their cues from their parents. As long as you don't lose sight of the real meaning of the occasion, neither will they.

Birthday Party Overload

When it comes to birthday parties, parents have been known to get more carried away than their kids, turning what should be fun into an exercise in one-upmanship. "First clowns, then ponies, and now my son has been invited to a party with a merry-go-round on the lawn," one father complained to me. "You feel obliged to buy expensive gifts, which the birthday child gets too many of. My kids are

---

A BIG-BUCKS BIRTHDAY GIFT

If you've been trying to figure out what to give your child as an unusual birthday gift, consider this money-smart idea: Buy your kid big bucks. You can buy sheets of uncut currency in $1 and $5 denominations from the U.S. Bureau of Engraving and Printing; 202-874-3316. For an order form and catalogue, write: The Bureau of Engraving and Printing, Mail Order Sales, Room 515-M, 14th & C St., S.W., Washington, DC 20228; 800-456-3408. Allow four to six weeks for delivery. If you're visiting in Washington, you can buy your bucks at the Bureau's Visitors Information Center at 15th St. and Independence Ave., S.W., from 8:30 AM to 3:30 PM, Monday through Friday.

TALES OF THE TOOTH FAIRY

Parents often ask me about the going rate for a tooth nowadays. Well, your kids can reasonably expect to get more than you did when you were a child. Depending on the rate of inflation in your household, anywhere from 25 cents to $1 a tooth would be appropriate.

Keep in mind, though, that the tooth fairy is an accommodating sprite who's happy to tailor her gifts to your wishes. Here's a selection of letters from readers who responded to a question I asked about whether the tooth fairy still makes nocturnal visits and how much she leaves behind.

- **The tooth fairy at our house pays $1 a tooth.** Our 8-year-old tries to get the rest of his baby teeth to come out so he can collect!

- **We pay $1 for each tooth**—as long as there are no cavities!

- **The tooth fairy brings $5 a tooth** at our house. This seems to be more than she brings my son's friends.

- **In our house the kids get $1 per tooth if it comes out during the week.** They'll get $2 per tooth if it comes out on the weekend. Both sets of grandparents "find" what the tooth fairy left at their house. So after all is said and done, if a tooth is lost on the weekend the child can reap up to $6 per tooth. Of course, all the money is deposited in their savings accounts and later transferred to their mutual funds for college.

- **We just went through this for the first time.** We have a box which the tooth goes into and it goes under the pillow. Conveniently, when the tooth is removed the box holds four quarters. My son, to guarantee a return on his investment, suggested that the tooth fairy could place the money right in the box.

  That is much more than I got as a child. I should have saved all those teeth and converted them now instead of when I was young.

- **No reply necessary:** What does the tooth fairy do with all those teeth?

- **In Oakland, Cal., during the 1920s, there wasn't a tooth fairy.** During the 1940s the going rate was 25 cents. In the 1990s the going rate is $1, my great-grandson informed his mother. His mother's reply: "No way."

- **The tooth fairy has visited my daughter, Elizabeth, for many years and always leaves her a very interesting coin.** She receives a coin with a picture of Queen Elizabeth on it. The value of the coin is not important to her, but the idea of a coin with her name on it makes her feel special. My husband and I collected the coins years ago while in England, and never realized how special they would become.

- **At our house the tooth fairy brings $1 per tooth, and the money goes into the kids' savings accounts.** My oldest daughter had to have nine teeth pulled within a few weeks for braces, so she got $10. P. S. It's harder to get the tooth fairy into the bedroom these days.

- **Before my 6-year-old daughter lost her first tooth, I cross-**

stitched a little "tooth fairy" pillow with a pocket on it, which is her special place for each lost tooth. She made a special request to the tooth fairy via letter to please leave her tooth behind because her daddy wanted to save it. Here is how the money added up on the last tooth:

First, my daughter charged her father $1 for each time he tried to pull it out. It took three tries, for $3. Then the tooth fairy left her $1 for the tooth—which she sold to Daddy for $1. Daddy owed her $4 (counting the three tries), but he didn't have change for a $5 bill and she got to keep the extra $1. So her last lost tooth cost the tooth fairy a total of $6.

The tooth fairy also leaves a little surprise, like a coloring book. As you can see, in our household the experience of losing a tooth is usually a big deal!

■ **I'm a pediatric dentist, so I collect lots of input from my little patients on what the tooth fairy left them for their lost teeth.** I've heard everything from ten cents to $20 for the first lost tooth (that's a wealthy tooth fairy). Five dollars a tooth is pretty common, and that surprised me. I'd say the most typical amount is $2 per tooth.

Almost without exception the children still put their teeth under their pillow at night and still fear the tooth fairy won't come if the tooth got accidentally lost or swallowed. [Note to kids: For the tooth fairy, lost and swallowed teeth are all in a night's work. Just leave a note instead.]

■ **My daughter's bottom teeth were coming in, but her baby teeth had not fallen out.** The dentist was going to charge me $64 to remove the teeth. I told my daughter if she could wiggle the teeth out herself, the tooth fairy would pay her half of what I would have had to pay the dentist. It took her two weeks of wiggling, but she made $30. All the kids at school wanted to use her pillow!

■ **When our son was young, the tooth fairy would leave 50 cents under his pillow and steal the tooth away.** Many teeth later, the tooth fairy forgot to come one night. Our son came to us, crying. We said to him, "You don't still believe in the tooth fairy, do you?" "No," he sobbed, "but I believe in money."

■ **Q. When did the tooth fairy first appear?** I always thought it was an American custom, but I have been told it was practiced in Italy in the 1940s.
A. It may have been, but the New York Public Library's reference desk tells me the custom most likely originated with the German tradition of placing a lost tooth into a mousehole or rathole.

According to the book, *Curious Customs*, by Ted Tuleja, people believed that when a new tooth grew in, it would possess the dental qualities of whatever creature found the old one—hence, the critters of choice were rodents, with their world-class pearly whites.

The principle of "fair exchange" was brought by German immigrants to America, where the tooth rat was replaced by the more palatable fairy—and the desire for hard molars with the expectation of hard cash.

even starting to compare the size of the party bags they bring home. Am I just a voice in the wilderness?"

Well, Dad, I'll join you to make a chorus of at least two. Perhaps what we need is a group called Birthdays Anonymous to support parents who want to withdraw from the party circuit. Some parents have made the break, and here's their advice on how to kick the habit:

Don't get hooked in the first place. You can solve lots of birthday problems (including too many gifts) by inviting fewer children. Young kids don't need a big blowout; asking the neighbor kids to drop by for cake and ice cream is excitement aplenty for both you and your child. One old rule of thumb is to invite a number of children equal to your child's age, with perhaps one more to grow on. One mom from Philadelphia simply held off on having nonfamily parties until her kids were in kindergarten. Then she held traditional at-home affairs with games of charades, penny pitch and pin-the-tail-on-the-donkey. By the time her children were in fourth grade, they were ready to invite a handful of kids for a sleepover or a matinee, and she was home free.

A variation on this is to have a big blowout every other year instead of annually, or perhaps for certain "milestone" birthdays—6, 10 and 13, for example. In the off-years, you can invite Grandma, Aunt Sis and all the cousins for cake and ice cream.

Be creative. If you must do something out of the ordinary, do it on the cheap. Take a group of kids fishing at a local pond; to a field for a pickup game of soccer or baseball; to a playground or a children's museum. Pack a picnic lunch.

Be radical. If you must have a crowd and don't want your children inundated with gifts, set a price limit of, say, $5 per gift. Or ask guests not to bring any presents. "We did that once and our friends told us it was seditious," laughs one father. "But we told them their children's company was the best present they could give."

In most situations, of course, your kids wouldn't show up at a party empty-handed. But there's no need to go overboard, either. For preschoolers it's sufficient to spend $10 per gift (plus batteries, if necessary). You can raise that to $15 as children get older, and $20 when they get to college. If the child in question is someone special—a best friend, a relative or a godchild, for example—add $5 to each of those benchmarks.

For older children or out-of-towners, gifts of money are appropriate (cash is better than a check as long as you're not sending large amounts) and so are gift certificates.

Birthdays on Holidays

When a child's birthday coincides with a holiday, you have two options: You can play it up, or you can play it down.

For example, you can play up the Christmas connection by making a tradition of celebrating with a party that has a seasonal theme—going ice-skating, or taking in a holiday movie or a local performance of "The Nutcracker," for example.

If you're too frazzled at that time of year, or worry about gift overload from party guests and Santa, play down the occasion by holding the party a month later to liven up the winter doldrums—or even six months later as a "half-birthday."

DEAR DR. TIGHTWAD

Q. For his birthday, my son wants to invite a half-dozen friends to go paintballing (the kids go to an outdoor course, divide up into teams, track each other and "fire" little pellets of washable paint). I don't object to the paint, or even the "shooting" part, so much as the price—$30 for each kid. I think that's a little steep for a birthday party, especially if you throw in the cost of pizza and cake. Would it be okay if we told his guests they had to pay their own way?

A. And maybe have them chip in for gas, too? Sorry but social niceties demand that whoever issues the invitation pays the freight. Guests should be treated at your expense, not theirs.

The most you could get away with without seeming ungracious (and cheap) is telling the kids that instead of bringing a gift, they should each contribute $10 to the cost of the outing.

If the cost is still too high, you could invite fewer guests or dispense with the pizza and cake. Or offer to take the kids paintballing some other time, when you can play the role of chauffeur rather than host and everyone can pay his or her own way.

As for the appropriate number of presents to buy, I pass along this spontaneous exchange between a seven-year-old and his 13-year-old brother:

Little brother: "I wish my birthday was on Christmas, so I get lots more presents."

Big brother: "You wouldn't get any more presents than you do now. If you get two birthday presents and ten Christmas presents now, you'd just get 12 presents if your birthday was on Christmas."

A Word of Thanks

I'm often approached by parents who confess guiltily that (like me, I confess guiltily) they have been lax in making their kids send thank-you notes for gifts they have received. I detect in their mea culpas the desperation of harried parents seeking reassurance that with so much else on their plates it's okay to skip the note, especially when a personal thank-you is only a convenient phone call away.

As an often-harried parent myself, I once would have been inclined to give that reassurance. But I've changed my mind. Every gift deserves a thank-you in some form, and a written note is the most desirable. It's worth nagging your kids to sit down and write one. Their expenditure of time is small compared with the large amounts of money lavished on them. Your objective is to make them feel so guilty that they'll eventually remember to send a note on their own—and will one day nag their own children to write to you.

Allowing for the fact that you are already stressed out, however, especially at holiday time, I'm willing to risk the ire of manners mavens and suggest a few rules of thank-you etiquette that will get the job done as painlessly as possible for you and your kids:

Thank-you notes should never be generic—they should always include a specific mention of the gift, plus a personal note on how the child liked it, or, if it's money, what he or she plans to do with it. But preprinted cards are acceptable. Giving your kids a nudge makes the job easier for them (and, by extension, for you). A tip of the pen to an editor friend of mine who tucks a pack of thank-you notes into the Christmas stocking of each of her kids. For young children, go ahead and address the envelopes.

A computer-generated card is acceptable, as long as it's personally designed, written and signed.

E-mail is fine, as long as the children do their own hunting and pecking on the keyboard. If the gift-giver is computer savvy enough to have e-mail, he or she will appreciate getting the message.

It's probably unrealistic to expect that kids will sit

DEAR DR. TIGHTWAD

Q. As the mother of three grown children, aunt of eleven and godmother of six, I have some questions about your advice regarding gift-giving. It strikes me that one of the aims of giving gifts to kids is to teach them how to receive thankfully and graciously. Maximizing the child's take does not strike me as a legitimate aim.

A friend of mine who has 17 grandchildren and limited means sends each child a birthday card with a dollar bill. Another, similarly situated, sends her grandchildren $2 bills, which the kids consider special. I suppose my husband and I could send our many nieces, nephews and godchildren the $20 for birthdays you consider appropriate, but that would come to about $1,000, which seems excessive, even if doable.

Just recently my 80-year-old aunt sent me a $5 bill for my 54th birthday. I spent it on a drink at Sardi's in New York, and wrote to tell her and remind her of our dinner there with her parents when I was 12.

A. Cheers to you and your aunt! Even at 54, you were probably tickled to get a few dollars of mad money on your birthday—and she was probably tickled to hear how you spent it.

Let me clarify that in my guidelines for giving—which cited $20 as appropriate for gifts to college-age kids, or "special" children, such as a relative or godchild—I didn't mean to imply that you were obliged to give that amount. The number was an upper benchmark, not a hard-and-fast rule. The aim is not to maximize the child's take, but to minimize your outlay.

It's fine to give less money—and even preferable. I've found that children genuinely appreciate any amount of cash. Especially for younger children, a couple of fresh new dollar bills mean more than a $50 check.

What most impresses me about your letter is that you took the trouble to write a thank-you note to your aunt. Such a courtesy is so often neglected nowadays, but it's still appreciated. Parents, it's worth nagging your children to make the effort—even if you just buy a package of pre-written notes and have the kids sign their name.

down on Christmas afternoon to pen their thanks for a gift they got that morning. But do have them get the job done before they go back to school.

And a note to gift-givers: Don't be miffed if the card is a little late. Assuming the kids (and their parents) aren't ingrates, they're probably just running behind. Playing a game of beat-the-clock takes the joy out of both giving and receiving.

Make the most of the thanks you get. One grandmother framed a note from her grandson and hung it on the dining-room wall—a painless yet effective reminder to him that such courtesies are appreciated.

Here's how one mom taught her 3-year-old to express her thanks: "We use construction paper and stickers to make thank-you cards. For example, I cut out an ice cream cone and our daughter is responsible for gluing it on to the paper and using stickers with the same theme to decorate it. I write something like, 'Thanks for the gift, it was really sweet!'

"It's corny, I know, but we've been doing this since she was 18 months old. Everyone loves receiving the cards since they are first and foremost a thank you. But they also show her progress in arranging items, coloring, and writing her name—not to mention being refrigerator art for the family."

KIDS' QUESTIONS

Q. "Can I buy Jenny a new bike for her birthday? She really wants one."
A. To young children who don't yet understand the idea of relative value, one gift costs about as much as another. So they might as well get what their friends want most.

Let your children down gently by telling them that a new bicycle is the kind of special present that Jenny's parents might like to buy for her. Then steer your kids toward smaller gifts with lower price tags.

If your children are older, tell them what you think is an appropriate price to pay for a birthday gift—in my opinion, $10 to $20. Kids may want to exceed that in the case of a special friend, but remind them that price isn't the only factor. The friend might be embarrassed by a gift that's too expensive—and the friend's parents might feel obliged to reciprocate, even if they can't afford it.

Older kids who are given the responsibility of buying birthday gifts with their own allowance money catch on quickly. "Instead of just going to the store and randomly selecting something, Luke thought a little more about the person he was buying for," one mother said of her 12-year-old. "In one case he remembered that his classmate was artistic, so he purchased drawing paper, colored pencils and markers. It was the recipient's favorite gift."

Q. "Can I spend my birthday money?"
A. In general, kids should be allowed to keep and spend the money they get as gifts. That's probably what the gift-giver would want, along with a report on what the kids bought. Nothing is less gratifying and more frustrating to a child than money that arrives in the mail and is

promptly whisked away by Mom or Dad.

But it's understandable if you don't want your 5-year-old dropping $50 at the toy store. So I offer the following guidelines, based on your child's age and the amount of the gift:

■ Preschoolers are allowed to spend gifts of up to $20 (when accompanied by you, of course), which would buy a character Barbie or an action toy. Anything above that is saved for another day. Another option: The little ones spend cash gifts; you save the checks.

■ Six to 12-year-olds, with more expensive tastes and a better-developed sense of how much things cost, get to spend gifts of up to $50.

■ Teens have discretion over gifts of up to $100.

Regardless of age, gifts over $100 demand some parental input. One dad whose son occasionally gets gifts of $200 from his grandmother requires that his son spend $50 to $100 on something he needs—a new winter jacket, for example. With an amount that large, gift-givers might consider consulting with you ahead of time to designate how the money should be spent.

Q. "I lost the $10 Aunt Barbara sent me. Can I do extra chores to make it up?"
A. Children have a responsibility to take care of their own money, so you're under no obligation to let them earn it back by doing extra chores. Nor should you require your kids to put an amount that small in the bank.

It's probably best to let them eat the loss and count on them to be more careful the next time. They probably will be if it's a check that has been misplaced. Eventually Aunt Barbara will notice that the check hasn't been cashed, and the kids will have to 'fess up.

Girl Scout Cookies & Other Sticky Situations

To look at the glossy gift-wrap brochure in the hands of that fresh-faced sixth-grader, you would never suspect the insidious means by which it got there. But one local newspaper took a behind-the-lines look at gift-wrap wars—how companies compete to have their product become the paper of choice of PTAs and other parent groups that raise money for schools. To win the hearts and minds of parents, companies battle it out not only with splashy designs but also with sniping at their rivals and, yes, even psychological weapons—in the form of muffin-and-croissant breakfasts for the parent group.

I've engaged in a few gift-wrap skirmishes of my own. Every year I'm in a friendly competition with the art director of *Kiplinger's* magazine because we both sell Sally Foster paper at the same time. We have our informal line of demarcation, with the art department on one side and editorial on the other, and our co-workers as the spoils of war.

The annual school fund-raising season traditionally starts with gift wrap on the fall, runs through Girl Scout cookies in winter, and winds up with candy bars or potted plants in spring. It's tough to tell who dreads it more—the parents who have to sell all this stuff, or the co-workers who see them coming. "You're a prime target, especially if you don't have kids," someone complained to me recently.

Unloading your annual quota of gift wrap—or cookies, candy bars, gourmet desserts, pizza kits and all the other things kids sell—is one of many situations that can result in a financial faux pas. Anticipating these awkward moments helps both you and your children avoid embarrassment and hurt feelings.

Take those fund-raising projects. Let me say in their defense that the schools, athletic groups and other organizations that sponsor them really need the cash. Over the years all those candy bars have sent thousands of kids on class trips and bought enough band uniforms to outfit the Russian army. Sometimes schools depend on fund-raisers to get money for their day-to-day operations. Lots of people actually like to buy high-quality gift wrap or fresh citrus fruit.

And some kids are born salespeople who thrive on the challenge. In California I once met a Girl Scout who was so good at selling cookies that she could sweet-talk Ron Popeil into buying a Veg-O-Matic. It's also true that with concerns about safety, kids (or their parents) often feel a lot more comfortable knocking on doors in office building corridors than along neighborhood streets.

But if colleagues in the workplace are tempting targets, they shouldn't be sitting ducks. I'd like to propose a truce in fund-raising wars at the office, with a code of conduct for sellers and suckers…er, buyers.

First of all, don't bring your kids to work. Sure, you'll be told that it's good for kids to participate in the

---

DEAR DR. TIGHTWAD

Q. Recently my son was invited to the movies. I talked to the other parent ahead of time, and we agreed that he would pay for the tickets while my son, Josh, paid for the popcorn. When they got to the popcorn counter, however, Josh announced, "I think I'd like to save my money." The other dad ended up buying the popcorn.

When Josh got home, I told him I was disappointed in him because he was supposed to buy the popcorn to share with Sean.
A. I hope (but somehow doubt) that Josh was equally economical about helping himself to

Sean's popcorn.

To avoid creating a foxy freeloader, you're going to have to work a little harder to drive home your point. Assuming that you gave Josh the money for the popcorn in the first place, he shouldn't have been allowed to keep it. If it was his money, he can use his savings to take Sean to the movies.

The next time your son is invited out, emphasize that buying popcorn is a requirement, not an option. And tell him that if he keeps this up, he'll get precious few return invitations.

effort so they can take on personal responsibility, gain self-confidence and learn about business. But let's face it: The real purpose of fund-raising is to raise money, not a child's self-esteem. Cute kids are just a convenient sales tool. Entrepreneurial kids (accompanied by their parents) can sharpen their skills without offending potential customers by setting up a table outside the local supermarket, for example.

As long as your employer doesn't frown on selling stuff at the office, it's okay to tap your co-workers on your kids' behalf. But follow these rules:

Avoid cyberclutter. Don't annoy your colleagues with general e-mail telling everyone what you're peddling.

Target your sales. Most effective are personal appeals to three groups of people: those who have expressed interest, those who have been customers in the past, and those from whom you have bought something.

Let the rest come to you. Post a signup sheet or notice in some central area. One mom set out a box of candy bars that her saxophonist son was selling for his band, along with this note: "Don't feel obliged, but feel free (and don't forget to leave $1)."

Don't exploit your position. The higher up you are in the office hierarchy, the less latitude you have. People who work for you shouldn't feel pressured to buy just because you're the boss.

Thank your colleagues for their support—and have your checkbook ready when they pay you a return visit.

Co-workers shouldn't feel obliged to buy anything, and parents shouldn't take offense at a polite, "no, thanks." In fact, Mom and Dad themselves should always have the option of saying "no, thanks" to sales efforts and fulfilling any money-raising obligations by simply writing a check.

On the Road

Fundraising may be a classic "sticky situation," but there are plenty of others that often catch parents unawares. Vacations, for example. Kids tend to want to overspend on everything from souvenirs to junk food, and parents' resistance is low. After all, they are on vacation, and they do want to avoid grumbling in the back seat of the car. But there are ways to keep the peace without busting the budget.

First, let me put in a good word for long car trips. Although parents dread the sound of sibling squabbling and the "Are we there yet?" chorus, it seems that children actually like family vacations.

In a survey of 300 children ages 7 to 12, the advertising firm of Saatchi and Saatchi asked the kids about their worst vacation experience. Most agreed with the response of one 9-year-old: "I don't think there could be a vacation I wouldn't like."

Children enjoy being with family—"Your parents seem nicer and less likely to punish you"—said one 8-year-old. And kids appreciate having a say in planning the trip: "Mom is cool—she always asks us where to go."

Take advantage of this good feeling to deal with money matters before they become a source of friction on the trip:

Lay out your game plan. Tell the kids what you're willing to buy in the way of souvenirs—maybe one T-shirt for each of them or postcards from each stop. They'll have to use their own money for anything else.

Collect inexpensive souvenirs that are easy to find and will still bring back pleasant memories of the trip after

---

DEAR DR. TIGHTWAD

Q. My 19-year-old son lives with his mother some distance away from me. My ex-wife told me she had given our son $200 toward books for college, but when he came to visit me he admitted he had spent the money on clothes and asked me for more. He had to have books, so I gave him another $200. I always feel pressured to give him money, but it's easy to get extravagant when I only see him once in a while and I have to compress years into days.

A. I sympathize with your situation, but letting your son manipulate you isn't going to improve it. It sounds like you and your ex-wife are on speaking terms, so next time talk to her in advance and tell her that you will pay for school books or other extra expenses. She'll probably appreciate the financial help, you'll get the satisfaction of spending money on your son, and he'll lose the opportunity to double dip.

DEAR DR. TIGHTWAD

Q. My brother, who is single, loves to buy presents for my two daughters, ages 10 and 7. The trouble is, his gifts aren't always in the best of taste. He goes for novelties, such as "gross-out" powder that turns your teeth black, and T-shirts with slogans that are slightly risque. I won't let the girls wear the shirts, but I feel guilty about getting rid of them.

A. Off-color teeth are one thing. Off-color shirts are quite another.

Let your brother have his fun with the gross-out powder. It's just the kind of slightly-naughty-but-not-forbidden treat that kids love and uncles are supposed to buy. But let him know that suggestive shirts are out of bounds because they cross the line between good clean fun and a dirty joke. If he must be a merry prankster, tell him to stick to whoopee cushions.

---

it's over—key chains, pins, or snow domes are a few that come to mind.

Give the kids their regular allowance ahead of time (something that's easy to forget in the rush of preparations). That way they have pocket money and won't have to bug you. To avoid wasting (or losing) money, they should bring only as much as seems reasonable to spend.

Buy off your kids with this "fine" solution to back-seat rowdiness: Give each child a roll of coins at the start of the trip. Each time one of the children gets out of hand, collect a coin. (Use the accumulated kitty to buy an occasional family treat.)

Before embarking on a 35-state road trip with their two children, ages 9 and 7, one mom and dad told the kids they'd pay for patches and postcards at stops along the way. The kids had to buy other souvenirs with their special vacation allowance of $1 per day. Another family makes it a point to include snacks and desserts in their children's travel budget. "We will buy no snacks or desserts unless it is our choice, not because someone has asked," said Mom. "It is amazing how this system has virtually eliminated whining for this or that souvenir or food item."

Guest Etiquette

You can't always buy peace among siblings. The Saatchi and Saatchi survey showed that as kids get older they appreciate companions their own age, so you may want to bring along a friend as a buffer if that's feasible.

But bringing along a friend (or accompanying someone else) brings up another financial issue: To what extent should the host finance the guest's visit, and how much spending money should the child bring? I'm puzzled by the reluctance of parents to discuss who's going to pay for what when their child is invited as a guest. Perhaps they think it isn't polite, or perhaps they take for granted that the whole excursion will be a freebie. Both assumptions are misguided, and parents who make them can put the host, and their child, in an awkward position.

So here, then, are my rules for invitation etiquette:

If your child is invited to accompany another child on a car trip, assume that the invitation includes the cost of transportation (and accommodations, if it's an overnight stay); assume that travel by air or rail is your responsibility. Ask the host parents how much your child will need for admission tickets or other costs. Far from causing embarrassment, raising the subject will clear the air.

If the host parents offer to pay for meals, tickets, or other expenses, accept graciously. But your kids should still have their own pocket money for incidental expenses.

If the guest's parents ignore the subject, it's perfectly proper for the hosts to bring it up, as in, "We'll be paying for Joanie's activities here at the beach, but there's a nice souvenir shop so she might want to bring some money just in case she sees something she likes."

Even if your child is lucky enough to be invited out by someone who's footing all or most of the bill, send

---

DEAR DR. TIGHTWAD

Q. My husband and I have no children, but we have four nieces and nephews. When the kids come to visit, they expect us to shell out for all kinds of goodies, and their parents (my sister and her husband) go along with it. For holidays and birthdays, they suggest gifts for the kids—usually expensive ones. We feel we're being taken advantage of.

A. Even if you love the kids dearly, you shouldn't have to pay dearly to keep them happy. Be specific about the limits of your generosity, as in, "Let's split the cost of this meal 50-50."

When your sister makes helpful suggestions about what the children want for their birthdays, tell her politely that you would rather choose your own gifts and surprise the kids.

---

your child with enough money to treat the host family to ice cream cones or breakfast out. Children need to learn the art of reciprocation. (See the kids' question on page 286.)

Remind children to abide by the host family's rules, to be helpful while they're houseguests, and to keep an eye out for something appropriate that they can send as a thank-you gift later.

Splitting the Tab

As a veteran of dozens of soccer matches and other athletic activities, I can attest that the real competition often occurs after the game, when the entire team descends on some hapless restaurant, confusion reigns and the grown-ups fight not to get stuck with more than their fair share of the bill. To win this contest, you have several options:

Skip the after-game meal (tempting but not always practical).

Suggest that you all go to a restaurant where everyone orders and pays separately (my personal favorite).

Swallow the cost along with your food, on the theory that over time it will all even out.

Volunteer to divvy up the tab and collect what everyone owes. That's a pain-in-the-neck job, but you get to stick somebody else—er, make sure no one tries to beat the check.

Dealing With Divorce

Take all the parent-child financial conflicts you can think of, multiply them by two, throw in a few more for good measure, and you have perhaps the stickiest issue of them all: kids and divorce. A marriage may end, but kids and money form the glue that will bind parents together. "Children of divorce know more about their parents' finances than any other group of children I've worked with," a family counselor once told me.

Conflicts fall into several categories:

The Santa Claus Syndrome

This is a common complaint of custodial parents, usually mothers, who resent it when their kids return from a weekend visit with Dad wearing expensive sneakers and new CD headphones, and chattering about their trip to the amusement park. Mom is sorely tempted to tell the kids that if their father is that well off, he can darn well afford to pay more in child support.

Bite your tongue, take a deep breath and, remember, criticizing your ex-spouse isn't going to work. Whatever bitterness exists between the two of you, your children can be fiercely loyal to both parents and will resist taking sides (although they're not above trying to exploit the situation to their advantage). "In a way, putting down the other parent is like putting down the child," said one family counselor.

Instead of going off on a tirade against your ex-spouse, tell your children that since the divorce your financial circumstances have changed, and that paying for day-to-day expenses doesn't allow a lot of room for extras. Kids sometimes have short memories, and may need a gentle reminder of the little extras you have purchased recently.

Also explain to your kids that parents have different ways of showing their love, and the absent spouse may simply be trying to make up for time he or she doesn't get to spend with the kids. It may leave you gritting your teeth, but when talking to your children you can afford to be generous to your ex-spouse. If you really have a beef with your ex, you should discuss it with him or her, not with the kids. And if he or she really is trying to buy off the children, they'll eventually pick up on that themselves. Counselors agree that children learn that a "real" parent is one who makes sure they brush their teeth, helps with homework and offers love and guidance—which can be both of you.

If you really think you deserve more money, take your former spouse to court and tell it to the judge. Better yet, couples can short-circuit future problems by addressing as many child-related financial issues as possible in the divorce agreement. Do your children have special needs or gifts that will require extra expenditures? Who's going to pay for piano lessons? Is summer camp still in the picture? If the kids are approaching driving age, who's going to pay for insur-

---

DEAR DR. TIGHTWAD

Q. My kids and I are always fighting about their messy rooms. I don't want to resort to bribery to get them to clean up, but what else can I do?

A. You could simply shut their doors. If you get along well with your children otherwise, and if the chaos doesn't seem to interfere with their schoolwork, think twice before you fight this battle.

But if the mess really bugs you, try cooperation rather than confrontation. Take the kids with you to buy brightly colored storage bins, labels and markers, and anything else that will make the job more appealing. Then set a time when you and they can tackle the clutter together, deciding what to toss and what to keep.

Sometimes children just need help getting organized and breaking down the task. Tell them, for example, to line things up on a shelf in size order or put them in drawers by category, or divide their room into quadrants and clean one square at a time.

Introduce them to the vacuum cleaner and the washing machine. But you can make the job fun, too, by letting them rearrange furniture or asking a friend to help (you provide the refreshments). Maybe they can even make a few bucks by selling castoffs at a yard sale.

DEAR DR. TIGHTWAD

Q. My daughter's friend, Diane, was taking pictures before playing in a school band concert. She asked if I would pick up the camera from the back of the auditorium when the performance started and hold it for her. I agreed—and then completely forgot to do it. When we looked for the camera after the concert, it was gone.

Even though the camera was inexpensive, I felt awful and replaced it with one that cost $20. But Diane's mother wouldn't let her keep it because she said it was Diane's fault the camera was lost. Did I handle this wrong?

A. Because you agreed to take charge of the camera, you were at least partly to blame for its loss. And the pictures are gone forever.

Your inclination to replace the camera was on target, and the price you paid was reasonable. Diane's mother obviously wants to teach her daughter to act responsibly. But it's also a valuable lesson for children to see adults admit that they goofed and make restitution. Call Diane's mother and try again.

ance? Who's responsible for college tuition? Margorie Engel, an author and speaker on families and divorce, recommends building into the divorce agreement a procedure for reviewing the settlement periodically through your lawyers to allow for changes in your children's health, growth patterns or emotional needs.

In the real world, rewriting divorce agreements often isn't an option, especially when child-support payments are spotty or nonexistent. If that's the case, get your kids to help brainstorm ways in which they can cut back on expenses or contribute money or sweat equity to the household. Said one divorced dad with custody of three children, "I don't hide the time and money pressures from my kids. We work together to do the household chores, and they no longer beg me for toys I can't possibly afford."

For children, the financial effects of divorce aren't always negative. As long as they're not burdened with the family's financial problems, they can be creative and responsible in finding ways to earn money and save up for the things they want to buy.

The Ransom of Red Chief Syndrome
This is a complaint of noncustodial parents, mainly fathers, who feel that they are already giving enough in

child support and resent the fact that their ex-spouse isn't accountable for how she or he is spending the money. They can't understand why the children always seem to be shabbily dressed and in need of money for some school or sports activity. They cough up more cash, but they feel like a chump.

Remember, kids aren't above manipulating a situation like this to their advantage. It may be that the $20 your daughter says she needs for the class trip was supposed to come out of her allowance, which she spent instead on CDs. One woman recalls that when her parents divorced, her younger brother managed to collect an allowance from both mom and dad. When her parents found out what was going on they put a stop to it, but only after a major shouting match with each other.

You need to get together with your ex-spouse and discuss, in civilized tones, what's going on. Do the kids need things that weren't budgeted for? If so, who's going to pay for them? Who should be responsible for taking the kids shopping for new clothes? One way to handle this is to arrange for both spouses to share more or less equally in child support. Under one system, both parents could draw up a budget for their children's expenses and open a special checking account, funded proportionately based on both their incomes. The

---

DEAR DR. TIGHTWAD

Q. I thought it was cute when my children, ages 7 and 5, decided to make money by selling their old toys at a yard sale. But I was horrified when some of the things they wanted to sell turned out to be gifts from relatives. Fortunately, they priced the stuff so high that no one bought anything. How should I handle this the next time?

A. Your kids are to be commended for their entrepreneurial instincts. But they also need to learn a thing or two about social graces, one of which is not to sell the gift they got last Christmas from Great-aunt Sally (especially if there's any chance at all that Great-aunt Sally will come for a visit).

Next time help them choose which items are okay to put on the block. And suggest a realistic selling price so they don't get too discouraged. If you suspect that deep down they don't want to get rid of their treasures, mention other ways they can make money—by selling artwork (of their own creation), or even those old standbys, lemonade and cookies.

checkbook goes back and forth with the kids, and both parents are responsible for handling expenses.

All this assumes that parents are still on speaking terms. In fact, family counselors recommend that parents make it a point to communicate regularly about their kids, even if it's just a phone conversation. "Make a list of the things you're going to talk about, and stick to it," advises one counselor. "If one of you deviates, the other can hang up."

If hang-ups become the rule, you might seek the services of a divorce mediator. (Contact the Academy of Family Mediators, 5 Militia Drive, Lexington, MA 02421; 781-674-2663.) As a result of mediation, one couple reached a written agreement that they and their teenage daughter would discuss extraordinary expenses. "The three of us would decide who could do what, and whether the thing should be bought in the first place," said the father. "We paid the mediator $900 to settle something $75,000 in legal fees hadn't settled."

You and your spouse may have split up, but you're both still parents with a common interest in how money is spent on your kids. Getting involved in a bidding war is a lose-lose-lose situation. Instead, ask yourselves how you'd handle things if you were still together.

The Cinderella Syndrome

This is a phenomenon of blended families in which one spouse shows financial favoritism toward his or her own children. (Members of the spouse's family, such as grandparents, can be guilty of this as well.) Parents who buy a toy or a shirt for their own kids but not their stepchildren risk creating a tremendous amount of ill will that could easily be avoided with a relatively small outlay of cash. When Margorie Engel remarried, her husband's mother "opened her arms to my two daughters," she recalls. "My kids got birthday cards and valentines just like her own grandkids did. They got checks, too. The checks were smaller, but the kids were never forgotten. It's not the amount but the thought."

In most cases, said Engel, stepfathers tend to step in and provide financial support even when they're not legally obligated to do so. But if at any time you feel that your kids are getting short shrift, you need to raise the point with your new spouse, who presumably is easier to communicate with than your former one was. Rather than simply complaining about the unfairness, it might be better to put your case in writing, listing expenditures on each child and suggesting ways they might be equalized.

At the other extreme, don't be infected by the Fairy Godparent Syndrome, in which an overeager stepparent showers the children with stuff in an effort to buy their affection. "It isn't going to work," according to Kenneth Doyle, a financial psychologist from the University of Minnesota. "The new parent is automatically seen as an interloper, and if that person comes on like gangbusters, it's going to look awfully crass." Give the children time, not money.

Turn page for Kids' Questions→

KIDS' QUESTIONS

Q. "Can we invite Kathleen to go to the movies with us this afternoon?"
(Asked with Kathleen staring longingly over your child's shoulder)
A. It's okay to extend a spur-of-the-moment invitation, but be prepared to pay for your guest. Neither Kathleen nor her parents have planned for the expense and might not have enough money on hand to cover it.

For future reference, tell your kids that if they want to take a friend on an excursion that costs money, they should call the night before to extend the invitation. That way you can tell the other parents if the treat's on you, or, if not, what the approximate cost will be. That gives them an opportunity either to decline gracefully or to send their kids prepared to pay.

Q. "When two grown-ups go out to eat, why does one of them offer to pay and the other say no? If someone wanted to buy lunch for me, I'd sure let them."
A. Plenty of grown-ups would love to accept an offer of a free lunch, too. But more than money is at stake here. You might call it a matter of table manners. Picking-up-the-check etiquette is something kids need to learn just as much as they need to learn not to slurp their soup or eat peas with a knife.

Explain to your children that treating a friend to a meal is a great idea. Maybe you'd do it because it's your friend's birthday, or as a way of saying thanks for something nice that he or she has done for you.

But it's always best to make clear ahead of time that you're going to pick up the tab. Making the offer on the spur of the moment often

puts the other person on the spot. Your friend doesn't know if you really want to pay or if you're just trying to be polite. That's why lots of adults turn down the offer of a free meal. Unless you've agreed in advance that one of you is going to treat, assume that you'll each be paying your own way.

If the other person strenuously insists on picking up the check, it's better to say yes than to make a scene over the spaghetti.

Q. "You told me to pay for the amusement park, but Mr. Haynes wouldn't let me. What should I have done?"
A. Before you scold your child for accepting some other parent's generosity, think about this: In any showdown between an adult and a child, the child's natural inclination is to back off. Teach your kids the art of reciprocation. If their host pays for their admission, your kid could offer to treat everyone to ice cream, for example. It may not be an even exchange, but making the gesture is what counts.

When your kids are invited on an excursion, assume the other family is only going to furnish transportation and that your kids will be taking care of their own meals and other expenses. If there's any doubt, discuss it with the other parents ahead of time. If they are going to pick up the tab, make sure your kids have their own pocket money to buy souvenirs or other extras—and to treat everyone to ice cream.

If you're the one who's issuing the invitation, you can avoid any misunderstandings by telling the parents what you intend to pay for. And when your guests offer to buy you an ice cream cone, don't turn them down.

Money-Smart Grandparents

When I first started writing about kids and money nearly ten years ago, grandparents were the subject of a question within a chapter. Now they get an entire chapter of their own, as befits their growing role in the financial lives of their grandchildren. Today's grandparents are healthier, wealthier and longer-lived, and they're notorious for their generosity. One survey found that in a typical month, about half of all grandparents buy gifts for their grandchildren. And the gifts are substantial—around $80 per grandchild for major holidays, about $40 for birthdays and $20 for lesser holidays such as Valentine's Day.

In my experience, grandparents are increasingly interested in longer-term largess, such as encouraging their grandchildren to invest in the stock market or helping to pay for the childrens' college education. In extreme cases, grandparents have taken on the role of surrogate parents in bringing up their grandchildren.

But there's far more to a grandparent's role in a child's financial life than giving the child money. When it comes to teaching about money, forget the generation gap—grandparents are right in sync with their grandkids.

Case in point: The second annual Stein Roe Young Investor Fund essay contest asked fifth, sixth and seventh graders, "Who in your life has been most influential in helping you learn about money and investing, and what have you learned?" Of the nine winning entries, three from each grade, five cited a grandparent.

287

For instance, Caleb Caudell's Great-Grandma Mary "believes that a person should save money to buy what he wants rather than use credit." Hillary Vervalin cited her grandpa's favorite expression: "Spend some, save some, give some." Steven Markowicz is "carrying on my grandma's reputation to save, invest and love the earnings." Said Sara Schuval, "What I have learned from my grandmother is that money invested will grow into more money, while money under the mattress will grow mold."

Spoiling the Kids Rotten

While Grandma's help is often welcome and appreciated—and sometimes even taken for granted—it also presents plenty of opportunities for conflict, or at least some awkward moments, among grandparents, their adult children and their grandchildren. Perhaps the two most common conflicts are polar opposites. On one side are parents who worry that grandparents are spoiling their grandchildren by showering them with too many goodies. At the other extreme are parents who take all those good-

---

DEAR DR. TIGHTWAD

Q. During the summer my children are often invited to spend a week with their grandparents. Should I expect Grandma and Granddad to pay for meals out and other activities, or should I send the kids with money to pay for themselves?

A. In general, the closer your relationship to hosts who extend an invitation, the more likely they are to want to pay your kids' way. So you could expect grandparents to cover more expenses than, say, a friend's parents.

In any case, you ought to feel free to broach the subject in advance with your parents or parents-in-law. Even if they insist on treating your kids, however, the children should still have their own pocket money for souvenirs and gifts (for more on financial etiquette for guests, see Chapter 16).

DEAR DR. TIGHTWAD

Q. After I had told my children they absolutely, positively could not have a new video game system, their doting grandparents arrived for a visit and presented them with one. I felt put on the spot and accepted the gift. But now I'm seething. I feel I should have stood my ground and turned it down. What do you think?

A. There are certain niceties that have to be observed in life, and accepting a gift graciously is one of them.

But don't let it end there. Stop seething and follow this three-step plan:

1. Set limits on the time your kids can spend playing video games.

2. Have a polite but firm talk with the doting grandparents (or aunt, uncle or godparent, as the case may be) and ask that next time they consult you before springing for a big gift. Tell them you'd like an opportunity to discuss what the kids need, want and are allowed to have.

3. Sit down and play a game or two with your kids, compliments of Grandma and Grandpa.

---

ies for granted, and even ask for more.

In the first situation, grandparents and their adult children need to strike a balance between the satisfaction grandparents get from buying stuff for the kids, and the parents' right to say enough is enough. After all, grandparents have been known to go overboard. For example, there was the grandmother who bought her granddaughter 55—count 'em, 55—new outfits, or the grandparents who sent their 5-year-old grandson his own television set and VCR.

Grandparents, feel free to be spontaneous with small gifts. Or if you're coming for a visit, arrive with plans to do something together—make a meal, bake a batch of cookies, have lunch at a burger restaurant. One grandma made a habit of picking up her grandkids at school and taking them out for "front-seat fries" (so named because whoever sat in the front seat got first dibs).

But consult with your adult kids ahead of time about major purchases. To keep gift-giving under control, one mom began sending her own parents toy catalogs, circling a selection of items with different prices, and letting Grandma and Grandpa choose what they'd like to give. "We've been getting great presents ever since," said Mom. Or parents can have their children keep a running wish list of things they'd like but won't necessarily get. On birthdays and holidays, gift-givers can take their pick.

Instead of trying to guess what her grandchildren wanted, one grandmother got into the habit of taking them shopping individually and letting them choose, setting a price limit of $100 for the teenage girls and $50 for the younger boy. "The girls shopped with an eye on price. I had to tell them that if it cost $5 or $10 more and they really love it, don't look at the price," she said. "My grandson, on the other hand, tried to talk me into everything. By the end of the day I was completely exhausted." But her shopping sprees had an ulterior motive: While the kids spent money, she spent time with the kids.

Taking Grandma for Granted

While some parents wish that grandparents would cut back, others apparently expect them to produce on demand. At birthday time the grandkids (or their parents) call Grandma to put in their order—sometimes an expensive item that's out of Grandma's price range. But Grandma worries that if she doesn't produce she'll be on the outs with her grandkids.

Grandma, stop fretting. If this ever happens to you, tell the grandchildren you'd prefer to surprise them with a gift of your own choosing. If they ask for something expensive, tell them that while you can't afford to buy it, you'll be happy to contribute to their own savings fund—or better yet, pay them for doing extra work around your house. You'll be giving them a lesson in deferred gratification—a gift that grandparents are uniquely qualified to give.

And don't worry about alienating your grandkids' affection. What children really love are grandparents who take an interest in their activities, joke with them, and create special occasions or share special interests that don't need to cost much money. One grandfather made a scrapbook of favorite comic strips he reads to the kids when they come to visit. A grandmother regularly sends her grandson newspaper clippings about her hometown hockey team, of which her grandson is a big fan.

One grandma started a tradition of sending her younger grandchildren storybooks with a homemade tape of her voice reading the story (the kids particularly liked her directives to "turn the page"). For her college-age granddaughter, she bought a computer and the two began exchanging e-mail messages.

The Check is in the Mail

Grandparents who live hundreds of miles from their grandchildren often send checks for birthday and holiday gifts, and then worry that money is too impersonal a gift. Are children disappointed when they don't get "real" presents?

Not on your life. I don't know many children above the age of 5 or so who turn up their noses at money. In the words of one 6-year-old, "Money is importanter than toys. I can buy things with it."

For very young children, checks aren't so much impersonal as they are useless. The kids can't play with them, spend them or cash them on their own. If you're giving a small amount of money—say, $5 or $10—consider sending cash, or at least enclose a couple of crisp

---

DEAR DR. TIGHTWAD

Q. I've heard some parents complain about grandparents who shower their grandkids with expensive gifts that the parents would rather their children didn't have. I have the opposite problem. My parents shower my kids with cheap trinkets that I'd rather they didn't have. They're broken within a day or two and I end up throwing them away. I don't want to hurt my parents' feelings, but I wish they'd just save their money.

A. Better yet, why not suggest that they save it in a bank account that you set up on the kids' behalf? Just tell them that the kids have enough stuff and don't really need anything else.

If your parents insist on buying trinkets that break, resign yourself to tossing them out. The gifts may not cost very much, but your parents are obviously getting more than their money's worth in satisfaction.

DEAR DR. TIGHTWAD

Q. Our grandson is an avid rock collector. For his ninth birthday, our daughter suggested that we buy him a rock tumbling kit for polishing stones. We did, and it set us back $109. Several months have passed, and he still hasn't used the kit. We really feel taken—especially after we went into a toy store recently and saw a toy rock tumbler for $29.95.

A. Taking the kit away from your grandson obviously isn't going to have much of an effect, so you might as well wait him out.

Because your grandson does collect rocks, your daughter's gift suggestion sounds like a thoughtful one that was made in good faith. Just because he hasn't used the kit yet doesn't mean that he never will. Maybe he just needs the right rainy afternoon with nothing else to do. Or maybe he needs help with what could be a complicated apparatus for a 9-year-old. Offer your services next time you visit.

There's a second lesson here. Grandparents understandably want to buy the best for their grandkids, but unless you can guarantee the children's interest it sometimes pays to get a less expensive item with a price tag that's more in line with the kids' attention span.

dollar bills with your check. One set of grandparents customarily sends each of their grandkids a $20 birthday check, along with cash equal to the child's age, up to a maximum of $10.

Depending on how much you send, make it clear that your grandkids should spend all or part of the money on something they like. Parents have a tendency to confiscate their kids' cash and checks for safekeeping, but what fun is that? My own mother is famous for the notes she encloses with money gifts for her grandchildren. A sample: "Dear Claire: This check is for your birthday. Have Mommy buy something for you, or you can save it to put in your billfold. Daddy can change it all into ones."

I'd also like to salute money-smart grandparent Mary McEwen of Nashville, Tenn., who won a contest with a wonderful suggestion for creating inexpensive yet memorable presents for her eight grandchildren. During the holidays, Mary makes a coupon book for each grandchild. Each book includes 14 coupons, one for every month plus bonuses for Valentine's Day and the child's birthday.

Each coupon is redeemable for $5—but that's not

the most valuable part of the gift. The front of each coupon is imprinted with words of wisdom from Mary, and the back has space for a thank-you note. To redeem the coupon, a grandchild must present it to Mary each month, recite the advice and tell her what it means. Then the kids have to complete the thank-you note on the back. When they're finished, they get the $5 gift. For $70, Mary gives her grandchildren a year full of fun, lots of great memories and painless lessons in money management and manners.

Leaving a Legacy

The ordinary routine of holiday and birthday gift-giving is one thing. But grandparents are also concerned about passing on a longer-lasting legacy to their grandchildren. "The older I get, the less important it is that my house be clean and ready for guests," said

---

BROACHING A TOUCHY SUBJECT

Your adult kids may find it hard to bring up the subject of *your* finances; aside from not wanting to confront your death, they don't want to seem nosy or greedy.

Yet they need to know the location of financial documents, provisions of your will, or plans for succession in a family business. In general, openness is better—things left unsaid or unconfronted in your life can become bombshells to family members in your will.

Consider naming one of your adult children as executor of your estate (although you may want to choose a neutral third party if selecting one child would strain family relationships or if you have doubts about your child's ability to fill the role).

You should draft a living will, which specifies your wishes regarding medical care you want in case of serious illness, and execute a durable power of attorney for both health and financial matters, so that your child is authorized to manage your affairs if you can't.

Note to adult children: If grandparents are reluctant to talk about their finances—a natural tendency among an older generation for whom money was a hush-hush affair—you can take a stab at it, but gently, to see if you get a response. You might mention that you've recently drafted or updated your own will. Or talk about a health emergency experienced by a friend or neighbor of your parents. Or send your parents copies of topical books or articles. "My mom always saves clippings for me, so it's time to turn the tables," says one woman.

Jacci Sutton. "You'll find me out in the mud with the kids instead." The kids are her seven grandchildren. Each summer Jacci and her husband, James, take two cousins at a time on boating and camping excursions and "mystery trips" on weekends. Grandma, a self-described computer hacker, keeps in touch with the couple's out-of-state grandchildren by e-mail.

Their grandparents, said Tommy and Teara, are "most definitely cool"—an assessment that will no doubt be reinforced when they get older and learn how their grandparents have given them a head start on their future. After discussions with their three grown children, Jacci and James decided that their estate should be split equally among all the grandchildren and the money earmarked for paying college expenses.

"It's not as if we're skipping over our children, because the grandchildren's needs are also their parents' needs," said Jacci. "We worked hard so that our kids could get a college education, so by relieving our children of that we are giving them something."

The Suttons have also arranged for automatic deductions from James's paycheck to be deposited into seven savings accounts, one for each grandchild, at their credit union. "It will be a little cushion for when they get to college," perhaps to pay for books or maybe a computer, said Jacci. The Suttons like these accounts because of a special insurance program offered at no cost by their credit union that would double the amount in the combined accounts up to a maximum of $5,000 if they should die. "We hope that our grandchildren will get the idea that this is how our family operates," said Jacci. "Each generation gives a boost to the next."

Gifts That Last a Lifetime

Giving a boost to the next generation can be as simple as buying shares of stock as a gift. Don't worry that the children will think you're an old fogy. Kids like to make money just as much as grown-ups do. Behind many a budding Wall Street investor is a grandparent who took the time to talk about his or her own interest in the stock market. In the Stein Roe contest, Amy Anderson wrote that her grandparents "have been a good example to me. They have an investment fund for each of their grandchildren. Instead of buying me an expensive toy for my birthday, they put money in my account. They then buy me something smaller for my birthday, but I know my future is

---

DEAR DR. TIGHTWAD

Q. Over the past five years I have given each of my three granddaughters common stock worth approximately $40,000 at today's prices. Because they were 13 to 17 years of age, I listed their father—my son—as custodian.

When I asked the girls, all of whom are now 18 or older, to change their accounts into their names only, I found they had no idea how much they had in their accounts. My son was very evasive when I asked him why the girls hadn't seen their shareholder statements.

Come to find out he has been selling the stock to pay expenses, and their accounts are down to approximately $2,000. I'm sure much of the money went for the girls' education, clothes, transportation and other needs. But my son has not offered an explanation or financial report.

I would like your opinion as to what we could do while keeping the family together. I feel deceived and betrayed by my son.

A. Your son's behavior may have been illegal as well as deceitful if he used his daughters' assets to pay his own expenses, or to fulfill his legal obligations to his children. In either case they could take legal action against him. But that would hardly keep the family together.

You—and other generous grandparents—might have avoided this situation by not being so trusting, even of a family member. If you had set up a custodial account under the Uniform Transfers to Minors Act (UTMA) or Uniform Gifts to Minors Act (UGMA), you could have named an institution, such as a bank or brokerage firm, as custodian. If there were any question of misuse of funds by a bank employee, for example, the bank would be responsible.

Since you intended to give substantial gifts to your granddaughters, it would have paid to set up a formal trust agreement. In such a situation, "I generally try to have two people as co-trustees—typically the grandmother, if the grandfather is making the gift, and one parent," said Martin Shenkman, an estate-planning lawyer and author of *The Complete Book of Trusts* (John Wiley & Sons). "If two people have to sign off on the trust's tax return, it's a lot harder for one of them to skip off with the money."

It's too late to take your son over your knee, and you may have to accept the loss to keep peace. But you can press for a better accounting, and rethink giving any more money to your son as part of your estate plan.

growing bigger every year."

For grandparents who want to help out with college bills, the easiest route is to pay the college directly. Direct payments for tuition, no matter how large, aren't subject to the federal gift tax. So you don't have to worry about limiting gifts to stay within the federal gift-tax exclusion, which is $10,000 per recipient per year, or $20,000 if your spouse joins in the gift. Since the money doesn't belong to your children or your grandchildren, you still control the assets, and have the flexibility to change your mind about how you want to spend them.

If you own appreciated assets, such as stocks, that you'd have to sell in order to raise money for college, you might consider making a gift of the assets to your grandchild. If your grandchild sold the assets, any capital gains would be taxed at his or her rate, not yours. In the case of a child who's still years away from college, grandparents might consider making a gift to the child through a custodial arrangement or a trust.

If you can't afford to foot the bill for tuition, don't worry. That's just one cost of college, and help is welcome on many fronts. You might buy your college-bound grandchildren a computer, pay for a trip home for the holidays or even volunteer your time to travel with them to visit schools before they make their selection.

The Second Time Around

Increasingly, grandparents are playing a more permanent role in the financial support of their grandchildren, with millions of children under the age of 18 living with their grandparents. Sometimes the stay is temporary—at least, grandparents hope it will be—when adult children come home to recuperate and regroup after a divorce, for example. But children, even grown ones, have a tendency to settle in. I once received a letter from a couple whose daughter and two grandchildren had come home for what was supposed to be a limited stay. "But as time goes on we find we are doing more and more to support our grandchildren, such as buying them clothes and paying for school expenses," they wrote. "We don't mind helping out, but we're not wealthy. How should we handle this?"

Once children have recovered their bearings emotionally, don't feel guilty about broaching the subject of their leaving. If you can't face that alone, have a third party, such as a financial planner, do it for you, or least be there to back you up. "You have to get it off an emotional plane and articulate what's best for the older people given their economic situation," said Robert Strom, who has developed a nationwide educational program for grandparents. "In my experience, adult children aren't insulted by this."

Grandparents who do end up raising their grandkids often face serious financial challenges, such as paying legal fees in custody battles or getting health insurance. In the case of health insurance, for instance, employers can set any policy they want as to who's eligible for family coverage, and often employers extend benefits to anyone who qualifies as a dependent under IRS rules—meaning, for one thing, that you provide more than half of your grandchildren's support for the year. Not every employer is so generous, however, and, if you're retired, medicare doesn't include dependents. For more information on grandparents raising grandkids, contact the AARP Grandparent Information Center, 601 E St. N.W., Washington, DC 20049 (202-434-2296); Grandparents United for Children's Rights, 137 Larkin St., Madison, WI 53705 (608-236-0480); Grandparents as Parents, P.O. Box 22801, Lakewood, CA 90714 (562-924-3996).

 **Turn page for Kids' Questions→**

KIDS' QUESTIONS

Q. "The sweaters Grandpa sends for our birthday every year are always too small. Can we ask for money this time?"
A. Asking for money is tacky, but suggesting that Grandpa send money in lieu of another gift is a reasonable request.

You can explain to him that as the kids get older it's difficult to buy things that fit and meet with their approval. If you don't want to make an out-and-out request for cash, suggest instead a gift certificate for a book, music or clothing store. Or remind Grandpa to include a gift voucher or some other proof of purchase so you can exchange the item for another size if it doesn't fit.

Who knows? Grandpa may actually be relieved. It's possible that for all these years the kids have been getting too-small sweaters or fire-engine pajamas because Grandpa felt obligated to send a gift but didn't know what to buy—and thought that sending cash would seem tacky. It isn't fair to let him keep frittering away his money on presents that aren't being used.

Remember, though, that kids should always thank Grandpa for his thoughtfulness, even if the sweater is too tight.

Q. Why does Grandma Pearl give bigger presents than Grandma Rose?
A. You might be tempted to say "Because Grandma Pearl has more money." Honesty is a good policy, but don't make too big a deal about any difference in wealth. You may be more sensitive about it than the kids, who are probably just being curious and not passing judgment. Remind them that the size of a present has nothing to do with the amount of love that comes with it.

Dr. Tightwad's Final Rx

Politicians and the media are obsessed with family values. Bookstore shelves are crammed with volumes advising your family how to acquire them. Americans, it seems, are on a crusade to find stability and set standards.

Inevitably those standards are going to involve money, because many of the values and virtues we want to pass along to our children touch on finances either directly or indirectly—thrift, self-discipline, generosity, responsibility, planning for the future. If children acquire those traits in the context of managing money successfully, they'll be able to use them to manage other aspects of their lives as well.

But no one can give you a secret formula for achieving family harmony or financial balance. The answer is within the grasp of any family. It's a matter of common-sense principles effectively communicated to your children. In the case of money, those principles include living within your means and recognizing virtue as its own reward. That so many families struggle with principles that seem so obvious is a sign of modern times, when outside influences and affluence can upset the delicate balance of family life.

My contribution, as Dr. Tightwad, is to offer suggestions on how to counter those outside influences. Some parents are already doing a great job and just need a pat on the back and a word of encouragement. Others have lost sight of basic values and need guidance about how to get back on track. Still others know exactly what they want to teach their children but are looking for practical suggestions on how to discuss sensitive issues involving money or answer awkward questions.

Dollars & Sense for Kids has tried to provide the pat on the back, the gentle reminder, the practical advice. Back in Chapter 1, I observed that when children ask their parents about money, parents are tempted to offer one of three responses: Yes, no or maybe. Here, in a nutshell, is my prescription for answering those questions more effectively:

- **Never say no** unless you mean it.
- **Never say yes** unless you want to.
- **Never say maybe** if you can think of a better response—and, having read this book, you can.

No, money doesn't grow on trees. But if early on you can plant the seeds of good money management and watch your children blossom into responsible adults, you'll have reaped a priceless harvest.

Index

A

AARP Grandparent Information Center, 297
Academy for Economic Education, 148
Academy of Family Mediators, 54, 284
Acorn Entrepreneurs: Visions of Young Enterprises, 195
ADR. *See* American depositary receipts
Advertising
  appealing to parents, 30-32
  Children's Advertising Review Unit, 64
  differences between sexes, 29
  food commercials, 74
  guides for parents and advertisers, 64
  teenagers and, 20-21, 27-29
  television commercials, 75-78
Allowances
  advances, 52, 129, 130
  age to start, 104, 114
  average amounts, 10
  budgeting, 119-120
  choosing a system, 128
  chores and, 109-115
  clothing allowances, 120-122
  determining amount of, 104-105
  donations to charities, 108-109
  expenses covered by, 110-112
  guidelines for, 12-13, 103
  impact of, 11-12
  investments, 18
  lunch money and, 130
  managing money, 106-108
  negotiating raises, 106, 129-130
  ParentBanc, 9-10,
  paying interest, 10-12
  rewards for grades, 122-124
  saving money, 18, 78-79
  scheduling payment, 127-128
  teenagers and, 210-211
  withholding allowances as punishment for bad behavior, 125-127
  for younger siblings, 129
American Association of Individual Investors, 155

American Board of Family Practice, 59, 221
American Century Giftrust, 161
American depositary receipts, 165
American Eagle, 96
American Express IDS New Dimensions, 159
American Express Retail Index, 35
American Numismatic Association, 95
American Savings Education Council
  Youth & Money Survey, 17-18
American Stock Exchange, 173
AMEX. *See* American Stock Exchange
Anti-counterfeiting measures, 97-98
ASEC. *See* American Savings Education Council
ATMs. *See* Automated teller machines
At-risk youth
  after school jobs and, 233
  teaching business skills to, 198-199
Auto insurance
  teenagers and, 211, 214
Automated teller machines
  explaining how they work, 144
  teenagers use of, 217-218

B

Babysitting, 231
Bankruptcy, 247
Banks
  certificates of deposits, 169
  children's ideas concerning, 22, 71, 135
  college students and checking accounts, 247
  co-signing an account, 141
  explaining bank machines, 144
  making withdrawals, 142-143
  opening a bank account, 140-143

origin of word, 93
  savings accounts, 169
  school banking programs, 33, 131-132, 138, 139
  teenagers and checking accounts, 203-204, 206-207, 218-220
  teenagers use of ATMs, 217-218
  Young Americans Bank, 32-33, 141, 206, 219, 249-250
Barron's, 150
Behavior
  "fine" system, 277
  rewards for, 130
  withholding allowances as punishment for bad behavior, 125-127
Better Investing **magazine,** 152
Better Than a Lemonade Stand, 195
Bidwell & Co., 164
Birthday gifts
  birthdays on holidays, 267-268
  from grandparents, 290-291, 298
  money gifts, 271, 291-293
  options for, 258, 263, 266-267, 271
  paying from allowance, 108
Birthday parties, 263, 266-268
Blue Chip Growth, 160
Blue chips, 151
Board games, 76-77, 79, 82
Books
  recommended reading list, 80-81
Borrowing
  from siblings, 86-87
  from your children, 86
Brokers, 163-166, 173
Budgets, 18, 207-209, 212-213
Bureau of Engraving and Printing
  amount of currency printed each day, 99
  big bucks as gifts, 263
  tour of, 101
Burger King
  programs for teenagers, 234

Business plans, 188
Businesses. *See* Careers;
    Entrepreneurship; Jobs
Buy Me That, 74

C

Capital gains
    from mutual funds, 204
Career academy models, 233
Careers. *See also* Entrepreneur-
    ship; Jobs
    avoiding cynicism, 52-53
    children's career choice
        survey, 180
    children's ideas concerning, 23,
        58-59
    understanding salaries, 56,
        57-58, 89
Cars
    expenses for teenagers, 211,
        214
CARU. *See* Children's Advertis-
    ing Review Unit
**Center for Applied Motiva-
    tion,** 52-53, 202
**The Center for Entrepre-
    neurship,** 197
Certificates of deposit, 169
Charities
    children being too generous, 88
    donations from allowances,
        108-109
    encouraging children to give, 79
    tax issues, 171
Checking accounts
    college students and, 247
    teenagers and, 203-204,
        206-207, 218-219
Child-labor laws, 197, 230
Children. *See also* College
    students; Teenagers
    child support, 49-50, 280-283
    financial conflicts resulting
        from divorce, 280-285
    grown children moving back in
        with parents, 248, 296-297
    money management and family
        values, 299-300
**Children's Advertising
    Review Unit,** 64
Chores
    allowances and, 109-115

enforcement of, 115-119, 281
    for preschoolers, 66
Communities in Schools, 234
Class trips, 222
Clothing
    allowances for, 120-122
    budgeting for, 208-209
    resisting pressure from
        children, 50-51, 85-86
    spending guidelines for
        preschoolers' clothes, 65
    teenage spending, 20
Coins
    acceptance of, 93
    categories of, 93-94
    coin collections, 95-96
    composition of, 92-93
    design of, 94-95
    dollar coins, 96
    doubled-die cents, 95
    gold coin, 96
    length of time in circulation,
        93-94
    number of new coins each
        year, 94
    value of old coins, 95
Collectibles, 174-175, 292
College
    earning scholarships, 230-231
    financial aid eligibility, 171
    grandparents' help with
        expenses, 294, 295
    saving for, 31, 204-205, 223
College students
    academic probation, 252
    checking accounts and, 247
    credit cards and, 243, 245-251
    money management, 243-245,
        253-254
    paying to retake failed courses,
        251-252
    providing spending money, 276
    sharing expenses, 236-237
Compound interest, 135-138,
    143
Conflicts over money, 43-51,
    54, 280-285
Consolidation loans, 251
**Consumer Credit Counseling
    Service,** 47, 219-220
Consumer Kids
    marketing conference, 30-32
Consumer Reports

Buy Me That, 74
Zillions, 26, 77
Contests
    letting children enter, 88-89
Continental currency, 99
Coogan law, 236
Co-signing accounts, 141, 249,
    250
Cost- plus pricing, 192
**Council of Better Business
Bureaus**
    Children's Advertising Review
        Unit, 64
Counterfeiting, 97-98, 101
Credit cards
    children's ideas concerning,
        21-22
    college students and, 243,
        245-251
    secured credit cards, 249-250
    teenagers and, 18, 204, 214-
        215, 217-218
    Young Americans Bank,
        249-250
Credit reports, 250, 252
Currency
    amount of money printed
        daily, 99
    big bucks as gifts, 263
    design of bills, 97-100
    engravers, 99
    history of money, 91-102
    identifying counterfeit bills, 101
    length of time in circulation, 99
    mutilated currency, 100
    redesign, 98
    value in other countries, 102
Current coins, 94
Custodial accounts
    advantages and disadvantages
        of, 170-171, 173
    mutual funds, 157, 159-161,
        163-164
    types of, 170

D

Dating expenses, 201-202,
    222-223
Debit cards, 219-220
Debtors Anonymous, 47
**Delaware Center for
    Economic Education,**

71, 185
Department of Labor, 195
Dimes
  history of, 92-95
Direct Investing, 166-167
Directory of Companies Offering Dividend Reinvestment Plans, 166
Directory of Mutual Funds, 155
Dividend reinvestment plans, 164, 166-168
Dividends, 173, 204
Divorce
  financial conflicts involving children, 280-285
Divorce mediators, 284
DLJdirect, 163
Dollars
  converted to francs, 102
  history of, 96-97
Doubled-die cents, 95
Dow Jones Industrial Average, 174
DRIP. See Dividend reinvestment plans
DRIP Investor, 166
Driving expenses, 211, 214

E

Edson, Tracy R., 97
Education
  encouraging entrepreneurship, 185
  financial literacy opportunities, 32-34
  mutual funds materials, 157-161
  saving for college, 204-205
  Stock Market Game, 150-151
  stock market Web sites, 167
Education Resources Institute, 246
  Eisenhower dollar, 93
Entrepreneurship. *See also* Careers; Jobs
  advantages of, 198-200
  business ideas, 184-187, 189
  business plans, 188
  child-labor laws, 197-198
  common mistakes, 191-194
  considerations, 193
  cost- plus pricing, 192

  encouraging children, 177-178, 183-184, 185
  fund-raisers, 179-181
  getting started, 187-191
  laws and regulations, 194-196
  legal issues, 196-198
  market approach pricing, 192
  personality traits involved, 181
  pricing, 192-194, 199
  raising cash, 188-189
  registering business name, 195
  resources, 195
  school programs, 182-183
  selling yourself, 189-191
  tax issues, 196-197
  yard sales, 190, 283
Equifax, 252
Estate taxes, 293
Etiquette
  guest etiquette, 278-279, 286, 288
  splitting the tab in restaurants, 279, 286
Experian, 252
Expressions and idioms, 101-102
Extracurricular activities, 230-231

F

Families
  children's money concerns, 55
  conflicts over money, 43-51, 54
  discussing family financial matters with teenagers, 205-207
  discussing family financial matters with younger children, 216
  financial conflicts resulting from divorce, 280-285
  gifts from grandparents, 24, 287-294
  grandparents' help with college expenses, 294, 295, 296
  grown children moving back in with parents, 248, 296-297
  investment clubs, 153-154
  money management and family values, 299-300
  money personality profiles, 44-46

  perceived favoritism, 54-55
  vacation spending, 275-277
Fast Cash for Kids, 181, 195
Fast-food workers, 233-234
FDIC. *See* Federal Deposit Insurance Corporation
Federal Deposit Insurance Corporation, 169
Federal Reserve Board. *See also* Jump$tart Coalition for Personal Financial Literacy Fed Challenge, 33-34
Federal Trade Commission, 217
Fidelity Magellan, 147
Financial literacy
  education opportunities, 32-34
  Jump$tart Coalition, 17, 24, 151
First Share, 167-168
First Start Growth, 159
Forbes, 150
Fort Knox, 96
Franklin, Benjamin, 101
Fund-raisers, 179-181, 273-275

G

Games
  board games, 76-77, 79, 82
  Stock Market Game, 150-153
  for teaching preschoolers money management, 67-68
Gender issues
  consumer preferences, 42
  consumption differences, 29
  differences in amount saved, 41
  investment choices, 43
  money management differences, 41-44
  wage differences, 42
Generation Y
  targeted by advertisers, 27-29
Geppetto Group, 202
Gift tax, 170-171, 295-296
Gifts. *See also* Toys
  birthdays, 258, 263, 266-268, 271
  children selling gifts they have received, 283
  cutting back on holiday gifts, 255-257
  emphasizing the meaning of religious milestones, 262-263

financing holiday gifts from
children, 261-262
gift registries, 257
gifts of time, 256-257
from grandparents, 24, 287-291,
298
money gifts, 24, 269, 271,
291-293
in poor taste, 277
Santa's role, 259-261
thank-you notes, 268-270
tooth fairy gifts, 264-265
trust agreements, 295
wish lists, 257-259
Giftshares, 160-161
Gold
gold coins, 96
history of money, 92
mining for, 96
price of, 96
Gold depository, 96
Government Money Market,
160
Grades
rewards for, 122-124
Grandparents
gifts from, 24, 287-291, 298
helping with college expenses,
294, 295, 296
investments for grandchildren,
294-296
money gifts, 24, 291-293
options for gifts, 290-291
overdoing gifts, 288-289
spending time with grand-
children, 294
supporting children and grandchildren, 296-297
Grandparents as Parents, 297
Grandparents United for
Children's Rights, 297
Great Seal of the United
States, 99-100
"Greenbacks," 97
Griffin Bacal, 28, 31-32
Grocery shopping
activities to occupy children,
72, 74
teaching preschoolers money
management, 63, 70
Growth funds, 154, 156
Growth Investor, 157
Guardians

naming in wills, 31, 55-56
Guest etiquette, 278-279,
286, 288
Guide to Dividend Reinvest-
ment Plans, 167
Guidebook of United States
Coins, 95

H

Half-dollars
history of, 94-95
The Handbook for No-Load
Fund Investors, 155
Handling cash
avoiding losing money, 83, 87
counting change, 89
tips for, 83
A Handy Reference Guide to
the Fair Labor Standards
Act, 195
Health insurance
coverage eligibility, 297
High School Financial
Planning Program
Survey, 204, 210
History of money, 91-102
Holiday gifts
birthdays on holidays, 267-268
cutting back, 255-257
financing gifts from children,
261-262
gift registries, 257
gifts of time, 256-257
money gifts, 291-293
Santa's role, 259-261
Secret Santa, 258, 262
thank-you notes, 268-270
wish lists, 257-259
Homeowners insurance
business pursuits clauses,
197-198
Honesty, 8
Household expenses, 87-88

I

Income funds, 154
Income tax. *See* Tax issues
Indianhead pennies, 95
The Individual Investor
Revolution, 166

Individual Investor's Guide
to Low-Load Mutual
Funds, 155
Institute for Higher Educa-
tion Policy, 246
Insurance
auto insurance and teenagers,
211, 214
coverage eligibility for health
insurance, 297
homeowners business pursuits
clauses, 197-198
obtaining sufficient life
insurance, 31
Interest
compounding, 135-137, 142
paying interest on allowances,
10-11
taxes on earnings by children,
165, 204, 232
Internet. *See also* Web sites
online brokers, 163
online buying, 35-37
Stock Market Game, 150-153
Invesco, 159-160
Investing for Life, 166-167
Investment Company
Institute, 155
Investments. *See also* Savings;
Stock market
children's ideas concerning,
22-23
family investment clubs,
153-154
filing tax returns, 238-239
gender differences, 43
for grandchildren, 294-296
risk taking, 48
starting an investment club, 152
for teenagers, 18

J

Jobs. *See also* Careers; Entrepreneurship
child-labor laws, 230
fast-food jobs, 233-234
filing tax returns, 238-239
full-time jobs and teenagers,
239
income tax withholding, 235
interviewing, 240-241

managing part-time earnings,
235-238
preparing resumes, 240
teenagers and, 225-242
tips for finding a job, 239-241
volunteer jobs, 229-231
**Jump$tart Coalition for
Personal Financial
Literacy,** 17, 24, 151
Junior Achievement, 197

K

Kaplan Educational center, 29
Kiddie tax, 140
kidstock.com, 166
KidsWay, 197
*Kiplinger's Personal Finance
Magazine,* 150

L

Legal issues
for businesses operated by
children, 194-198
child-labor laws, 197, 230
contracts with minors, 197-
198, 206
teenagers and ATM debt,
217-218
teenagers and credit card debt,
217
*The Lemonade Stand:
A Guide to Encouraging the
Entrepreneur in Your Child,*
195
Letter engravers, 99
Liberty Head nickels, 95
Life insurance
obtaining sufficient coverage, 31
**Low Cost Investment Plan of
the NAIC,** 167
Lunch money
allowances and, 130
Lynch, Peter, 147

M

"Mad money," 101-102
Market approach pricing, 192
Marketing. *See also* Advertising
kids and, 20-21

Marriage mediators, 54, 284
Matching savings, 132, 137
McDonald's
programs for teenagers, 234
Mediators
marriage and divorce, 54, 284
Merrill Lynch, 18, 204
Minimum wage, 237
Mint Act of 1792, 96
Monetta, 160
Money
origin of word, 93
Money, 150
Money personality profiles,
44-46
Money record worksheet,
106, 124-125
Money safety
avoiding losing money, 83, 87
tips for handling money, 73, 89
Money-market funds, 169-170
Moneypaper, 167
*Moneyskills: 101 Activities to
Teach Your Child About
Money,* 66-67
*Moody's Handbook of
Common Stocks,* 148
Morningstar Mutual Funds,
155
Mutilated coins, 93
Mutilated currency, 100-101
Mutual funds
advantages of, 154-157
custodial accounts, 157,
159-161, 163-164
growth funds, 154-155
income funds, 154
kid-oriented funds, 157-161
money-market funds, 160,
169-170
no-load funds, 156
reading mutual fund listings, 158
resources for tracking funds,
155
risks involved, 169-172
Roth IRAs, 228, 238
tax issues, 204

N

NAIC Advisory Service, 152
Nasdaq, 173

**National Association of
Investors Corp.,** 152, 167
**National Child Labor
Committee,** 230
**National Council on Economic
Education,** 185
**National Credit Union
Administration,** 169
**National Foundation for
Teaching Entrepreneurship,**
198-199
Netstock Direct, 166
New Dimensions, 159
New York Stock Exchange,
173
Newspaper carriers, 197
**Nickelodeon/Yankelovich
Youth Monitor**
allowance survey, 10, 105
Nickels
history of, 92
Nike, 29
The No-Load Fund Investor,
157
No-load mutual funds, 155,
156

O

One Share of Stock, 168
One Up on Wall Street, 147
Oppenheimer Funds, 43-44
Opportunity wage, 237

P

**Parent Encouragement
Program,** 107-108
ParentBanc, 9,
Parents
children's influence on
spending, 25-27
conflicts over money, 41-51,
54, 280-285
consistency in parenting, 54
co-signing accounts, 141, 142,
249, 250
grown children moving back in,
248, 296-297
guides for monitoring and
explaining advertising to
children, 64-65

impact on children's attitude toward money, 39-41
influence on teen spending, 201-202
resisting pressure from children, 30-32, 50-51, 57-58, 64-65, 70, 85-89, 216, 220-221
resisting sales pressure, 35
responsibilities to children, 31
strategies for, 7-9, 13-16, 28
teaching children money management, 51-53
teaching children the concept of limited funds, 57-58
teaching honesty, 8
telling children their salary, 56
Peer pressure, 83-84
Pennies
history of, 94
Penny stocks, 147
Picture engravers, 99
Preschool children
teaching money management, 61-70
Prom expenses, 201-202, 222-223
"Proof" coins, 95
Proxy votes, 154

R

"Red Book," 95
Restaurants
splitting the tab, 279-280, 286
treating children, 10
Resumes, 240
Retail sales
teenagers and, 231
Retirement
Roth IRAs, 228, 238
saving for, 31
Revere, Paul, 98
Revolutionary War
continental currency, 98
Rewards
for good behavior, 130
for grades, 122-124
money rewards, 128
to preschoolers for completing chores, 66
Roth IRAs, 228, 238
Royce Giftshares, 160-161

S

Saatchi & Saatchi
Kid Connection, 35
Salaries
children's understanding of, 56-58
Sales tax
for children's businesses, 196
Sandwich coins, 93
Santa, 259-261
Save for America, 33, 131-132, 139
Savings. See also Investments; Stock market
from allowances, 18, 78
allowing children to spend their savings, 144
certificates of deposits, 169
choosing a system, 138-140
collectibles, 174-175
for college, 31, 204-205, 223
compounding interest, 135-136, 142
co-signing accounts, 140, 141
differences among siblings, 42
encouraging saving, 131-133
gender differences, 41
goals, 133-135
making withdrawals, 142-143
matching savings, 132, 137
opening a bank account, 140-142
for retirement, 31
Save for America, 33, 131-132
savings accounts, 22, 169
school banking programs, 33, 131-132, 138, 139
setting goals, 208
teenagers' college savings, 204-205
School banking programs, 33, 131-132, 138, 139
School fund-raisers, 179-181, 273-275
Secret Santa, 258, 262
Secured credit cards, 249-250
Securities Industry Foundation for Economic Education, 150
Self-employment tax, 187, 196
Shopping
grocery shopping activities, 63, 70, 72, 74
resisting pressure from children, 85-86
Silver
history of money, 92-93
Silver dollars
history of, 93
Small Business Administration, 196
Smart Credit Strategies for College Students, 251
Smart Money, 150
SMG2000, 150-153
Social security numbers, 31
Software
recommended list, 80-81
Spending
age related, 25-27
allowing children to spend their savings, 144
children's influence on parent's spending, 25-27
clothing, 20, 120-122, 208-209
marketing and, 20-21
statistics, 25, 27
teaching money management, 33
vacations, 275-277
Spending plans, 207-210, 212-213
Split stock, 149
Splitting the tab, 279-280, 286
Standard & Poor, 148, 150
Stein Roe Young Investor, 157
Stock market. See also Investments
blue chips, 151
brokers, 163-166, 173
children most likely to invest, 145
children's ideas concerning stocks, 22-23
custodial accounts, 170-171, 173
direct purchase plans, 164-166
dividends, 153, 173
Dow Jones Industrial Average, 174
family investment clubs, 153-154
investments for grandchildren, 294-296

low-cost investing, 161-168
minimum entrance require-
    ments, 164-168
mutual funds, 154-161
online brokers, 163, 164
penny stocks, 147
picking stocks, 147-150
principle of a market, 146
proxy votes, 154
reading stock listings, 149
risk involved, 169-172
selling stock, 166, 173-174
split stock, 149
starting an investment club, 152
Stock Market Game, 150-153
stockholder benefits, 173
teenage investments, 18
Web sites, 167
Summer businesses. *See*
    Careers; Entrepreneurship;
    Jobs
Suretrade, 163
Susan B. Anthony dollar,
    93, 98

T

Target, 27
Tax issues
children's tax rates, 171
co-signing accounts, 141
custodial accounts, 170
dividend and interest earnings
    for children, 165, 204, 232
donations to charities, 171
filing tax returns, 238
gift tax, 170-171, 295-296
income tax for earnings from
    children's businesses, 196
income tax withholding, 235
kiddie tax, 140
money as a gift, 31
mutual funds, 204
pennies and sales tax, 94
Roth IRAs, 228, 238
sales tax for children's
    businesses, 195-196
self-employment tax, 196
tax forms required for
    children's businesses, 196
teenage earnings and, 232
unearned income and, 204
Teach Your Child the Value

of Money, 52, 136
*The Teenage Entrepreneur's
    Guide,* 188
Teenage Research Unlimited,
    27, 41-42, 215, 226
Teenagers. *See also* College
    students
allowances and, 210-211
budgeting, 207-209, 212-213
checking accounts and, 203,
    206-207, 218-220
class trip expenses, 222
clothing allowances, 120-122
credit cards and, 18, 204,
    214-215, 217-218
dating expenses, 201-202,
    222-223
debit cards for, 219-220
differences in amounts saved
    between boys and girls, 41
discussing family financial
    matters, 205-207
driving expenses, 211, 214
extracurricular activities,
    230-231
fast-food jobs, 233-234
filing tax returns, 238
finding a job, 239-241
full-time jobs, 239
income tax withholding, 235
managing part-time earnings,
    235-238
misunderstandings about
    money, 202-207
parents' influence on spending,
    201-202
paying jobs and, 225-241
preparing resumes, 240
resisting pressure from,
    220-221
Roth IRAs for, 228, 238
saving for college, 204-205
succeeding in business,
    241-242
underachievers, 202-203
volunteer jobs, 229-231
wage differences between
    genders, 42
A Teen's Guide to Business,
    181, 195
Television. *See also* Advertising
advertising, 75-78
teaching preschoolers money

management, 64-66
Temper Enrollment Service,
    167
Thank-you notes, 268-270
Time Warner, 180
Tooth fairy gifts, 264-265, 269
Toys. *See also* Gifts
gift registries, 257
resisting pressure from
    children, 85-86
returning broken toys, 89
for teaching preschoolers
    money management, 66, 68
television commercials, 75-76
Trans Union, 252
**Treasurer of the United
    States**
responsibilities of, 100
Treasury Department
design of coins, 94-95
responsibilities of Treasurer
    of the U.S., 100
Trust agreements, 295

U

UGMA. *See* Uniform Gifts to
    Minors Act
*Ump's Fwat, an Annual
    Report for Young People,*
    148
Uncurrent coins, 94
Underachievers, 202-203
Uniform Gifts to Minors Act,
    170, 295
**Uniform Transfers to Minors
    Act,** 170, 295
U.S. Mint
address, 94
design of coins, 94-95
determining composition of
    coins, 92
redemption of mutilated coins,
    93-94
tours, 101
USAA First Start Growth, 159
UTMA. *See* Uniform Transfers
    to Minors Act

V

Vacations
guest etiquette, 278-279, 288

spending, 275-277
Value Line Investment Survey, 148, 154
Value Line Mutual Fund Survey, 155
Videotapes
recommended list, 81
Volunteer jobs, 229-231

W

The Wall Street Journal, 174
Washington, Martha, 98-99
Washington Post, 151
Web sites. *See also* Internet
buying stock directly from companies, 166
Jump$tart Coalition, 24, 151
Kiplinger financial calculators, 22
online brokers, 163, 164
online buying, 35-37
stock information, 166-167
Washington Post, 151
Web Street, 163-164
What Makes You So Special?, 83
Wills
naming guardians, 31, 55-56
revising, 31
Worksheets
money records, 106, 124-125
teenager spending plans, 212-213
World Wide Web. *See* Internet; Web sites

Y

Yard sales, 190, 283
Young Americans Bank, 32-33, 141, 206-207, 219, 249-250
Young Entrepreneur, 197
Young Investor, 157
Youth & Money Survey, 17-18
Youth and Work Program, 230
Youth Money Matters, 167

Z

Zandl Group, 27, 29, 42, 221
Zap awards, 77-78
Zillions: Consumer Reports for Kids, 26, 77